Elite?

Elite?

A Christian Manifesto for Youth Sports in the United States

ADAM D. METZ

CASCADE Books • Eugene, Oregon

ELITE?
A Christian Manifesto for Youth Sports in the United States

Copyright © 2018 Adam D. Metz. All rights reserved. Except for brief quotations in critical publications or reviews, no part of this book may be reproduced in any manner without prior written permission from the publisher. Write: Permissions, Wipf and Stock Publishers, 199 W. 8th Ave., Suite 3, Eugene, OR 97401.

Cascade Books
An Imprint of Wipf and Stock Publishers
199 W. 8th Ave., Suite 3
Eugene, OR 97401

www.wipfandstock.com

PAPERBACK ISBN: 978-1-5326-0379-2
HARDCOVER ISBN: 978-1-5326-0381-5
EBOOK ISBN: 978-1-5326-0380-8

Cataloguing-in-Publication data:

Names: Metz, Adam D.

Title: Elite? : a Christian manifesto for youth sports in the United States / Adam D. Metz.

Description: Eugene, OR : Cascade Books, 2018 | Includes bibliographical references and index.

Identifiers: ISBN 978-1-5326-0379-2 (paperback) | ISBN 978-1-5326-0381-5 (hardcover) | ISBN 978-1-5326-0380-8 (ebook)

Subjects: LCSH: Sports—Religious aspects—Christianity. | Athletes—Religious life. | Sports—Psychological aspects. | Sports—Sociological aspects.

Classification: GV706.42 .M47 2018 (print) | GV706.42 .M47 (ebook)

Manufactured in the U.S.A.   OCTOBER 19, 2018

All Scripture quotations, unless otherwise indicated, are taken from the Holy Bible, New International Version®, NIV®. Copyright ©1973, 1978, 1984, 2011 by Biblica, Inc.™ Used by permission of Zondervan. All rights reserved worldwide. www.zondervan.com. The "NIV" and "New International Version" are trademarks registered in the United States Patent and Trademark Office by Biblica, Inc.™

Scripture quotations designated NRSV are from the New Revised Standard Version Bible, copyright © 1989 the Division of Christian Education of the National Council of the Churches of Christ in the United States of America. Used by permission. All rights reserved.

To Mary Beth, my lifetime companion and best friend. You make my life better every day, and I can't imagine a better partner for watching our children play.
And to Grandpa. I love sports because of you. Go Browns!

"Beneath that thin, shiny layer of elite spectator sports is a system that is troubled, if not failing."

TOM FARREY, *GAME ON*, 21.

Table of Contents

Acknowledgments ix
Chapter 1: Just a Game 1

PART ONE: *A Theology of Sports*

Chapter 2: Playing Games: A Theology for Sports 17
Chapter 3: There Can Be Only One: A Theology of Competition 33
Chapter 4: Sports as a Spiritual Power 57

PART TWO: *The Youth-Sports Industrial Complex*

Chapter 5: Children at Play: The Power of Youth Sports 79
Chapter 6: From Playgrounds to Hallowed Grounds:
    The Industrialization of Youth Sports 91
Chapter 7: Youth Sports and Sports Ministries 108

PART THREE: *Ministering to the Youth Sports Industrial Complex*

Chapter 8: Finding the Prophetic Voice of the Church in Youth Sports 125
Chapter 9: "I Want to Be Like Mike":
    Spiritual and Identity Formation in Young People 142
Chapter 10: Youth Sports as Missional Frontier 157
Chapter 11: Redeeming Youth Sports 171

Epilogue 183
Bibliography 185
Scripture Index 195
Name/Subject Index 197

Acknowledgments

In writing this book I have learned much about sports and faith and the relationship between the two. I have also learned a great deal about the incredible circles of support and encouragement that surround me. I haven't won an Academy Award and this is no acceptance speech, but it is a helpful time to pause and outwardly thank some of the people who were vital in helping bring this book into existence.

I usually skim through these acknowledgments and see the shout-outs to the authors' families without giving it much thought, but now that I'm writing a book of my own I have a better appreciation for how much thanksgiving there is to share with my family. Mary Beth, you have been so gracious in giving me the space and support to see this through, and I am a better person because of you. Clark, Clementine, and Cecilia, you are excited to see this in print, and I'm grateful for your patience. If it wasn't for you, this book would have never been written. Always know: I love to watch you play. All three of you gave me opportunities to keep the ideas of this book rooted in the experiences of the real world.

In writing this book, I have been reminded of all that my parents did for me when I was a kid, and I have never told you enough—thank you for watching me play!

Thank you, Alum Creek Church family. Thank you all for being patient with me through this long process. You are simply the best church family I could hope for. Thank you for supporting me in doing what I love, embracing my shortcomings, and lavishing encouragement on my family constantly. You are truly a blessing.

This entire project owes its genesis to Dr. Craig Detweiler, whose class helped inspire this convergence of interests that continue to lead me to new places. Thank you for your constant support of my work.

Acknowledgments

From the outset, I was committed to making this book speak to as many people as possible. To that end, I enlisted a group of readers who have proved to be a vital sounding board throughout this process. Your commitment to me and this book is more encouraging than you will ever know. Special thanks to Dr. Megan Birk for providing an outsider's perspective. Your questions pushed me to think more deeply, and your suggestions made for a better finished project. Stuart Rogers, you also proved to be a tireless reader whose input was more valuable than I am able to convey to you. Mark Spence, thanks for encouraging me the past several years as these ideas were first formulating, I appreciate your friendship and thank you for your encouragement. JP Conway, you also remained a steady voice of encouragement and reassurance that this message is an important one to pursue—thank you! Chris Harrell, thank you for making time to work through the early drafts; your encouragement has been inspiring. Thank you to everyone else who took time to be part of the reading team: Brian, Julie, Mark, Karen, Matt, Tammy, and Robert.

Dr. John Mark Hicks, you provided insightful feedback for chapter 3 and have remained another bedrock of encouragement for my work. Your theological influence on my thinking is undeniable, and your dedication to working as a pastor for pastors is more valuable than you can know.

My good friends and brothers, Nate and Dion—I love you guys and your influence has helped shape every part of this book. Our text thread often gets me through the day.

Through my years at Alum Creek, I have had the wonderful blessing to watch over scores of teenagers whom I have watched play all kinds of sports. I have loved to watch each and every one of you play. Thank you for putting up with me through the years, and to my most recent group of kids—I love all of you and am thankful I get these years with you.

As I write about in this book, I can't help but think of the many people whose paths I have crossed because of sports. To my old coaches, Jeff and Carlos, you helped make sports enjoyable enough for me that I still want to play them all these years later. Thank you to all the parents, who have indulged me with conversations about youth sports these past several years. There is a long list of coaches, officials, fellow parents, and (of course) young people that I know and have known because of sports. You have all helped shape my understanding of this world, and it is because I have had such wonderful experiences that I want others to see sports for the good that it can be.

1

Just a Game

Somewhere in the basement of my house, sitting amidst cobweb-tinged shelves crammed with Christmas decorations, suitcases, half-full cans of paint, and boxes of pre-digital-age photographs is a storage container full of my childhood mementos. Most people, I think, have the same kinds of boxes full of the same kinds of keepsakes. The relics vary, of course, as each one of us has our own unique mementos directly tied to our own unique childhoods. As years have turned to decades, I have watched what was once a collection of several such boxes moved from my parents' house shrink to this one small container. As childhood memories fade like dreams, the collection of must-have memories has been slowly weeded down to the few trinkets most directly tied to the most enduring of my personal recollections. Inside the storage container is a potpourri of items that are as eclectic as a *Jeopardy!* category: the first Bible I was ever given, a baby blanket my mom made for me, a stuffed Cat in the Hat given to me by my great-grandmother one year for Christmas, and even copies of my elementary school grade cards.

Through each family move and every paring down of these mementos to a smaller box, among the reminders of my childhood that I seem to have had the most difficult time parting with is a 1989 Defiance Boys League baseball runner-up trophy. With the exception of a brief foray into both basketball and football (each for one season), the sports of my youth were baseball and soccer. Although my hometown of Defiance, OH, has become a kind of haven for professional baseball talent, I was a case study in mediocrity who never won a championship and was excited just to be on a team that won more games than we lost. The one exception to my entire experience of youth sports was this 1989 Boys League baseball team. Too many years have passed for me to remember all the details of the championship game and the season itself is even foggier in my memories, but I do remember that we overachieved in finishing second place. My old baseball coach Buhrer recently reminded me that we lost the championship game, but it ended under protest due to a base running interference call. Later, the protest was upheld, the game was replayed from the moment of the interference call, and we lost. Again. Even in the midst of that season's disappointing conclusion, I can still remember swelling with pride at having had such a successful season. It may have been a small league with a small number of teams in our small town, but the feeling of victory was anything but small. Back then you only got trophies if you finished in first or second place. It felt as though we had done something and that I was a part of something. It was one of the rare times in my youth that I felt as though I had accomplished something. For a ten-year-old boy, that is just about the best feeling you can ever hope to have.

Even now, far removed from my experiences in youth sports and in addition to the many memories I have of playing soccer and baseball, I have memories of playing basketball and football at my school even though I only played those sports for one season. When I take a step back, it seems ludicrous that these experiences are equally embedded within my memory bank alongside other more important memories like my wedding day, the birth of my children, and my baptism. While these memories of playing sports may not be as important as my other memories, I would be lying if I said they were any less vivid. These memories do, however, seem less absurd in light of former United States President Bill Clinton sharing his memories of playing church league basketball in Arkansas. "One night I was the leading scorer on our team. I scored sixteen points in a church league game, never before or since . . . and I nearly dunked the ball!"[1] If, after serving two terms as the President of the United States, Bill Clinton can still remember scoring sixteen points in a meaningless church league basketball game, then I feel at least partially justified for hanging on to my second-place Boy's League trophy for all these years. It is difficult to overstate the significance sports plays in the lives of young people.

When I wasn't playing sports, I was watching sports. Cheering on my teams to win championships (which they seldom did) and celebrating their victories with my peers was a big part of my experience growing up. In

1. Merica, "Bill Clinton Relives His Athletic Glory Days."

many ways, my playing sports felt like a connection to the professionals that I loved to watch on television. It is difficult to disentangle memories of my youth from either playing sports or watching my favorite teams play sports. It would be disingenuous to say sports were a hobby for me, something I enjoyed in my leisure time, and nothing I took too seriously. If I am being honest, sports has been a big part of who I am for a long time.

When cheering for a losing team, a better man might just shrug his shoulders and say, "We'll get them next year," and move on to weightier aspects of life. I'm not proud to admit that when the Indians lost the World Series in 1997 I was in a bad mood for a week, or that I had trouble sleeping the night before the Cubs-Indians World Series Game 7 in 2016. I would feel like a better Christian if I could dismiss the fact that these memories had a truly formative effect on my life. What kind of holy man or holy woman gets rattled from the results of a sporting contest? Probably the kind that holds on to a baseball trophy from when he was ten years old. The reality, however, is that in 1997 and in 2016, when the Indians lost the World Series, it affected my mood for several days and has remained emblazoned among my most significant memories. I had a wonderful childhood and often recall many fond memories, but I have held on to that Boy's League trophy for all these years because something special happened on that day.

This is the same realization that Catholic philosopher Michael Novak ponders in his classic book on sports and religion when he asks of himself (perhaps half-pondering and half-confessing), "How could I be forty years old and still care what happens to the Dodgers?"[2] Novak's question was provoked by reflecting upon professional sports, but today's world of amateur sports, particularly among young people, provides a rich opportunity for revisiting careful, critical reflection on the role sports play in our society.

Sports are taking over the lives of families with young athletes in unprecedented fashion. It has gotten so out of control that the Tennessee State legislature had to pass a law in 2017 that forbids school sports teams to mandate practice on holidays, weekends, or religious holidays.[3] This book is written for Christians who feel unprepared for and at a loss to deal with a youth sports scene that seems to be spiraling out of control.

Seven years ago, I innocently walked into a new stage of my life with sports when my wife and I signed up our four-year-old son, the oldest of

---

2. Novak, *The Joy of Sports*, xi.

3. Cook, " Tennessee Law First To Address Sports Parents' Desires To Sit Kids For Religious And School Holidays."

three, to play T-ball in our local community league. The subsequent years have seen all three of our children involved in a variety of sports: baseball, softball, basketball, football, swimming, soccer, and dance (so far). Suddenly, my wife and I have become confronted with new realities of sports that I never had to deal with in my bygone sports days: paying league fees, regularly buying new equipment for our constantly-growing kids, managing practice schedules for three different children, dealing with the diverse personalities and styles of coaches, making decisions as to which leagues to sign up for, and the ever-present reality of the politics present in youth sports. The logistical challenges are real, but they often pale in comparison to the unique psychological and spiritual challenges that come from being a sports parent. Now I am learning to consider things like how much pressure I put on my children to succeed in athletics, how my behavior from the sidelines and from the stands affects them, how to find a healthy balance between inactivity and over-scheduling, and the spiritual impact sports' schedules have on their identity formation. As we dove headfirst into the experience of youth sports, we found countless parents who are struggling with many of the same challenges we were.

As much as we try to tell ourselves and our children that sports are just a game, the effects and ramifications that accompany sports seem impossible to dismiss as simply just a game. My children know that I have held on to that Boy's League trophy all these years. They are also aware of how all-consuming their sports' schedules become with each passing season, and they are increasingly aware of the financial burden sports become to our family's budget. Some of my fondest memories and some of our best family time have occurred around sporting events. My purpose in writing this book is not to dismiss sports in their entirety. As we will see, I believe sports have a crucial role in our lives and, especially, in the lives of young people. However, when we stop and consider how much of our time, money, and attention sports demand, it is difficult to dismiss them as just a game. Christians must begin to take more seriously the implications of their involvement in sports, and my hope is this book will offer a significant step forward in doing that.

JUST A GAME?

On one hand, this familiar refrain serves as an important reminder for amateur athletes and sports fans everywhere as to the proper place of sports in life. To remark, "It's *just* a game," is to remind participants and spectators alike that the game is not the most important experience in a person's life. This declaration suggests that sports lack the significance and sophistication of the world's more serious matters like politics, religion, education, science, or economics. Sports, according to this line of thinking, exist as a welcome respite from these much more complex and significant matters. During the contentious 2016 Presidential election, I often turned to sports radio because I knew most of the talk-show hosts would avoid political conversations. People are seldom comfortable in the mingling of politics and religion, but the mixing of sports and politics or religion is often viewed with similar angst.

On the other hand, to minimize the importance of sports in this way seems to woefully understate the actual experiences that both athletes and spectators have during sporting contests. Beyond that, it seriously undermines the effect sports do have on the most significant and complex aspects of culture. When American gold and bronze medalists John Carlos and Tommie Smith thrust their black-gloved hands into the air atop the Olympic podium in Mexico City in 1968, were they part of *just* a game? Do over 100,000 fans show up on a Saturday afternoon to watch *just* a game? Do families enroll their toddlers in sports clinics and their teenagers in elite sports leagues to play *just* a game? Can a teenage girl who bursts into tears as she walks across the field to play the final game of her high school career be convinced that this is *just* a game?

As hard as we may try to sell the idea to our athletes (and to ourselves) that their chosen sport is just a game, all other evidence surrounding the game seems to indicate that they are much more. Few realities carry the same cultural swagger in the United States that sports do. CBS pays the NCAA over one billion dollars a year to broadcast the NCAA Men's Basketball tournament on its family of networks every March. Celebrity athletes are paid millions of dollars for the clothes they wear, products they use, and food they eat. Cities often look to sports for justification of their status as a major city—"the more teams you have . . . the more major league you are."[4] When we regularly read news reports of parents assaulting other parents in the stands of their children's sporting events, witness coaches berating game officials at youth leagues, and hear about countless cheating scandals involving everything from birth certificates to performance enhancing

---

4. Delaney and Eckstein, "Public Dollars, Private Stadiums, and Democracy," 13.

drugs at nearly every level of competition, it is difficult to sell the message that sports is *just* a game.

Playing Games in the United States

The desire to minimize the role of sports and games in the lives of young people is rooted in the notion of play. Philosophically, play is often said to be *autotelic*—an action done simply for its own sake. In *A Brief Theology of Sport*, Lincoln Harvey describes play as "radically non-productive, a passing event in which time, energy, and skill are invested for no apparent reason."[5] This is fully on display when children are told by their parents, "Go play." Upon returning from play, the children's parents are not expecting a full report or even to see evidence of what the children's play accomplished because play, in and of itself, fulfilled its goal. British theologian Robert Ellis pushes the notion a bit further by suggesting play is more than simply an end in and of itself, but that it is something that we enjoy for its own sake—something he describes as *autocharatic*.[6] The next chapter dives into the nuances of this conversation, but at this point suffice it to say that both descriptions, whether trying to frame sports as *autotelic* or *autocharatic*, are simply sophisticated ways of describing sports as just a game.

Athletic scholarships have become the treasure at the end of the rainbow for countless families caught up in the youth sports arms race, and in large part, pursuing them has come to dictate much of the way in which youth sports operates. If playing sports is intended to be *autotelic*, then playing sports in hopes of one day earning a scholarship betrays the very nature of play. The pilgrimage to elusive scholarships is beginning to occur at earlier ages and is accompanied by more intense specialization. Furthermore, the life of American families increasingly beats to the rhythm of sports commitments to the detriment of all their other social connections—especially their faith communities. Families can't load up their SUVs every weekend, drive hundreds of miles, check into hotels for weeks at a time, spend tens of thousands of dollars a year, and then try to convince their children that their sport isn't that important. Quite the contrary, as a father who expects to pay $90,000 on his son's basketball career told author Tom Farrey, "If a kid comes up to you and says he wants to be a doctor, do you tell him he's not smart enough? Or that it's too expensive? Do you

---

5. Harvey, *A Brief Theology of Sport*, 68.
6. Ellis, *The Games People Play*, 266.

shoot that dream down? Or do you try and help him attain it?"[7] While professional and big-time college sports have long included elements clearly distinct from backyard play and neighborhood sports, the line between professional and recreational continues to blur even within youth sports. Youth sports operating under titles of club, academy, premiere, select, elite, and travel are robbing sports of their *autotelic* and *autocharatic* functions and are making them the means toward a prestigious end.

Although less than one percent of college players will ever have an opportunity to play sports professionally[8] and only two percent of high-school players receive a Division 1 scholarship,[9] playing sports as children is still one of the most common social experiences in the United States. Family-friendly movies from the 1990s, *The Sandlot* and *The Mighty Ducks*, glamorize the glory days of backyard baseball in Southern California in the 1960s and the world of youth hockey, respectively. More recently, the movie-turned-successful-television-series, *Friday Night Lights*, is set against the backdrop of Americana on display in Friday-night high-school football in Texas. These shows have been so well-received, in part, because they are set against the backdrop of life scenarios that are so relate-able to a large number of the general population. While an infinitesimally small group of athletes ever plays sports at the highest levels, the race to get there takes up an inordinate amount of time and attention from families throughout the country.

Evidence of children's games pervades every community in the United States: from basketball courts to baseball diamonds, from soccer fields to swimming pools. In 2004, the co-host of the cable morning show *Fox and Friends*, Brian Kilmeade, published the book *The Games Do Count*, a collection of firsthand reflections on playing youth sports by some of America's best known celebrities and most successful politicians. As the famous running back for the Cleveland Browns, Jim Brown, says in the Foreword: "We're all human beings and the experiences we have playing sports as kids are indelibly written on our minds, and although we grow up, we never grow past them."[10] Youth sports are so fundamental to the American psyche that they have long been integrally tied to its educational system. Whether one is a sports fan or not, completely avoiding exposure to them is nearly

---

7. Farrey, *Game On*, 23.
8. Manfred. "Here are the Odds your Kid Becomes a Professional Athlete."
9. O'Shaughnessey, "8 Things You Should Know about Sports Scholarships."
10. Brown, "Foreward," ix.

impossible in the United States. Novak recounts comments made by James Weschler that aptly describe those who do not relate to sports: "The country seems divided between those caught up in the frenzy [of sports] and those who could not care less. In many places, the latter must feel like aliens."[11] It is this ubiquity of the sporting experience that helps make it such a powerful force within American culture.

Playing Games in Church

In the earliest days of organized sports in the United States, Christians often struggled to reconcile their faith with sports. Sports were most often grouped with games and other recreational experiences that were regularly seen by Puritan ministers as frivolous and counter-productive to the Christian ethic. Reflecting on this early antagonism towards sports among Christians, Robert Higgs writes, "Historical records do reflect a suspicion of recreation that today strikes us as ludicrous."[12] As sports and games grew in their popularity and became more organized, however, they proved to be an unstoppable cultural force that led many Christians to adopt the philosophy, "If you can't beat them, join them."

The late part of the nineteenth and early part of the twentieth centuries saw the inception and rapid burgeoning of Christian ministries that focused specifically on sports. Capitalizing on the popularity of sports, these parachurch ministries used sports as a chief socializing agent by which to proselytize non-Christians. It is difficult to overstate the turnaround of the church's impression of sports over this time period. Shirl Hoffman summarizes: "It was a remarkable reversal: in the span of a half-century, large segments of the Protestant community, long society's self-appointed suppressors of play, had overcome their suspicions and done an about-face on the sports issue."[13] Incredibly, what once was a chastised and despised activity of American culture became legitimized to the point that the church not only accepted it, but began using it as a platform for evangelism. While sports may be just a game, they also have become a setting where countless people have been introduced to the stories of Jesus and many have made lifelong commitments to him as their Savior.

---

11. Brown, "Foreward," xi.
12. Higgs, *God in the Stadium*, 8.
13. Hoffman, *Good Game*, 102.

Organizations like the Fellowship of Christian Athletes (FCA), Athletes in Action (AIA), and, probably the most widely known, Young Men's Christian Association (YMCA) have emerged as significant institutions, uniquely serving at the intersection of the Christian faith and sports. More recently, universities have begun to offer degree programs in sports chaplaincy, mega-churches have built on-site athletic facilities and created roles for full-time recreation pastors to manage their sports leagues and facilities, and additional sports ministries continue to emerge and thrive—the most successful recent example being Upwards Sports. During this time, sports have been seen largely as theologically neutral and simply a means to an end (sharing the gospel). These organizations have tended to focus on the platform created by sports participation rather than on various ethical and systemic aspects of the sports themselves (more on this in chapter 8).

Within the last decade or so, Christians have begun to take more seriously the role that sports play in society and the relationship they have with the Christian faith. Professional sports and big-time college sports in the United States (most notably football and basketball) have evolved into exceptionally powerful economic forces. Professional sports teams often play in stadiums that were constructed with publicly-funded tax money, and owners often leverage the significance of the local team by threatening to move if tax issues are voted down. Chronic Traumatic Encephalopathy (CTE) has awakened the nation's conscience when it comes to the head trauma many athletes regularly subject themselves to, and it has prompted critical reflection on a host of related ethical issues. Racial disparity among professional sports league personnel, coaches, administrators, and owners helps keep professional sports at the forefront of conversations regarding race relations in the United States. Although the United States government passed Title IX in 1972, which marked a major move forward for women's equality with men in sports, there remains a constant uphill battle for gender equality across the sports' spectrum. These issues and many others have helped the church awaken to the fact that, while it is important to keep sports in its proper place, it is clearly much more significant than just a game. Although professional sports receive the majority of critical attention, youth sports most directly affect the lives of the majority of young people. For that reason alone, it is one area most in need of serious theological and pastoral reflection.

Elite?

THE UBIQUITY OF YOUTH SPORTS AND THE MINISTRY OF THE CHURCH

Walk through the parking lots of superstores, trendy shopping malls, or fast-casual food chains that comprise the American, suburban landscape, and it will be nearly impossible to pass through an aisle without seeing a parked SUV or minivan that, along with their child's number, dons stickers of allegiance to some local or regional youth sports team. The evidence of just how big youth sports in the United States has become is everywhere. Teams can be seen checking into hotels in cities throughout the country, team caravans are on nearly every highway and interstate (especially holiday weekends), and tournaments are held at parks and gymnasiums in almost every town and city. Advertisements for tryouts, leagues, and tournaments can be spotted in front of schools while teams are constantly fighting and politicking for use of their community's fields and open spaces. They can even be seen on television as it is common to see high school football games broadcast nationally, and ABC has broadcast the Little League World Series since 1962. In a 2013 article, authors Bruce Kelley and Carl Carchia aptly capture the breadth of youth sports, "Youth sports is so big that no one knows quite how big it is."[14] Furthermore, ESPN journalist-turned-youth-sports-activist, Tom Farrey, acknowledges, "For the largest number of kids, sports are their primary organized activity outside of school."[15] Considering this nearly ubiquitous experience among young people, it is imperative for the church to provide a critical look at the implications this world has on the faith of young people.[16]

Sports have been a dynamic part of every community I have been a part of: from Defiance High School in Ohio, to Lipscomb University in Tennessee, and, especially over the past fourteen years, in Columbus, Ohio.

---

14. Kelley and Carchia, "Hey, Data, Data—Swing!"

15. Farrey, *Game On*, 14.

16. Clearly, not every young person plays organized sports. There are countless other hobbies, interests, and extracurricular programs available for young people: Boy Scouts, Girl Scouts, music, art, drama, outdoor education, computer programming, gaming, among countless others. In focusing on youth sports, this book is not making the case that sports are somehow more significant or beneficial than other hobbies or extracurricular programs. Countless non-sports-related school clubs and programs deserve more attention and participation, and many of these kinds of opportunities would be better supported if not for the popularity of youth sports. The world could use more young poets, outdoor adventurers, musicians, and computer programmers, but that is another subject for another day.

Personally, I have turned to sports as a means to stay healthy and active, as a way to promote a healthy lifestyle within my children, and I have experienced a social component in sports that brings communities together in a way that almost nothing else does. My family has made great friendships through our experiences in sports, we have a better appreciation for and connection to our community than we would if we did not participate in our neighborhood's sports programs, and through my work as a high school football official, I have been able to serve my community in a unique and meaningful way for over fifteen years.

My experience in youth ministry for the past twenty years has provided a window into the many challenges that sports present to Christian families whose children play sports. The continuing evolution of elite and travel sports leagues provide a more complex backdrop against which families are facing increasingly difficult challenges regarding their commitment to sports. Participating in sports seems to have become more challenging for Christian families over the past several years. There is a growing number of leaders from across academic disciplines and throughout a variety of sports-related fields who are beginning to sound the alarm that there is much about youth sports in the United States that needs attention and reform.

My love for sports and theology, my dedication to my family and to God, and my experience in vocational ministry led me to write this book. Having studied youth sports over the last several years, it has become clear many people share the same concerns and frustrations. I have lost count of the number of times I have struck up a conversation with parents whose child is caught up in a sport, and they feel a mixture of feelings ranging from fear to frustration, and anger to exhaustion. Countless parents are looking for someone to talk to about the challenges their family faces with their sports commitments. In many ways, I am writing this book to let these parents know they are not alone.

I write this book as an aging athlete who struggles, but longs, to find the time to be more physically active. I have run two half-marathons, enjoy playing catch and shooting hoops with my children as often as I can, spend Friday nights in the fall officiating high school football games, help coach my children's sports teams, and fill much of my free time with various kinds of sports-related activities. I write as a parent who knows firsthand the financial pressures and stressful time commitments that accompany having active children in sports. I write as a Christian who takes my faith seriously, desires to be a godly leader within my family, and who regularly feels at least some tension between my commitment to Jesus and my commitments to sports. I write as a pastor of a small church who works with teenagers and has watched countless families with children at one time or another come face to face with the feeling of having to choose between serving God and serving sports.

AT THE NEXUS OF SPORTS AND FAITH

It has become clear to me that Christians have mostly participated in sports without significant reflection on the implications to their faith. This is not so much an indictment, but rather an observation. The church has offered very little critical theological reflection until recently, and the purpose of this manifesto is to bring much needed attention specifically to the world of youth sports. There are two extremes between which I will be navigating. At one end, it is easy to blindly accept sports as it is and ignore its many shortcomings (an extreme most often on display in the church today). At the other end, an overreaction to the other extreme is to sweepingly dismiss everything about sports and ignore its many positive attributes. As we will see, the flaws in youth sports today are seldom in the sports themselves but embedded within the systems and practices that have been built up around them.

This book is divided into three parts, and each part addresses a unique aspect of some of the more pressing issues in the relationship between youth sports and the Christian faith. Part 1 presents the theological framework of the book. Chapter 2 offers a theology of sports rooted in the concept of play and originated in the creative order described in Genesis 1–2. Chapter 3 provides a theological foundation for understanding the oft-neglected topic of competition and highlights the proclivity towards sin that is embedded in many competitive environments. Competition has been a central player in the growth of club, select, elite, and travel youth sports. Chapter 4 focuses on the social entities that make up youth sports. Relying on the work of pioneers like Walter Wink and William Stringfellow, this chapter explores the implications of counting sports among the spiritual powers. Understanding sports as a spiritual power helps parents understand why they often feel helpless and without a voice in the face of existing youth sports programs.

Part 2 focuses on the current state of youth sports in the United States. Chapter 5 provides a broadly-painted picture of contemporary institutions, organizations, and governing agencies ruling the world of youth sports. President Eisenhower once warned the country to guard against the military-industrial complex, and chapter 5 applies Eisenhower's words to the sociological juggernaut that the youth-sports industry has become. Chapter 6 considers some pressing implications the industrialization of youth sports is having on Christians and their communities. Chapter 7 describes some of the unique contributions parachurch sports ministries have made to the youth-sports industrial complex in the United States over the past century while also suggesting some theological blind spots these same groups have perpetuated.

Part 3 focuses on some pastoral implications for the church as it engages the youth-sports industrial complex. Chapter 8 reflects on the prophetic role the church has in youth sports and encourages Christians to seek out ways they can minister to young people who are often overlooked and neglected by the current practices of sports leagues and organizations. Chapter 9 tackles one of the key issues at stake in the lives of young people: spiritual formation. As teenagers navigate the challenging years of adolescence, few activities or experiences are as formative as sports. This chapter discusses the challenges that sports present to families and suggests ways that our children can strive to "be like Jesus" and not only to "be like Mike." Chapter 10 offers a new vision for how Christians engage in sports by seeing sports as an important gateway into local communities. Too many Christian families are allowing sports to alienate themselves from their local community through travel leagues and elite teams, rather than seeing sports as an opportunity to more deeply invest themselves within their existing community. This chapter encourages Christians to commit to their neighborhood and recreation leagues and envisions a world where Christians see their local community as a primary mission field.

Chapter 11 concludes by offering practical ways Christians who love sports can best serve God with passion. The opportunities for Christians to participate in the youth sports machine are numerous and offer meaningful ways to establish vital connection with the local community. Sports provide one of the richest environments for Christians to live life alongside their fellow neighbors and citizens. Christians should be just as deliberate in participating in sports as they are in every other aspect of life. With this book, I hope to encourage Christians to seek a way to live out their love and passion for sports in a way that embraces playfulness, engages their community, embodies spirituality, and never supplants their identity in Christ.

PART 1

A Theology of Sports

Pondering how Greek thought and philosophy might relate to Christianity and the Bible, the early church father Tertullian famously asked, "What does Athens have to do with Jerusalem?" Following Tertullian's lead in approaching the topic of youth sports, we might ask, "What does the Little League World Series or high school football have to do with Jerusalem?" Although few cultural practices are more universal than sports, the church has seldom provided thoughtful reflection as to how sport relates to the core theological doctrines of the church.

It has been common for Christian athletes and sports ministries to latch on to some of Paul's athletically-inspired Bible verses as encouragement and justification for sports. Actual, critical engagement between sports-related topics and the Bible, however, has been rare from the most revered theological circles as much as sports ministry leaders. The tide is beginning to turn, though, and in recent years Christian theologians and Christian scholars from disciplines related to sports have begun to address this neglected topic. Before turning our attention specifically to youth sports, Part 1 focuses on the broader theological concerns that are prompted by the playing of sports, like the role of play in creation, the relationship between play and Sabbath, the role of competition, and the systemic challenges created by the powers that manage sports. Before answering the many difficult pastoral questions prompted by sports, we must first undertake the challenging and exciting task of theology.

2

Playing Games: A Theology for Sports

On October 30, 2002, after the Cleveland Browns handed the New York Jets their fifth loss in seven games, Jets coach Herman Edwards went on a postgame rant that, thanks to social media, has become a famous part of sports lore. The outspoken head coach of the New York Jets was asked about his team's inability to win. He responded with a sound bite that continues to be played today on sports networks and seems to be on everyone's list of "Most Memorable Postgame Press Conferences of All Time."

> This is what the greatest thing about sports is. You play to win the game. Hello! You play to win the game. You don't play just to play it. That's the great thing about sports. You play to win. And I don't care if you don't have any wins, you play to win the game. When you start telling me it doesn't matter, then retire. Get out, because it matters.[1]

In many ways, Edwards's statement, "You play to win the game" is nothing more than an updated version of the more famous credo, "Winning isn't everything; it's the only thing." This famous statement is usually attributed to former Green Bay Packers head coach Vince Lombardi, but more accurately can be attributed to former college football coach Red Sanders.[2] Regardless of the origin of the quotation, the statement, along with the ethos it represents, has stood entrenched among the most precious and true of all alluring American myths. A dynamic example of the scope of this American belief came during Donald Trump's 2016 campaign leading up

1. Herman Edwards, NFL postgame interview, October 30, 2002.
2. Overman, "Winning Isn't Everything. It's the Only Thing!," 81–85.

to his election as President of the United States. Throughout the campaign, one of his most oft-recited critiques of the United States was that, "We don't win anymore." This posture of winning at all costs seems to be a natural derivative of American exceptionalism itself.

Herman Edwards's reductionist belief that "we play to win the game" is easier to stomach in reference to professional athletes whose "play" has become professionalized, but it seems as though Edwards's philosophy has equally won the day in youth sports. Winning and losing are clearly crucial aspects of sports, but to limit the purpose of sports to the outcome of its contests is to severely undermine a much deeper philosophical and theological rationale that so enamors us to our games. Note the tension between Edwards's rant and the leader of the modern Olympic movement, Pierre de Coubertin, who opened the 1908 Olympic Games in London with this famous statement, "The important thing in the Olympic Games is not to win, but to take part."[3] Competition has come to serve as the foundational and organizational principle of sports at all levels in the United States, and it has done so largely to the detriment of play. Because it is my assertion that competition has replaced the spirit of play, and that theology has a role in both explaining and repairing this breach, it is vital to understand the differences between play and sport. This chapter seeks to establish a theological purpose of sports beyond competition by beginning with an investigation into the theology of play.

PURPOSES AND OBJECTIVES IN GAMES

Although the specific objectives of games vary, nearly every game has an objective similar to football as stated in the first rule in the National Federation of High Schools Football rulebook: "The game is won by the team which accumulates the most points."[4] In all the baseball games and soccer games I played in my youth, we were always trying to score more than the other team. In most of those games, the other team scored more than us, but I can honestly say that in those games when my team won, the game seemed more fun. In one sense, it *is* more fun to win than to lose (as is often stated), but something more dynamic than fun seems to be at work in those games. A more accurate description is that winning seems more satisfying

---

3. Quoted in Lynch, *Let Them Play*, 18.
4. Colgate, 2016 NFHS Football Rules Book, Rule 1, Article 1.

and even fulfilling. The game feels more right when we win. Thus, in that manner of speaking, we do play to win the game.

It would be absurd to watch two opposing teams playing to lose. Equally outrageous would be watching one team trying to lose against another team playing to win.[5] Even the famous consummate-losing opponent of the Harlem Globetrotters, the Washington Generals, played to win. While Globetrotter basketball games have always been one-part sporting event, two-part show business production, at the heart of the show was always a basketball game between a gifted basketball team full of players with over-the-top skills and a competitively average counterpart devoid of the Globetrotter flash. Everyone who ever watched a Globetrotters game knew the Generals would lose. With the notable exception of January 25, 1971 when the Generals actually did defeat the Globetrotters 100–99, the Generals lost an astounding 14,000 times in their famous matchups against the Globetrotters before the Globetrotters dropped them as their regular opponent in 2015.[6] Although the Generals were expected to lose (and to some degree were actually paid to lose), the plausibility of the game required their effort. As NBC Sports columnist Joe Posnaski writes, "The team's purpose was to PLAY the Globetrotters, the purpose was not to LOSE to the Globetrotters. Weird as it sounds, the Generals were always playing to win."[7] Thus, the integrity of any game (even if a team is expected to lose) is directly tied to the players upholding the stated objective of a game: winning. While the Washington Generals always played to win the game, they also played in order to entertain the spectators. In reality, there are many reasons why we play.

Every game is governed by rules of play, and inherent in the rules of play is a stated objective. The objective in most sports is to score more points than the opponent, the objective in the board game Monopoly is to amass a larger fortune than the other players, and the objective of the video game Angry Birds is to kill all the green pigs. On one level and in concert with Coach Edwards's postgame remarks, these objectives speak to the reason behind playing. More realistically, however, I may play soccer

---

5. This is exactly what happened in a 2002 soccer match in Madagascar. In protest of what they believed to be a biased officiating call in a previous match, the Stade Olympique l'Emyrne soccer club scored a world record 149 own goals against AS Adema. The final score was 149–0, and angry spectators demanded their money following the game. Reuters, "Team Repeatedly Scores Own Goals to Protest Refs."

6. McKenna, "How Red Klotz, 14,000-Time Loser, Beat the Harlem Globetrotters."

7. Posnaski, "Loser's Lament."

to improve my physical health, play Monopoly with my family because it is raining outside, or play Angry Birds on my phone because I am waiting for my dentist appointment. There are objectives that govern the rules of play, but in a broader sense, there are more fundamental purposes that lead us to play. It is the reason why 90 percent of young people would rather play for a losing team than sit the bench for a winning team.[8] For all the focus on winning and losing, at the heart of all sports and games is the desire to play.

PLAYING SPORTS

Embedded in the very linguistics of sports in the English language, the phrase "playing sports" illustrates a relationship between play and sports. All sports have some affinity to play, but not all play is manifested through sports. Sports, as with games, introduce structure to play in varying degrees. Although play does not cease being play with the implementation of structure, the nature of play is altered. Oxford theology professor Robert Ellis argues that, "in play we are creators while in sport we are creatures."[9] Sports is differentiated from play in the participants' submission to established or agreed-upon structures, and the freedom from structure and rules is most often what draws us to play. As a result, sports embodies a distinct manifestation of play and, at a more complex level, precludes itself from some widely held assumptions regarding play.

For example, two of Roger Callois's well-known criteria for play do not easily reconcile with the most developed examples of sports: the idea that play is both unproductive and free.[10] Almost every parent can relate to rolling a ball back and forth with their toddler. It is a clear example of play: free of any inherent objective beyond the enjoyment and fun of the moment (free and unproductive). However, as the toddler continues to develop both physically and mentally, the act of rolling or tossing a ball back and forth with a parent might expand (depending on the social environment and developmental capacity) to the inclusion of a bat, a field, a glove, and eventually will be accompanied by rules and new objectives like hitting and catching the ball. Ultimately, the child's play might evolve to include even more complex rules regarding the scoring of runs, holding runners on base, throwing balls and strikes, and perhaps concluding with learning

---

8. O'Sullivan, "Why Kids Quit Sports."
9. Ellis, *The Games People Play*, 141.
10. Caillois, *Man, Play, and Games*, 9–10.

the nuance of a balk. What originates as a free and unproductive game of catch evolves into a more complex game (along the lines of sociological traditions) with stated objectives and a less free environment. For example, in order to play in a game with others, the child must learn that shortstops play in the infield between second and third base and not wherever he or she "freely" may choose to play. Thus, the increasing of structure and the lessening of freedom does not necessitate that play stops functioning in a given activity; however, it seems that the nature of play drastically changes as it becomes more structured.

Ellis lists four features that distinguish sports from play and provides a helpful designation between the two: "sports is a form of bureaucratized play," "sports is play dictated by the element of *agon*/competition," "sport is an embodied contest of physical and mental exertion," and playing sports requires skill that can be refined by practice.[11] Described this way, play is a broader category over which sports can be categorized and subsequently all manifestations of sports at all levels may not maintain the characteristics of play. Although a local Little League baseball game resembles a professional baseball game in that anyone can tell they are playing the same game, the extent to which the lives of professionals revolve around their games (not to mention the increased stakes of the outcome of the game) illustrates that, somewhere along the line, play evolves into something different. At some point the participatory game which appeals to only family and friends of the players, develops into, according to the metaphor used by Drexel University professor Ronald Bishop, "a spectacle [that] helps viewers forget their troubles."[12] Interestingly, it seems with the industrialization of youth sports the "spectacle of sports" no longer exists exclusively in the world of professional sports.

John O'Sullivan is a former collegiate and professional soccer coach who has taken on the mission of transforming youth sports in the United States and has become one of the leading voices in addressing the broken system.[13] In 2014 he published the groundbreaking book *Changing the Game*, a title that he has also assigned to his organization that advocates for change in youth sports. He begins his bestselling book by describing two

---

11. Ellis, *The Games People Play*, 127–29.
12. Bishop, *When Play was Play*, 41.
13. O'Sullivan presented a TED talk on the subject of youth sports in 2014 entitled "Changing the Game in Youth Sports" and is available, along with many other important resources, at the Changing the Game website, changingthegame.com.

very different soccer games that were occurring simultaneously at a local park. Notice the presence of play in one game and the absence in another in this familiar scene.

> The other day as I lay on the sideline soaking up some fall sun and watching my six-year-old daughter's soccer game, I could not help but smile. As the girls laughed and giggled their way up and down the field, trying and failing, falling and getting up, I was witnessing pure joy and exuberance. The parents clapped and cheered, the coaches hustled to keep the ball in play, and everyone involved doled out high fives and cries of "great game" to players on both teams. When my daughter's teammate scored, her teammates all gave her hugs. Then all the girls on the other team gave her a hug. This was youth sports in its quintessential form: pure, unadulterated fun for everyone.
>
> Then I glanced at the field next door, where some ten-year-old boys were playing. As the boys threw themselves about, the parents screamed and yelled to "get up," "get back," "pass it," "shoot it," "hustle!" The coaches screamed at the players, everyone screamed at the referee, and no one was smiling. Unless, of course, there was a goal, at which point the goal scorer would glance to the sideline to see if mom and dad approved. At the same time, the guilty party on the opposing team would put his head down and sulk back to the kickoff while receiving the third degree from his coach and the accompanying groans and moans from the "home fans."
>
> As I sat there, I could not help but wonder: Where did it all go wrong? How did we get from here to there? When and why did we take the joy and romance out of youth sports between the ages of six and ten? Is anyone here watching my daughter's game looking across the way and saying, "I want this experience to become like that?" The answer is a resounding no.[14]

I would add to O'Sullivan's list of questions, "When did they stop *playing* sports?" Anyone who has watched youth sports games can relate to his description. The fervor, passion, and even insanity that has long been associated with sports at the highest levels seems to have matriculated down to younger and younger games.

This experience highlights the need for deeper reflection on the purpose behind playing sports. At one time or another in their experience of youth sports, most parents ask themselves, "Why are we doing this?" Robert Ellis provides a helpful framework for engaging the Christian Scriptures

---

14. O'Sullivan, *Changing the Game*, 3–4.

and shifts the focus to the broader subject of play. As Fuller Seminary professor Robert Johnston writes in his important book on play (a foundational project upon which much of Ellis's argument is built), "The evidence for 'play' in the Bible is extensive."[15] Johnston highlights the neglected use of play in the Bible including its use by the authors of the Wisdom Literature, the way it is embodied in the regular cultic feasts and celebrations of Israel (particularly Sabbath), and how it is exemplified within the friendships of Jesus as told in the Gospels.[16] It is important to establish a solid theological framework for understanding play before moving on to some of the specific challenges created by today's youth-sports industrial complex.[17]

PLAY AND THE BIBLICAL NARRATIVE

The Mosaic Law gives attention to many intricacies of the Israelites' personal lives: dietary restrictions, business transactions, sexual conduct, personal hygiene, and even specific instructions regarding women's menstrual cycles. Considering all of this attention to their personal lives, it is striking that Israel was not given a single instruction regarding their practices of recreation. While it would not be possible for any text to provide explicit teaching on every aspect of the innumerable complexities of a given society (not even the United States law code), the ubiquity of play in culture (specifically, sports) makes the Bible's silence noteworthy. Gary Warner, a longtime sports-ministry leader notes that the neglect is not limited to the Old Testament, "If one wishes to point a finger at God for leaving anything out of the New Testament, it could be in the area of play."[18]

Within the creation narrative, two purposes of God's chief creation emerge: work and rest. The male and female were created in God's image, *imago dei*, and they were given a job to do, "to work and take care of [the Garden]" (Gen 2:15). There is great significance in realizing that work was part of God's creative intent before the Fall. Yale professor of theology Miroslav Volf speaks directly to the place of work in the creation account.

---

15. Johnston, *The Christian at Play*, 123.

16. Johnston, *The Christian at Play*, 83–124.

17. See chapter 4, "Play: A Biblical Mandate," in Johnston, *The Christian at Play*, 83–124, and chapter 4, "Play and Sport: Initial Theological Explorations," in Ellis, *The Games People Play*, 123–64.

18. Warner, *Competition*, 196.

> The account starts with the statement that "there was no man to till the ground" (Gen. 2:5) and concludes with the statement that God sent the first human pair out of the garden of Eden to "till the ground from which they were taken" (Gen. 3:23) . . . It is therefore correct to say that, according to Genesis 2, the work of human beings belongs to the very purpose for which God originally made them.[19]

Following Adam and Eve's sin, work becomes challenging as personified by the toil and sweat of the Genesis 3 curse, but the pre-Fall purpose remains: humans have been imbued with the purpose of work.

Although God created the man and the woman to work, and work has a central place in the purposes of God for his creation, work is not presented as if it is their sole purpose. God also works in his creative actions in Genesis (Ellis refers to God's work in creation as "working play"), but even God is not limited to the task of working.[20] "By the seventh day God had finished the work he had been doing; so on the seventh day he rested from his work" (Gen 2:2). In bearing the image of Yahweh, the man and woman do find their purpose in work, but they are also created to rest. Bound up in the Old Testament reality of Sabbath rest was both rest and worship. While it pushes too far to extract worship from the Old Testament's understanding of work (none of these categories exist exclusive of the others), the Sabbath emphasized a time specifically devoted to worship.

The Torah prescribes a six-day work week followed by a mandatory Sabbath day, creating a six-day/one-day rhythm that permeates all of the Old Testament. Enumerated among the Ten Commandments, the Sabbath stands as a foundational principle for Israel rooted in the two chief events in Israel's history: the creation of the cosmos (Exod 20:11) and God's deliverance of Israel from the Egyptians (Deut 5:15). Incidentally, both of these events also serve as chief inspirations for Old Testament worship. Tim Keller, former pastor of Redeemer Presbyterian Church in Manhattan, believes Sabbath holds the world in check. "Work is not all there is to life. You will not have a meaningful life without work, but you cannot say that your work is *the* meaning of your life."[21] Eugene Peterson reflects on the Sabbath stating, "Without Sabbath, in which God goes beyond the workplace (but not away from it), the workplace is soon emptied of any sense of the

---

19. Volf, *Work in the Spirit*, 127–28.
20. Ellis, *The Games People Play*, 148.
21. Keller, *Every Good Endeavor*, 40.

presence of God and the work becomes an end in itself."[22] Thus, work and rest have a kind of symbiotic relationship with each other.

The dual categories of work and rest help describe a vast majority of human activity. Work includes accounting, landscaping, the assembly line, plumbing, household duties, upper management, and countless other examples of vocations and chores in which we are contemporaneously "tending and taking care of the Garden." Rest includes, but is not limited to watching television, sleeping, reading, meditating, praying, journaling, singing, and countless other activities of relaxation and reflection that help remind us of the presence of God. While these two categories do cover a multitude of human endeavors, there still remains a great number of activities (activities that are among what Johan Huizinga considers "the most fundamental in life"[23]) that do not fit neatly into either category: sports, video games, board games, hiking, making crafts, drawing, camping, photography, art, and running to name a few. These activities are labeled as recreation, play, hobbies, or leisure and fall into a kind of gray area of overlap that seems to exist between activities we consider to be work or rest. Except for a small percentage of professionals, soccer is not considered work; but, at the same time, it seems impossible for something that is so physically demanding to be considered rest. A video game lacks the physical and mental strain of work but stimulates the mind with constant flutters of activity that also seem to negate it from being considered Sabbath rest. Thus, this twofold division between work and rest creates a false dichotomy that remains insufficient in their descriptions of many human activities. While creating definitive categories by which to describe all human activity is a frivolous exercise, the lack of direct biblical teaching regarding play makes such categories helpful and illustrates the overlap that play shares in the two worlds that are mentioned in the biblical narrative—the world of work and the world of rest.

As one category of humanity's chief activities, play is manifested throughout culture in countless ways, but few playful activities are as ubiquitous in culture as sports. Sports were a significant part of the societal backdrop at the time of the New Testament yet Jesus never mentions anything remotely connected to sports. With the exception of some athletic metaphors, Paul ignores the topic as well. First-century foot races and boxing do prove to be some of Paul's most frequently used metaphors (1

---

22. Peterson, *Christ Plays in a Thousand Places*, 116.
23. Huizinga, *Homo Ludens*, 28.

Cor 9:24–27, Gal 2:2, 5:7, Phil 2:16, 2 Tim 2:5, 4:7), but as New Testament scholar Everett Ferguson acknowledges, "Such metaphorical language was part of the stock-in-trade of popular philosophers and moralists and need not indicate any extensive firsthand acquaintance by Paul or others with the games."[24] In reality, "Scripture neither explicitly condones nor endorses informal play," a fact that leads Hoffman to imply, "the New Testament authors considered it to neither confer special advantage nor post a substantial threat to the spiritual vitality of early adherents of faith."[25] Catholic theologian Alois Koch goes as far to conclude, "The effort to justify today's sport from the biblical writing is understandable, but in my opinion a waste of effort."[26] The Bible's ambivalence remains confounding, especially when one considers the fact that the infamous gladiatorial games were increasing in popularity contemporaneously in Paul's life (and subsequent Christian leaders would speak out loudly against them) and the ancient athletic contests were often accompanied by sacred rituals.[27] Although the presence of athletic language in the New Testament has led many Christians, especially within the athletic community, to readily see an unequivocal embrace of sports in the Bible, the teachings remain far from explicit. It is more realistic to see a high level of scriptural ambiguity towards sports and play and a lack of a smoking-gun text that unilaterally condones or condemns sports. Instead, this ambiguity encourages us to further explore the theological evidence as it relates to the subject of play.

THEOLOGICAL REFLECTIONS ON PLAY AND SPORT

Establishing definitions is an essential, first task for any theological reflection. In the case of play, such an endeavor proves to be a challenge from the outset. This challenge is illustrated in the title of one contemporary treatment of play by sociologist Brian Sutton-Smith: *The Ambiguity of Play*.[28] James Evans Jr. writes, "The near universality of play as a human practice makes a simple and definitive summary difficult if not impossible."[29] Play is such a fundamental aspect of social behavior that setting out to identify it

---

24. Ferguson, *Backgrounds of Early Christians*, 92.
25. Hoffman, *Good Games*, 25.
26. Koch, "Biblical and Patristic Foundations for Sport," 99.
27. Ferguson, *Backgrounds of Early Christians*, 94.
28. Sutton-Smith, *The Ambiguity of Play*.
29. Evans, *Playing*, 2.

seems rather self-evident. In much the same way, when the United States Supreme Court found it difficult to articulate a specific definition for pornography in a 1964 U.S. Supreme Court obscenity case, Justice Potter Stewart famously concluded, "I know it when I see it." This same principle seems applicable to the subject of play as it remains challenging to provide a precise verbal definition, but it is rather obvious to recognize in action.

For many decades, Johan Huizinga's work *Homo Ludens*, has been a chief authority on play. The title of Huizinga's book highlights the centrality of play to the human condition. Authors Bado-Fralick and Norris reflect on his use: "We are defined not merely as *homo sapiens*—rational beings—we are *homo ludens*—beings that play."[30] Play deserves serious critical attention because it is so ubiquitous to the human experience. In David Miller's book, *Gods and Games*, published in 1970, he suggests that play was beginning to emerge as the definitive metaphor for the American mythos.

> We may be witnessing a mythological revolution, turning toward a new frontier in which leisure, meditation, and contemplation are potentially dominant. Instead of work being our model for both work and play, play may be the model for both our games of leisure and our games of vocation. Play may be the mythology of a new frontier.[31]

While the driven, traditional, hard-working culture that often propagates workaholism remains an unquestioned part of America's corporate culture, Miller's comments also bring to mind the way many of today's most successful companies have become known for their playful and creative work spaces. For example, note how Google describes its own work environment: "Our offices and cafes are designed to encourage interactions between Googlers within and across teams, and to spark conversation about work as well as play."[32] Mashable.com recently highlighted "13 Playful Work Environments that Reinvent Office Space" including foosball tables at Skype, bicycles at Living Social, and a two-story slide at Box.[33] Interestingly enough, while it seems that some of the working culture in America is recognizing the importance of playfulness, one area of life that has come to display a *less* playful environment is sports!

---

30. Bado-Fralick and Norris, *Toying with God*, 127.
31. Miller, *God and Games*, 138.
32. Google, "Our Culture."
33. Hiscott, "13 Playful Work Environments that Reinvent Office Space."

Components of Play

Originating in the 1930s, Huizinga's definition still provides a pertinent framework from which to begin. "Play is a *voluntary activity* or occupation executed within *certain fixed limits of time and place* according to *rules* freely accepted but absolutely binding, having *its aim in itself* and accompanied by a feeling of tension, joy, and the consciousness that it is *'different' from 'ordinary life.'*"[34] Within Huizinga's definition of play, there are clear distinctions between the activities of work and rest described in the previous section. Whereas work is a necessity of livelihood and was the first command given in Eden and Sabbath was a weekly mandate complete with extensive regulations, play is a "voluntary activity." Huizinga explains that, "Play to order is no longer play: it could at best be but a forcible imitation of it."[35] Whereas work and rest are rooted in the real world of everyday tasks and limited by physicality, play takes the player into an alternate reality with its own unique rules and dynamics as illustrated by the "other worlds" of athletic fields, ice rinks, playgrounds, volleyball courts, wrestling mats, half pipes, video games, and board games. Sports and video games are managed by their own specific timekeeping rules and devices, and many board games contain a sand-filled hour glass by which the player is taken out of "real time" and transported into an alternate world, not only spatially, but also through the game's own unique timekeeping practices. The Jack Norworth song that has become baseball's anthem, "Take Me Out to the Ball Game," illustrates this poignantly in its line: "I don't care if I ever get back."[36] Play takes place quite literally, in a socially constructed other world and finds its purpose within itself. According to Huizinga, "It is rather a stepping out of 'real' life into a temporary sphere of activity with a disposition all of its own."[37] In other words, there is an overt transcendence on display in the manifestation of sports.

More than a decade following the original publication of *Homo Ludens*, the French sociologist Roger Caillois would posit his own qualities of play building on Huizinga's foundation and subsequently contributing another invaluable resource on the subject of play. Caillois believed play was marked by six qualities: free, separate, uncertain, unproductive,

---

34. Huizinga, *Homo Ludens*, 28. Emphasis mine.
35. Huizinga, *Homo Ludens*, 7.
36. Norworth, "Take Me Out to the Ball Game."
37. Huizinga, *Homo Ludens*, 8.

governed by the rules, and constitutes make-believe.[38] Although there is clear overlap with Huizinga's definition of play, Caillois sought to establish his six qualities in order to expand the swath of activities that Huizinga's work included. He believed Huizinga's discussion neglected too many of what he believed to be pertinent manifestations of play. Caillois goes on to further delineate the broad spectrum of playful activities into four different types of games: *agon* (competitive games like football, billiards, or chess), *alea* (games of chance like roulette or lotteries), *mimicry* (games of simulation like playing dress up or pretending to cook with toys), and *ilinx* (vertigo inducing games like merry-go-rounds or roller coasters).[39] While our attention pertains to the broader subject of play, it is specifically the subcategory of the *agonic* contests that finds the most direct relevance to the discussion of sports. This chapter focuses on the theological framework of the broader understanding of play, while the next chapter will address the theological implications specific to the subcategory of *agonic* play.

Amidst the overlap of Huizinga's and Cailois's descriptions of play, a general consensus of some of the definitive attributes of exactly what play is have widely been reiterated. In one example, Catherine Garvey describes characteristics that are "widely cited as critical to its definition," and mentions the following: play is pleasurable and enjoyable, play has no extrinsic goals, play is spontaneous and voluntary, play involves some active engagement on the part of the player, and play has certain systematic relations to what is not play.[40] This consensus helps illustrate that the initial statements regarding an ambiguity of play are relevant mostly to peripheral activities. Although it may be difficult to adequately put into words exactly what constitutes play (and what does not), most people recognize it when they see it. Non-academics and academics alike agree that play involves the related concepts of fun,[41] smiling,[42] laughing,[43] and not taking things too seriously.[44] With all of this in mind, play can be defined as *those games*

38. Caillois, *Man, Play, and Games*, 9–10.
39. Caillois, *Man, Play, and Games*, 14.
40. Garvey, *Play*, 4–5.
41. Bad-Fralik and Norris, *Toying with God*, 107–36.
42. Garvey, "The Natural History of the Smile" in *Play*, 17–23.
43. Johan Huizinga notes that "the purely physiological act of laughing is exclusive to man." Huizinga, *Homo Ludens*, 6.
44. David Miller begins his book with a playful parable that he hopes reminds the reader (and himself) that even in the theological task we must not take ourselves too seriously. Miller, *Gods and Games*, 2–4.

and activities (or the process of creating games and activities) that are participated in by one's own volition, for the sole purpose of fun and enjoyment, regularly inducing smiles and laughter, and governed by its own set of rules and guidelines—rules that are often changing and evolving as the game or activity progresses. Admittedly, the definition glosses over complex issues that would require a more thorough study of play (such as the pedagogical function of play in childhood development,[45] the relationship between play and war,[46] and the fact that play can be serious[47]), but it remains definitive enough for our purposes here and to aid our theological inquiry.

Play as Essential

The quest to establish a definitive description of play must not lose sight of the significance of play itself. As psychologist David Elkind acknowledges, "Play is not a luxury but rather a crucial dynamic of healthy physical, intellectual, and social-emotional development at all age levels."[48] This echoes the language of purpose explored above in the commentary on Genesis regarding work and rest. Not only should play be seen as some kind of sentimental notion of Edenic purity, it is physiologically essential to our healthy growth and development as human beings. Religious professor Lonnie Kliever summarizes three widely accepted purposes of play: play helps us learn (an essential educational device is even called "role *play*"), play has an essential social element (building teamwork and abiding by socially constructed rules), and play has an impressive element (it is how we articulate fun and beauty).[49]

With all due respect to Coach Herman Edwards, "Young people do *not* play just to win the game." We can give Coach Edwards the benefit of the doubt and assume he was referring exclusively to professional sports, but this win-obsessed culture has matriculated into the lifeblood of youth sports so deeply that play often seems to be a distant memory. Young people need to be assured that they are free to play sports, just to play them—not for success, popularity, scholarships, varsity letters, or to play on a more prestigious club next season. Sports are one of the few places in

---

45. See Elkind, "Play, Learning, and Development" in *The Power of Play*, 87–168.
46. Huizinga, "Play and War" in *Homo Ludens*, 89–104.
47. Huizinga, "Play and War" in *Homo Ludens*, 5–6.
48. Elkind, *The Power of Play*, 4.
49. Kliever, "God and Games in Modern Culture," 40–41.

their high-stakes, standardized-test-driven-world, where young people still get to play. No wonder Jerry Lynch observes of sports, "Without the fun, they are done."[50] The purpose of play is complex and multi-faceted as much as being essential to the human condition. In other words, because we are human, we play.

LET THEM PLAY

While there are countless games and activities that fall under the rubric of play, no single manifestation of play has garnered the attention, participation, and power of sports. As Novak writes in his well-known homage to sports, "Sports are our chief civilizing agent. Sports are our most universal art form. Sports tutor us in the basic lived experiences of humanist tradition."[51] Nearly forty years ago, longtime sports journalist Frank Deford was one of the first to suggest that the power of sports was establishing itself as a new religious denomination. "While churches struggle with problems of declining attendance, falling contributions and now even reduction in membership, Sportianity appears to be taking off."[52] The contours of sports culture in the United States that Deford was writing about in the 1970s was but a fraction of today's sports industrial complex. This chapter has focused on play and sports in the broadest sense, but the rest of this book focuses on ways in which contemporary sports have come to betray the purpose of play within the burgeoning area of contemporary youth sports.

Chap Clark, a professor at Fuller Seminary and prolific youth ministry author devotes an entire chapter of his book *Hurt 2.0: Inside the World of Today's Teenager* to the topic of sports (a notable exception to the general neglect by the youth-ministry community). He writes, "Sports (including dance) are no longer about fun, exercise, experience, and play. They are about competition, winning, and defeating an opponent. Sports are no longer child's play; they are a grown-up dog-eat-dog reality."[53] When my son played tee ball, the players seldom knew the score or even if their team had won or lost. Like the girls in O'Sullivan's story, they just had fun. It was quite a contrast from my son's team a few years later when players burst into tears after losing their tournament game or would slam down their bat after

50. Lynch, *Let Them Play*, 129.
51. Novak, *The Joy of Sports*, 27.
52. Deford, "Religion in Sport."
53. Clark, *Hurt 2.0*, 104.

striking out. A few years of development make quite a difference. More parents and coaches need to be reminded of the words of sports parent guru, Jerry Lynch. "The first thing we must all learn to do is how to free ourselves so we can step away, get out of the way, and simply *let them play*."[54]

While play serves as the initial inspiration for sports, the impulse that most readily fuels it is competition. While many corporate environments seem more welcoming of the spirit of play than ever before, younger and younger athletes are faced with competitive realities that were once delayed until later stages of development. Somewhere along the line, the cap was taken off the tube of competition and some people involved in youth sports are trying to figure out how to get it put back in the tube. While a theological discussion of sports and play has proved challenging, the next chapter investigates the woefully neglected topic of competition and considers the great temptation that it is for athletes of all ages.

---

54. Lynch, *Let Them Play*, 16.

3

There Can Be Only One: A Theology of Competition

The first time I ever saw grown men fight was during a church league basketball game. I don't remember any of the details of the fight, and I doubt I would consider it more than a tiff if I were to witness it today, but it made such an impression on me that I have never forgotten it took place. My friends who are basketball officials assure me that some of the worst games they have ever officiated were in church leagues. I have played in meaningless volleyball games at church camp and watched them unfold into tense shouting matches ending in players storming off the court. Countless poems and songs have been written extolling the great feats that have been accomplished by a beloved in the throes of their passionate love, but the one motivation that may just have the power to supplant even love is the desire and hunger for victory.

In the previous chapter, we saw the intimate relationship between play, sports, and competition. As play evolves and develops, competition is introduced in varying degrees. This chapter will revisit the topic of play in searching for a working definition of competition, discuss the evolution that takes place as one moves from free play to more structured play, and consider the ways that competition is impacted by this evolution of play. A theological investigation of competition explores the central question: Was competition created by God and inherent in the creation, or was it a direct result of the Fall? This chapter explores the role competition has in helping foster both vices and virtues.

Elite?

INSIDE THE FISH BOWL OF COMPETITION

Few aspects of culture are as entrenched in the ethos of the United States as is winning. Every major sport has its own format for establishing its champion and each format is enmeshed in various degrees into the fabric of U.S. culture. People host parties on Super Bowl Sunday (a de facto national holiday) to watch the NFL crown its king. The brackets for the NCAA men's and women's basketball tournament have achieved an iconic status that is honored every spring. Champions are determined by the long succession of playoff series in professional basketball and hockey leagues, and the Fall Classic—the World Series—still maintains a prominent spotlight as the leaves change their color and summer gives way to autumn. Sports like golf and tennis have their major tournaments and additional showcases are held for other non-team sports throughout the calendar year. The scene of confetti falling from the sky while Queen sings "We are the Champions," and the head coach hoists a trophy overhead is such a familiar one, it is difficult to imagine an alternate picture of winning. Even the answer to the question, "What are you going to do now that you've won?" has become a part of this winning lore in America. "I'm going to Disney World!"

The enduring popularity of the World Series[1] helps reinforce the oft-cited platitude that "nothing is as American as baseball and apple pie." With all apologies to purists throughout the country, however, there indeed may be one thing more fundamental to U.S. culture: the World Apple Pie Eating Championship. Held during the Johnny Appleseed Festival in Brunswick, OH, on September 13, 2013, Joey Chestnut ate a record 4.375 three-pound apple pies in eight minutes.[2] The essence of Americana is not exemplified in this specific event per se, but in the quintessential desire for unbridled competition that helps spawn such events. The competitive hunger of Americans helps drive the existence of this contest, as well as the better known Nathan's Hotdog Eating Contest that has occurred at Nathan's Coney Island location annually since 1972. Demonstrating the confluence of sport, hotdogs, competition, and patriotism is the fact that this world-famous contest occurs on Independence Day and is aired on ESPN. Here is a sentence deserving reflection: Citizens of the United States love to compete so much that we hold contests to see who can eat the most food the fastest.

---

1. The television ratings for the 2016 World Series between the Cleveland Indians and Chicago Cubs were the highest they had been in fifteen years. For ratings summary see: Brown, "Baseball Is Dying?"

2. As reported by Major League Eating.com.

There Can Be Only One

Competition is the essence of the United States. It undergirds the economy, determines local and national politics, creates our most famous celebrities, and plays a major role within the academic environment. It is difficult to find one corner of U.S. culture that isn't dominated by some kind of competition. There is a National Spelling Bee, the Academy Awards, Billboard's music charts, the *New York Times Best Seller List*, reality-television shows, cooking-show competitions, game shows, and prizes and awards for just about every type of profession. In a paper presented at the Christian Business Faculty Academy conference in 2004, authors Yvonne Smith, Sharon Johnson, and Erik Hiller state, "Competition is everywhere and just as fish don't notice the water, we seldom notice it."[3] From the time when babies first enter the world, they are immediately baptized into a competitive environment. Even while in utero, there are competitions to see who can guess the baby's name, gender, or due date. Take a moment and do an Internet search for "baby contest" for an example of just how competitive the world is from the very moment we are born. After the competition for cutest babies, the real competition begins as to which baby will be first to walk, talk, stop using a bottle, or get out of diapers—and all of this is before standardized testing! Competition is so ingrained in the American psyche that it turns out to be a challenging topic to address.

In the beginning of his book, *Competition*, Gary Warner illustrates the tenuous relationship between Christians and competition in sports with this story.

> A well-known coach of a professional sports team, known for his pre- and post-game prayers and "chaplains" on the sidelines, invited an FCA staff member to lunch. It was the week before an important game, and the coach asked about the weaknesses of a player on the opposing squad. The FCA man said the player had none. The coach retorted that every man has weaknesses. The FCA staffer's reply was that the player was a close friend . . . and he would not share weaknesses even if he knew some. End of lunch. Next day the FCA man went to the team's practice and discovered his press pass, issued by the coach, had mysteriously been canceled. He has not heard from the coach since.[4]

Competition can bring out the best and worst of the human race. When the objective is to win, inevitably, all participants will have to consider the

---

3. Smith, Johnson, and Hiller, "God of the Games," 3.
4. Gary Warner, *Competition*, 12.

extent to which they are willing to go in order to win. In most games the lines between gaining an advantage fairly versus gaining an advantage unfairly are extremely small. Specific rules help guide the ethics of the game while playing, thus precisely delineating the line between fair play and cheating. Faking a handoff in football is legal, but sneaking a player off the sideline is not. However, especially in more ambiguous aspects like college recruiting, the ethics are less definitive. What promises might a coach make to a player? What might a coach say about another program? Herein lies countless opportunities for ethical dilemmas and the realistic struggle with the role of competition.

Surprisingly, even though competition is such a fundamental part of the modern world and poses real questions for Christian ethics, the topic has drawn relatively scant attention from serious theological circles. Three Christian business professors astutely describe the role competition plays among several important groups: "Business people assume competition, sociologists deplore it, sports psychologists adore it, and theologians ignore it."[5] In researching this topic thoroughly for this book, I have concluded that two of the most prevalent aspects in society, sports and competition, are also two of the most neglected areas of study within contemporary theology.

Lying at the heart of a theological discussion of competition is the paradoxical difficulty of whether or not a competitive environment can be cultivated where virtues are promoted and vices are not perpetuated. Self-control, one of the fruits of the Spirit (Eph 5:23), remains a crucial practice that must dictate the experience of competition. Jesus's teaching, "The last will be first, and the first will be last" (Matt 20:16) seems to directly contradict the contemporary notion of competition. Can you imagine that Bible verse hanging in a locker room? Culture within the United States has come to inhabit a win-at-all-costs ethos that has become especially prevalent in today's youth-sports culture. While any theological study of competition will be inherently complex, this chapter offers some important observations regarding competition and ends by suggesting how Christians can participate in competitive activities cautiously and surreptitiously.

---

5. Smith, Johnson, Hiller, "Gods of the Games," 2.

There Can Be Only One
THE EVOLUTION OF PLAY

Any exploration of competition must wrestle with the relationship between competition and play. Before turning specifically to this topic we must first acknowledge some parameters within which this study of competition is presented. In another paper presented by Christian business professors, Sharon G. Johnson and Galen Smith highlight the diverse nature of competition, "We discovered that part of the complexity (and contentiousness) of the discussion surrounding competition is that it is defined in so many different ways between various fields of study (for instance, economics versus psychology), and between authors in the same field of study."[6] Ideally, the concepts of competition within sports as it relates to theology will bear relevance beyond sports, but the study that follows should first be applied to examples of athletic competition.

Within the U.S. context, it is impossible to separate the idea of competition from sports. Warner says, "Competition, as America defines it, is play intensified; play related to another's play with more than mere fun the essence."[7] Hoffman explains the essentiality of competition to sports this way: "Rid sport of competitor's mutual striving for a prize available only to one of them and you change it into something entirely different."[8] Higgs and Braswell use a humorous cartoon to further illustrate the relationship: "[A priest] lectures young boys that in church league, it is not a matter of whether one wins or loses. 'What is the point, then?' asks one of the players. 'I forget,' admits the priest."[9] I wonder if the two guys I saw fight in a church league game ever saw that cartoon. Without competition there are no winners and losers, and it seems as though we have difficulty watching sporting events without a declared winner and loser. In the title of his book, Francesco Duina even calls winning "an American obsession."[10] Consider the four major professional sports leagues in the United States: baseball and basketball games never end in ties, football games almost never end in ties,[11] and in 2005 the NHL adopted an end-of-the-game shootout to

---

6. Johnson and Smith, "Perspectives on Competition," 5.
7. Warner, *Competition*, 28.
8. Hoffman, *Good Game*, 145.
9. Higgs and Braswell, *An Unholy Alliance*, 249.
10. Duina, *Winning*.
11. College football games adopted an overtime format that would end ties beginning with the 1996 season. In contrast, NFL games can still end in a tie—and every time one does, another national debate erupts about whether or not the NFL should do

determine the winner of a game that would otherwise end in a tie. A 2014 *Time* article suggests a major reason professional soccer fails to achieve more widespread popularity in the United States is the frequency of ties.[12]

Competition can be seen in the evolution of playing catch in the backyard with a parent to competing with a team, against another team, on a designated field. It is also illustrated in the evolution of running around aimlessly as a toddler with no objective, then running to avoid being tagged "it" by another playmate, then running a set distance on a marked course, and finally running against other runners in relation to timed completion of the race. Competition represents a progression of the objective of play. Whereas play may involve scoring points, competition requires scoring more points. Whereas play involves running, swimming, or jumping, competition requires running and swimming faster and jumping higher or farther. Warner describes competition as essential to athletic performance: "Athletic performance does not reach the highest level of excellence, and records are not shattered, by those who want to play, only by those who want to compete."[13] For this reason, it is often noted that the definition of competition is rooted in striving together, rather than being set against one another. Indeed, runners most often run their fastest time when they are running against equally swift competitors. World records are not set in the Olympic qualifying heats, partly because the runners are conserving energy, but also because they are not running against the fastest runners. The closer the race (the more competitive the race is), the harder they run.

While the essential nature of competition may not be inherently antagonistic, it is comparative. Even when we are competing against ourselves for a better time, we must consider our previous outcomes for the sake of comparison; competition requires comparing two or more entities. Most often, competition demarcates "us" and "them," and the chief objective is always for "us" to defeat "them." Beyond competition being essentially comparative, it also conveys a sense of shortage or limitation.[14] A person always competes against another team or person for a prize, position, or award that both teams cannot achieve. For that reason, in situations where "everyone gets a trophy" the idea of shortage or limitation is absent and an

---

away with ties. The 2016 season saw two games end in a tie, and the debate lives on. The national debate seems to reiterate: Americans hate ties!

12. Faris, "Why America Doesn't Like Soccer, and How that Can Be Changed."
13. Warner, *Competition*, 73.
14. Johnson and Smith, "Perspectives on Competition," 6.

important component of competition is lacking. A 2013 *Sports Illustrated* article provides an apt mantra for describing the heart of competition, "There Can Be Only One."[15]

Competition and the Betrayal of Play

While competitive play still aims to be pleasurable and enjoyable (both essential elements of play), there seems to be some inconsistencies between competition and some of the other characteristics of play.[16] The higher up the competitive ladder one goes, more rules are necessary to govern the conduct and organization of play and the lines between competitors are more clearly delineated. Play has no extrinsic goals (we play just to play), but competition upholds stated, innate goals like running a faster time and scoring more points than opponents. Play is spontaneous and voluntary, but competition becomes more structured within increasingly complex games, leagues, and tournaments.

In some ways, competition represents the beginning of the institutionalization of play by enhancing the complexity of the rules that govern play. Caillois writes, "Rules are inseparable from play as soon as the latter becomes institutionalized."[17] This institutionalization occurs within the games themselves as well as within the governing structures that manage the game. Allen Guttmann, in the book *From Ritual to Record*, describes this institutionalization as having been codified through the modern quantification of sports.[18] Statistics and records have allowed for the quantification of play furthering the challenge of demarcating where a game or sport stops being play. As leagues become more sophisticated in their structure and administration, the playful elements of sports are jeopardized. Consider the evolution and institutionalization of play in the following example from a typical community youth baseball and softball league.[19]

15. Kluwe, "There Can Be Only One."
16. Garvey, *Play*, 4–5.
17. Caillois, *Man, Play, and Games*, 27.
18. Guttmann, *From Ritual to Record*, 51.
19. This example is given from the Westerville Baseball and Softball League (WYBSL) in Westerville, OH. My son and my oldest daughters have played in this league for several years, and I have coached in this league. This well-run and well-organized community-based baseball and softball league is representative of comparable sports leagues throughout the country.

Elite?

At the age of five, boys and girls are introduced to the games of baseball and softball with a game that resembles both, but is clearly different from both: tee ball. The children hit a softer version of a baseball off of batting tees and no score is kept. Fielding gloves are worn, any casual fan recognizes the field as a baseball or softball field, there are four bases laid out in the shape of a diamond, there is a home plate, and batters must run to first base before an infielder touches the base runner or base in possession of the ball. Tee ball, however, serves only as an introduction to the more complex games of softball and baseball. Tee ball is for children; there are no adult tee ball leagues. The players will eventually master hitting the ball off of a tee and advance to hitting the ball thrown from an adult pitcher before children pitch to children in more advanced leagues. Additional rules are added each year as children progress to the next, more advanced level of the league. Eventually, the children play baseball and softball with their full complement of rules.

This evolution speaks to the growth and development of children and their acquiescence to the more complex sport. As the children are introduced to these more complex rules and tactics of the game, the leagues become more sophisticated. Early on, all players receive a participation trophy, but as players move on to more advanced leagues, scores are recorded, divisions are established, tournament brackets are created, individual statistics are recorded, and champions are crowned. In other words, success and recognition become scarcer and more elusive. The objectives advance from hitting and catching a ball (often called "the basics"), to getting the other team out, to scoring more runs than the other team, and, ultimately, to finishing first. This description of the growth and development track for youth baseball and softball reflects the experiences most young people have when they grow up playing sports in the United States. Describing the evolution of play in this manner makes it is easy to see the challenge of determining the point at which sports abandons the markings of play.

The institutionalization represented in this youth baseball and softball example is but a microcosm of the larger institutionalization that dramatically shaped youth sports in the United States during the twentieth century. Steven Overman argues, "The reform efforts of the Progressive era that set out to control the leisure time of children and adolescents culminated in the institutionalization of play and games. In the final reckoning, play has been deemed too important to leave to youth. Play must be supervised and controlled."[20] Overman describes in detail the intentional efforts that were made by leaders in the United States to use sports in order to promote achievement and success in their children (a value they hoped would carry on in their children beyond the realm of sports).[21] Tom Farrey, a journalist-turned-youth-sports-advocate, describes how the institutionalization of sports is affecting children at younger and younger ages. "As recently as 1995, 8 was the average age that boys began playing organized sports (it was 10 for girls). Now, 8 is the age at which more than a few of them begin to compete for national titles."[22] By the time boys are eight today, some of them will have had five years of organized soccer before the "average boy" would have started in 1995. That is too much of a head start for parents to miss out on; so youth leagues begin and travel teams are formed at younger and younger ages: a youth sports arms race is underway.

The driving force behind getting children to compete at earlier and earlier ages is the competitive instinct of their parents. I've lost track of the number of times I have overheard parents express their fears of "letting their child get behind" or their commitment to "get their child ahead" in sports by getting them start earlier or having them play organized sports more often. Parents are enrolling their four-year-olds in their first soccer camp, already looking ahead to how they can best ensure their child can compete for a spot on the high school team. Somewhere along the line, competition has overruled play as the guiding principle of sports.

The Best of the Best

This quintessential comparative nature of competition results in constantly looking for new opponents with whom to compare and compete. Overman describes how this comparative ethos has become second nature to parents, "Parents are concerned with how their children fare in school, but are less interested in what is learned than in how the child measures up to other children."[23] In sports language, parents have become less concerned with how well their children are learning the basics of a sport (or whether they are enjoying it!) than how they stack up to other children in the league or even their national rankings. The technological and communication revo-

---

20. Overman, *The Protestant Ethic and the Spirit of Sport*, 252.
21. Overman, *The Protestant Ethic and the Spirit of Sport*, 249–66.
22. Farrey, *Game On*, 159.
23. Overman, *The Protestant Ethic and the Spirit of Sport*, 257.

lutions of the twenty-first century have provided an even larger format for this insatiable desire to compete (not to mention a larger sampling with whom to compare our children's abilities). Many are no longer satisfied by having their child be the best player on the block or in the community league—now parents can get caught up in *national* rankings.[24] A quick online search brings up AAU basketball clubs nationally ranked as early as nine and ten year olds and in the third grade!

Over-invested parents and adults help create and maintain competitive systems to feed their own competitive appetites. Starting their children at such early ages, their competitiveness leads them to sign up their children for the most competitive sports leagues, take them to the best trainers and coaches in the area, and drive or fly to the most competitive tournaments. Being able to tell fellow parents that your child is a national champion, played in a national tournament, or has a national ranking has become part of keeping up with the Joneses of suburban America. I am amazed at the depth of knowledge that parents show regarding their children's teams and opponents. Not surprisingly, parents often use first-person pronouns when talking about "our" team or "our" upcoming tournament or game. In a recent blogpost, John O'Sullivan remarked on parent's rising involvement in their children sports, "Youth sports has become less a tool to educate children about sport and life, and more often a place where parents go to be entertained by their kids."[25] All of this, under the auspices of competition, is helping to bring the experience of sports for many children far away from the intention of play.

The evolution of play described in my community's softball and baseball league illustrates the need to allow for a natural hierarchy built into any description of competition. Competition functions differently at the Olympic level than it does in a neighborhood pickup game, and it must be treated differently. This distinction in levels of competition can be illustrated in the example of a summer family gathering. It is quite common for members of a family to gather around an erected volleyball net in order to play a game that has some semblance of volleyball. The game is often egalitarian and inclusive as all members of the family who want to play, from youngest to oldest, get the chance to play together. It is clear to all outsiders that the

---

24. For a brief overview of the history of ranking youth amateur basketball players in the United States and the impact it can have on players and their families, see Chapter 8 in George Dohrmann's exposé on the grass roots basketball machine in Southern California: *Play Their Hearts Out*, 112–19.

25. O'Sullivan, "The Adultification of Youth Sports."

family is playing some manifestation of volleyball, but the score is loosely kept (if kept at all), the youngest children are often given special help and altered rules, and good fun is had by all.

At some point, it is also common for the children and lesser-skilled players to be removed from the court so that the other players can play a "more competitive game." The rules of the game become more strictly enforced, score is kept more rigidly, play is noticeably more intense, and fun is still had by all—but a different kind of fun. Clearly these two examples of competition are related, but they are not the same experience. Furthermore, both these examples differ from an interschool, varsity match where neutral third-party officials enforce even stricter adherence to rules and spectators fill the stands. A more detailed investigation of this hierarchy gets us beyond our purposes here, but sports-ministry pioneer Greg Linville provides a helpful summary with what he calls the "Progressive Intensity Levels of Competition."[26] The least intense activities Linville labels "Play," and then progresses upwards to "Playful Games," "Games," "Athletics," "Recreational Sport," "Varsity Sport," and finally "Professional Sport." In summarizing, Linville expresses the potential competition has for taking sports away from their intended purposes: "As sporting commitment and activity increase, they are inherently accompanied and influenced by heightened levels of potentially negative strength and power. Each step taken up the ladder of Progressive Intensity Levels of Competition further reduces the likelihood of obtaining competition's goal of fun, enjoyment, fulfillment, or even fitness."[27] As we advance in competitive levels, our purposes in some way change.

Competition is so pervasive and unavoidable that to dismiss it as unequivocally contrary to Christian virtue is a clear overreaction to the moral and ethical challenges it does pose. Moreover, to dismiss competition as unilaterally unethical on these grounds is as illogical as dismissing sex or money because of the moral challenges they can create. At the same time, even though competition is such an integral part of the world, Hoffman forces reflection, "For those who are willing to see, the dissonance between competition and Christianity remains."[28] Harvey echoes Hoffman's point, stating simply, "[Competition] can prove difficult for Christians."[29] Rather

---

26. Linville, *Christmanship*, 4–5.
27. Linville, *Christmanship*, 5.
28. Hoffman, *Good Game*, 145.
29. Harvey, *A Brief Theology of Sport*, 101.

than allowing competition to get a theological free pass simply because it is so pervasive, its pervasiveness demands critical attention just like the complex and controversial issues provoked by matters of sex and money. As should be clear by now, there is no denying the fact that competition is a fundamental aspect of culture in the United States, and its familiarity serves only to complicate the quest for finding its proper theological place.

A THEOLOGICAL INQUIRY INTO COMPETITION

Although the main focus of this study of competition is on its role in sports and because the Bible offers little in the way of direct teaching regarding sports, a theological inquiry into competition will have to wrestle with the broader aspects of competition. Harvey reiterates a point that was made earlier: "A review of the literature finds little evidence of theological engagement with the question of sport."[30] The Bible does have a good deal to say in considering competition more broadly. At the heart of a theological inquiry into competition is whether God built competition into the very fabric of Eden, or if it was instead collateral damage resulting from sin entering the world. In support of the former perspective is the fact that there is an irrefutable evolutionary element of competition evident within nature, or as Bruce Sanguin describes, "Struggle is part of the evolutionary cycle."[31] Human beings are the product of competition from the very beginning as conception occurs when one sperm defeats the millions of other sperm in order to fertilize the ovum.

At the same time, however, there seems ample evidence to also affirm Hoffman's conclusion, "Competitive sports, competitive politics, competitive business—anything competitive is always treacherous ground for Christians to tread, for it threatens to realign human relationships and sever bonds of fellowship that their faith enjoins them to project and nurture."[32] It is the infatuation with competition (and the related experiences of success and achievement) that drives the use of performance-enhancing drugs, compels coaches to skirt rules and regulations, and helps reinforce a social caste system within too many high schools across America. Anything that separates the world into "us" versus "them" is not easily reconcilable with the Christian narrative.

30. Harvey, *A Brief Theology of Sport*, xiii.
31. Sanguin, *Darwin, Divinity, and the Dance of the Cosmos*, 105.
32. Hoffman, *Good Game*, 164.

There Can Be Only One
Competition and the Bible

The Bible is a collection of literature that at times exemplifies competitive elements, and at others seems at odds with them. A survey of competition in the Bible begins where all theological inquiries begin—"in the beginning." Genesis chapter 2 presents the theological foundations for the chief purposes of humans on display in Genesis: to work, rest, and play. It is not hyperbole to suggest that competition permeates all three realities today, and the crux of the matter is whether or not that is the way God intended it to be. Reflecting on the creation narrative in Genesis 2, Old Testament scholar Walter Brueggemann summarizes, "The destiny of the human creation is to live in God's world, with God's creation, on God's terms."[33] Determining the role of competition in the world is to pursue whether or not competition is a part of "God's terms." While I believe too many proponents who argue that competition is inherent in creation are too quick to assume the affirmative, there are certainly clues that allow for the potential of seeing a built-in, Edenic system of competition that was present in the beginning.

The Edenic narrative is presented as a place of complete harmony, peace, and cooperation within and among the creation. In their study of competition, Smith, Johnson, and Hiller reach the following conclusion regarding competition in Eden, "We could find no Scriptural basis for thinking that competition, per se could not have been present in Eden. Adam and Eve may well have raced each other, played dunking games in the water, or vied to see who tended more trees that day."[34] Although Genesis fails to provide any explicit language of competition that definitively establishes it as part of creation, neither does any of the language preclude the existence of an original, built-in, competitive environment.

Such an allowance, however, is just that. It pushes the text too far to follow retired NFL quarterback and Christian, Frank Reich, in seeing the subduing and ruling mandate given to humanity as some kind of godly, competitive edict. In Eden, the first humans were called to subdue chaos and not one another.[35] For Reich to conclude, "We were created to compete," seems too presumptuous of what the text is conveying.[36] While

---

33. Brueggemann, *Genesis*, 40.
34. Smith, Johnson, and Hiller, "God of the Games," 9.
35. Thanks to John Mark Hicks for suggesting this point.
36. Reich, "Competition and Creation."

competition may not be a direct antonym of harmony, we seldom think of a competitive environment as a harmonious one. Etymologically, competition is rooted in the idea of striving together, but in Eden what obstacles created the need to strive? Higgs states succinctly that "in play we commune with nature and others," "in sports we compete with nature and others," and at the very least competition is less Edenic than play.[37] If competition can be experienced in a way that enhances play and does not dehumanize the players, we can conceive of a healthy, godly role of competition. We have certainly all had experiences with competition that have left us feeling fulfilled, accomplished, and whole. It is hard to assign these competitive experiences as immoral, and there remains enough ambiguity in the opening chapters of the Bible that we cannot definitively rule out the presence of competition from within God's original creation.

Less ambivalent, however, are the negative overtones of numerous examples of competition that follow in Genesis. What began with the harmonious relationships in Eden turns into a collection of archetypal stories of competition and rivalry: Cain and Abel's competing sacrifices (Gen 4:4–5), Sarah and Hagar's competing fertility (Gen 21:8–10), Jacob and Essau competing for their father's blessing (Gen 27), Joseph and his brothers competing for their father's favor (Gen 37:3), and, frequently, Yahweh competing with false gods for the hearts of his people. Although it may be inconclusive as to whether or not competition existed in the Garden of Eden, the potential for wickedness and perpetuating evil inherent in competition becomes an unavoidable part of the early patriarchal narratives. It is important to see that, from the very beginning of Scripture, it is a spirit of competitiveness that sows disharmony and alienation among God's people in the shadow of the Edenic paradise. In this context, competition almost appears to be an essential byproduct of the entrance of sin into the world, dramatically affecting the way humans relate to one another. Sin has provided the obstacles and the environment within which competition is needed.

This fact notwithstanding, throughout the biblical narrative God's people, and God himself, are regular participants in competitive activities. Israel's armies regularly compete with foreign armies under Yahweh's divine guidance. Elijah competes with the prophets of Baal for the honor of God atop Mount Carmel (1 Kgs 18:16–46). God's prophets regularly compete with the false prophets regarding their "word of the Lord." The classic messianic curse given by God to the serpent in Genesis 3:15 is given

---

37. Higgs, *God in the Stadium*, 3.

in the language of competition: "he will crush your head, and you will strike his head." Here there will be a clear winner and loser! Thus, to label competition as inherently evil and disregard its place in the Christian life is to ignore these examples in the Bible. When sin enters the world, the adversarial nature of competition is easier to justify within the archetypal realty of good versus evil—a story that has been told and retold in countless ways ever since.

At the same time, to unilaterally justify competition according to this line of thinking betrays, to a large degree, the parameters and context of the competition in these examples. Each example above maintains that God was clearly on one side or the other as his very holiness was under attack. In each instance, God was with or was pleased by Abel's sacrifice, Sarah, Jacob, Israel, Elijah, and most intimately, Jesus. Biblical examples of competition most often speak of good competing against evil and the favor of the Lord resting on one side or the other. This might move us to believe competition remains a viable option for Christians as long as we can determine that we are battling evil.

Consequentially, it is noteworthy how often sports teams vilify their opponents. While this may be done respectfully, it is also often the case that the opponents are caricatured as less deserving of winning or even as less respectable citizens. This all points to our innate desire to want our winning to be justified and illustrates the tendency of competition to dehumanize our opponent. After the 2016 NCAA National Championship football game when Clemson defeated Alabama, in his postgame interview Clemson quarterback DeShaun Watson said, "This is what God wanted." Competition is so much easier to justify when we know we are on God's side! The biblical examples of competition are most often good competing against evil in the name of the Lord.

Moreover, when the Bible does address competition and is not dealing with matters of good and evil, the teachings resemble Jesus's words, "The last will be first and the first will be last" (Mat 20:16). This is hardly a principle for winning a competition. As a matter of fact, it is challenging to see any competitive element in the ministry of Jesus that was not a manifestation of good versus evil. Although, in a way, Jesus competed against the devil in the desert through temptation, the twelve apostles did not compete for their spots as apostles, and Jesus never suggested a duel, a race, or even a debate to confirm or establish the presence or favor of his Father. Rather, as journalist Tom Krattenmaker vividly portrays, Jesus's ministry exemplified a counter-competitive ethic.

> What seems beyond doubt, however, is that the loaves-and-fishes story teaches believers that God's salvation is universal, a "championship" granted to all who believe, not just those strong enough or powerful enough to out-do a rival for the eternal prize . . . This is not to say that sports are bad, but to demonstrate that at their core, they operate according to rules and values radically different from central themes of the religion of Jesus.[38]

Thus, when focusing on sports or economics it seems quite problematic to determine God's presence being in one team and not on the other or in one country or company and not another. In a recent provocative article in *Sports Illustrated*, Mark Oppenheimer highlights the impasse that exists for Christians attempting to establish a positive, theological perspective of competition. He writes, "Jesus' message is not exactly neutral towards winners and losers. The Bible is clear that he preferred the loser. The Bible is filled with pages that extol the weak over the strong and the poor at the expense of the rich."[39]

The central question of whether competition is inherent in God's created design for the world or if it is a byproduct of sin entering the world remains far from settled. Because play is a contrived reality, the role of competition takes on an added complexity that deserves additional attention. Moving beyond the biblical text itself, there does seem to be some positive justification seen in the evidence from within the created order of nature (natural revelation). Regardless of whether or not it was God's intended purpose, there is ample evidence from the Bible that God and his people took part in competitive activities. The vast majority of these activities served the direct purpose of glorifying God or defending God against an adversarial evil. It is impossible for anyone to live a life without taking part in some kind of competitive activities. Therefore, the focus of this inquiry into competition must move beyond the question of whether or not to compete, and focus instead on the matter of *how* Christians are to compete. Far from simplifying the situation, however, the matter of how competition relates to ethics and spiritual growth brings with them another set of complications.

---

38. Krattenmaker, *Onward Christian Athletes*, 172.
39. Oppenheimer, "In the Fields of the Lord."

There Can Be Only One

HWJC? (HOW WOULD JESUS COMPETE?)

In a hyper-competitive culture like the United States, the quickest and easiest way to achieve a large platform is by winning. America loves winners! It is not surprising, therefore, that Christian publishers have been eager to publish memoirs and instruction manuals from successful players and coaches. The path to victory, however, is often filled with ethical landmines that are too often ignored by Christian athletes and coaches (not to mention spectators).[40] Higgs's critique gets at the challenge that faces those who defend competition, "What is especially puzzling and worrisome today is the way more and more ministers seem to find less and less difference between the ferocious spirit of sports and the tender fruits of the holy spirit [sic]."[41] The moment Christians stop realizing an innate tension between the "killer instinct" often spoken of in sports circles and Paul's message, "But the fruit of the Spirit is love, joy, peace, patience, kindness, goodness, faithfulness, gentleness and self-control" (Gal 3:22–23), is the moment they have sold out to an American gospel of sports and competition. Sports are not inherently inconsistent with the Christian ethic or overtly sinful. However, Christians must acknowledge there are challenges to the Christian ethic inherent in athletic competition and be more cautious and discerning in their involvement in sports. Oftentimes, the gospel according to sports and competition in America is nothing more than a perpetuation of a kinesiologically-clothed prosperity gospel.[42]

In his book on competition, Warner reflects on the epiphany he received when he realized that many of the manifestations of sports he was witnessing actually ran counter to the Bible's teachings.

---

40. Unfortunately, there are numerous examples of Christians who have been successful in athletics while also facing accusations of ethical shortcomings. Here are three very public examples all involving college football. In 2011, two of the most prominent, revered, and respected college football coaches, both outspoken Christians, were terminated from their high profile head football coaching positions at two of the most prestigious universities in the country: Jim Tressel at Ohio State University (accused of lying to the NCAA during program investigations) and Joe Paterno at Penn State University (accused of helping cover up—or at least ignoring—known accusations of sexual child abuse by an assistant coach). In 2016, Baptist-affiliated Baylor University, endured a major scandal involving rape by football players and administrative cover-up that eventually cost the jobs of their head coach, athletic director, and university president. Ironically, they hosted the annual Symposium on Faith and Culture in November 2015 which focused on sports and Christianity.

41. Higgs, *God in the Stadium*, 322.

42. Krattenmaker, *Onward Christian Athletes*, 72.

> I began to consider the point that should Jesus pay us a return tomorrow, he would not consent to be some combination of Norman Vincent-Peal-Billy Graham-Joe Namath for the Oakland Raiders. He might just say, instead, football had gotten to be a little much. He might just say that organized sports for our children is detrimental to the health and growth of our children. He might just remind us that there is more to life than throwing a ball or watching it be thrown. He might not play our game.[43]

Warner made those remarks reflecting on sports in the 1970s. Imagine his reaction today! Such a perspective sounds absurd to the sports-saturated ears of today's sport-obsessed culture, but its absurdity simply furthers the point of how much our culture has bowed down before the idolatry of sports. While we may feel, far from calling us away from sports, God is actually our motivating factor for competing in sports, Christians still must be able to have honest conversations regarding how competition is affecting their spiritual growth and development.

Many of the ethical quandaries that arise in sports are rooted in their appeal to the ego. In an essay devoted to "Sport as Pastoral Opportunity," Catholic theologian Bernhard Maier directly addresses the temptation sport poses to the ego: "The wolf in sheep's clothing is a sports egoism vested in a form of humanism. But it really constitutes a reciprocal tolerance of egoism."[44] Pride is the sin that C. S. Lewis labeled "The Great Sin" because he believes it "leads to every other vice" and represents "the complete anti-God state of mind."[45] Pride is essentially competitive and is competitive by its very nature."[46] While it would be irresponsible to sweepingly equate pride with all competitive activities, it is equally irresponsible to understate the risk of temptation that Christians participating in competition are putting themselves. Warner emphasizes the significance of taking competition seriously for Christians. "Since the nature of both organized sport and pride is competitive, the only sure way to health is to work through competition and not remain apathetic about it or refute it."[47] Competition is a dynamic reality that all Christians who participate in sports must take seriously.

---

43. Warner, *Competition*, 194.
44. Maier, "Sport as Pastoral Opportunity," 212.
45. Lewis, *Mere Christianity*, 109.
46. Lewis, *Mere Christianity*, 109.
47. Warner, *Competition*, 127.

There Can Be Only One

The scene in 1 Kings 18 of Elijah standing alongside his water-drenched altar with the prophets of Baal can be seen as a biblical example of competition and an example of competing on behalf of the righteousness of God. However, the competitive environment within the created realm of play seems to be another experience of competition altogether. At one level, it seems easier to justify playful competition because it *is* just play and the consequences can be limited to that world. Attempting to confine playful competition to the world of play gets to the heart of the challenge, though. More often than not, the competitive fire of a game affects spectators, coaches, and players beyond the game. At the end of their study, Johnson and Smith provide a balanced yet realistic conclusion for Christians wrestling with competition, "Our research has led us to be both less sanguine about the supposed benefits of competition and more sensitive to the possible harm of competition."[48] Competition is so ingrained within the American psyche that it often receives a moral "free pass" from Christians. While the outright rejection of any acceptable Christian ethic of competition goes too far, it seems as though it is far more common for Christians to blindly accept it with a total lack of any ethical considerations.

THE SPIRIT OF COMPETITION AND THE SOUL OF YOUTH SPORTS

In his lengthy book *The Protestant Ethic and the Spirit of Sports*, Steven Overman explores the interrelationship that capitalism, competition, and theology (specifically, Reformed theology) have had in the United States. He refers to "Calvinism's agonic view of life as a constant struggle in which few rise to the status of the elect."[49] Calvinism, capitalism, and competition all go hand-in-hand, according to Overman as he examines the ways these three ideologies helped shape sports and games in the United States. A leading voice in the discussion of theology and sports, Joseph Price, conjures Reformed theology in discussing the definitive example of competition in U.S. sports: the NCAA Basketball Championship in his essay, "The Final Four as Final Judgment."[50] With its 68-team format, more than any other sporting event in the country, it embodies the competitive mantra,

---

48. Johnson and Smith, "Perspectives on Competition," 9.

49. Overman, *The Protestant Ethic and the Spirit of Sports*, 115.

50. Price, "The Final Four as Final Judgment: The Cultural Significance of the NCAA Basketball Championship," 171–81.

"There can be only one." For Price, the basketball tournament provides a fitting example of a Reformed understanding of faith, judgment, and the elect. Although Overman and Price caricature Reformed theology and rely too heavily on Max Weber and other social analyses of Protestantism in the United States, I think they do show at least a propensity within the Reformed tradition to readily embrace competition.

In many ways, the NCAA basketball tournament stands as the hallmark of the industrialization that took place in U.S. sports throughout the twentieth century. According to Overman, it was a relentless and unharnessed competitive environment in the late-nineteenth and early-twentieth centuries that helped drive the industrialization of the country. Alongside business, agriculture, government, and other social realities, the effect this competitive drive had on sports is unmistakable.

> A vulgar form of Social Darwinism reinforced the prevailing view of life as a struggle for survival. The competitive ethos carried over into sport, where it found an ideal setting in which to be played out. American sport embraced open competitiveness and defined itself in the process. What started out as casual play and gentleman's games inevitably became contests where winning was indeed the only thing.[51]

While a refined theology of competition remains elusive, the fact that Christians, Reformed or otherwise, have come to terms with their participation in competitive sports is obvious. The Bible verses on Tim Tebow's eye black, post-game midfield prayers, and kneeling in end zones following a touchdown are all poignant examples of the accord with which Christians have come to view the relationship of faith and competition. Furthermore, as sports were undergoing their twentieth-century industrialization, Christians began to see another biblical justification for competition that often coincided with sports: competing for Christ. As sports leagues became more prominent in communities throughout the United States (often initiated and organized by local churches and parachurch organizations), Christianity began a burgeoning relationship with sports in the United States. Chapter 8 explores Christian sports ministries in more depth.

---

51. Overman, *The Protestant Ethic and the Spirit of Sports*, 235.

There Can Be Only One
SOME CONCLUSIONS ON COMPETITION

This chapter has examined many aspects of competition and much work remains for Christians moving forward in their consideration of sports. Although competition is an unavoidable force and provides an important conduit for progress, it is not without the potential for significant ethical and moral conflicts. Having addressed many of the challenges competition presents, it seems prudent to offer at least some definitive statements regarding competition in bringing this chapter to a close. First of all, for Christians, competition neither can be unilaterally dismissed as pagan nor blindly embraced as if ordained by God. Inevitably, those of us who profess Christianity will be contributing members to countless systems and experiences of competition throughout our lifetimes. Many experiences within these competitive environments do not promote an ethic consistent with the life of a disciple of Jesus Christ.

What makes the discussion of competition in sports unique is that the entire experience is contrived. In considering the ethics of sports and games we are dealing with matters that can be entirely avoided. Sport is not a matter of life and death. Everyone competes in sports because they want to, not because they have to, and so we should be especially cautious if these contrived experiences are antagonistic to our faith. More simply, Jesus said, "If your right eye causes you to stumble, gouge it out and throw it away. It is better for you to lose one part of your body than for your whole body to be thrown into hell. And if your right hand causes you to stumble, cut it off and throw it away. It is better for you to lose one part of your body than for your whole body to go into hell" (Matt 5:29–30). Christians must be more cautious about how competitive environments, like sports, shape our identities. Some Christians may need to hear, "It is better for you to not play sports and subject yourself to the temptation of competition than for your whole body to go into hell."

Balance and humility remain essential for Christians as in all things. Gary Warner describes how competition can promote one of the very virtues that it so often challenges.

> Those who would advocate eliminating all competition in favor of play would destroy one potential plus for competition: that competition in itself can be a strong force for nullifying pride. Competition shatters illusions. If one always opts for play, he may become a victim of self-delusion and self-inflicted pride. One can fantasize

himself to any height of excellence, and there is no danger. One never has to prove himself if he always plays.[52]

Proverbs 27:17 states: "As iron sharpens iron, so one person sharpens another." It is not a stretch to believe this sharpening can come in the shape of competition so long as play remains the dominant value. A gifted runner often posts his or her best time when challenged by another gifted runner. Competition is often the catalyst and motivation for progress. In 1997, the IBM computer, Deep Blue, defeated the world champion Gary Kasparov in a chess match that many people believed would mark the end of serious pursuits in chess. However, to the contrary, a recent article makes the case that computers have actually made humans better at chess.[53] When competition escalates, so do other participants within the competition. In appealing to God's natural revelation (as revealed in creation), it seems evident that God has ordained some level of competition by which aspects of creation function.

There is no denying the fact that competition can promote the pursuit of excellence among competitors—something that draws us to sports in the first place. Lincoln Harvey offers a unique interpretation of competition that speaks to this idea. He argues for sport as "liturgy of contingency," where winning embodies life *ex nihilo* and losing represents death.[54] Competition becomes the real-life drama depicting the life-and-death, spiritual struggle described in Romans 7:7–25 that all Christians know so well. It explains why we like to win so much and hate losing. Harvey writes, "It also explains why close competition is better than a one-sided match. We want to live the reality of life and death together. That is why we love it when a game is settled only at the closing stages: a last-minute goal, a last-second touchdown."[55] As ticket prices to college football games highlight—we would rather watch our favorite teams play closely contested matches against evenly matched opponents (these games always demand top dollars) rather than play inferior opponents that lead to lop-sided scores.

Havey's next point provides the critical balance when he considers the effect sin has on sports. He says, "Fallen sport too easily becomes a form of idolatrous self-worship, nothing less than the denial of our genuine contingency by confusing ourselves with God and beginning to offer worship to

---

52. Warner, *Competition*, 128.
53. Norris, "How Computers Made Humans Better at Chess."
54. Harvey, *A Brief Theology of Sport*, 88–100.
55. Harvey, *A Brief Theology of Sport*, 109.

ourselves."⁵⁶ In defending competition in sports, it is important to add the caution that engaging in competition is subjecting oneself willingly to the seductive temptation of pride. Competitive activities bring competitors in close proximity to what C. S. Lewis describes as "the real black, diabolical Pride."⁵⁷ The "thrill of victory" can become just as addictive and destructive as any other vice or addiction.

As an example, my son's basketball team recently lost a game when a last-second shot from the other team failed to go in the basket, but the game official made a questionable call. (It was a bad call!) The fouled player, who happened to be one of my son's best friends, stepped up to the free throw line, made the first free throw, and thus won the game for his team. I was surprised to see how angry my son was at having lost this game. It proved to be an apt illustration of the challenges brought about by competition. My son found it difficult to put into words why he was so angry, but much of his anger was directed at the game official who called the foul. (As a high-school football official, I have made my share of unpopular calls, so I know this experience well!) He even found it difficult to be happy for his friend who made the game-winning shot. The basketball game was a community league made up of two teams of local ten-year-old boys who were brought together in ten games over the course of two months. No one beyond the families and friends of these teams knew who won or lost any of their games, and yet the pain, frustration, and other emotions were as real as any other emotions these children experience. This common story illustrates how competition can dehumanize participants (like the referee or opponents), fracture relationships (like my son and his friend), and encourage a lack of empathy. Certainly, this was a "life lesson" for my son and is an apt illustration for how competition can help to positively build character. At the same time, when we only focus on the positive attributes of competition, we ignore the equally problematic aspects.

A final point regarding competition relates to the next chapter about the spiritual powers. The incredible power and interwoven relationship competition has to nearly every aspect of society makes it a perfect partner of the spiritual powers. Competition is pervasive and powerful, and it is difficult to overstate its power and place in the world. Competition is a kind of spiritual power and the force that drives imperialistic nations to war, greedy

---

56. Harvey, *A Brief Theology of Sport*, 103.
57. Lewis, *Mere Christianity*, 113.

companies to oppression, and politicians to mudslinging and muckraking. Competition is intimately related to power.

The spiritual powers are at their most dangerous when they are in competition with one another. Competition is the fuel that gives them their power. Perhaps competition was created as a good and helpful reality by which the powers were to function. Competition drive athletes towards a higher level of performance, fuels positive economic growth, and has an irrefutably crucial role within nature. However, as we will see in the next chapter, these powers have all been affected by the Fall.

In Mark 2, the Pharisees set out to compete with Jesus's authority regarding the Sabbath as they challenged him and his disciples regarding their collecting grains. Jesus responds with his well-known statement, "The Sabbath was made for humankind, and not humankind for Sabbath." (Mark 2:27, NRSV). This statement proves to be paradigmatic regarding how humans interact with the spiritual powers. The powers, like the Sabbath, have their God-ordained, created role within the world. However, as the powers begin competing among themselves and with humans, they become discontent with their place and usurp the role of master. More times than not, competition is their fuel of choice. A much-needed message to parents of young athletes today requires a modern-day twist on Jesus's teaching: *"Sports were made for humankind, and not humankind for sports."* The spiritual power of youth sports has betrayed its soul through an incessant reliance on competition. The next chapter will consider the implications of understanding sports as a spiritual power like economics, politics, and militarism before turning to the implications this all has specifically on youth sports in the United States.

4

Sports as a Spiritual Power

This chapter may seem to be far afield from what you expected to read when you picked up a book about youth sports. Discussions of politics, economics, and spiritual powers hardly seem relevant to the world of scoring goals, dribbling balls, and coaching strategies. However, as you read through this chapter I want to lay out the case for understanding sports as a spiritual power and argue that understanding sports this way helps explain much of what is happening in today's world of youth sports. The better we understand the power structures that are at work within our social fabric, the better prepared we are to address problems as they manifest themselves in our everyday lives. You probably have chosen to read this book because you agree there are many problems with youth sports today or you may be finding it hard to navigate your family through the hectic and challenging world of youth sports. The previous chapter ended by proposing: "Sports were made for humankind, and not humankind for sports." Many people in the United States have lost sight of this, and we are not able to get to the heart of the problems in sports until we begin dealing with it is as a spiritual problem.

We will be delving into some deep theological waters in order to find our way to the intersection of sports and the powers. The chapter begins with an overview of a theology of the powers highlighted by the significant contributions of Hendrik Berkhof and the important subsequent work of Walter Wink. Additionally, this summary of the powers utilizes insight from the works of William Stringfellow and Karl Barth. In moving the discussion towards sports, the chapter considers Stanley Grenz's more recent treatment of the powers as "structures of existence." Having summarized a theological perspective of the powers, the chapter ends by presenting specific examples of the ways in which sports in the United States functions as one of these spiritual powers.

A THEOLOGICAL OVERVIEW OF THE POWERS

The spiritual powers are not an overly familiar concept to many Christians, so perhaps a contemporary illustration will prove helpful in getting started. On Wednesday June 2, 2010, my family and I sat down to watch the Detroit Tigers play the Cleveland Indians on television. We watch the Indians play as often as we can and because they play the Tigers over twenty times a year, this was a typical summer night in the Metz household. One of the Indians' radio announcers often says, "The great thing about baseball is that you never know when you might witness history." June 2, 2010, happened to be one of those nights as the Tigers pitcher Armando Galarraga was pitching exceptionally well. He entered the ninth inning with a perfect game on the line as he had not allowed a single base runner through twenty-four batters. Galarraga got the first two outs in the ninth inning and was one out away from pitching the twenty-first perfect game in the history of Major League Baseball and the first in Tigers history.[1]

The Indians batter Jason Donald hit a groundball that was fielded by the first basemen who threw back to the pitcher covering first base and appeared to beat the runner. The umpire, Jim Joyce, however, called Donald safe and the perfect game was spoiled. Instant replay was not used by MLB in 2010 so there was no recourse to overturn the call, and the game became one of the most infamous in professional baseball's history. As soon as Joyce went to the locker room he asked to see the replay, and he realized immediately he had blown the call. Joyce requested to meet with Galarraga and offered him a tear-filled apology in the locker room that night telling him he felt almost as bad as when his father passed away. His face was quickly on television sets across the country bemoaning his mistake. He and his children even received death threats.

To simply correct the error and award Galarraga the perfect game seems like it would have been the right thing to do. Debate raged after the game as to whether or not the call should be reversed, but commissioner

---

1. A perfect game in baseball is when a pitcher does not allow a single base runner in an entire game, getting twenty-seven outs consecutively.

Sports as a Spiritual Power

Bud Selig released a statement that MLB would look into instant replay more seriously, but the call would not be overturned. As Joyce entered the same Comerica Park to umpire the final game of the Tigers-Indians series the next day, he was greeted with a standing ovation as Galarraga presented him with the lineup card in a moving show of sportsmanship and forgiveness. Even with this shared experience that an injustice had taken place, the vast majority of people were willing to forgive the umpire's error as "part of the game" or "just the way things are." Some people refer to sporting deities while others refer to the "powers that be," but this sense that there is something greater involved in our games than the individuals that comprise them resonates with the Bible's teaching of the spiritual powers.

In extolling the sovereignty of Jesus Christ as the image of God and agent of creation, Paul proclaims, "For by him all things were created: things in heaven and on earth, visible and invisible, whether thrones or powers or rulers or authorities; all things were created by him and for him" (Col 1:16). Mennonite scholar John Howard Yoder claims "few realms of biblical thought have until recent years been so resolutely ignored by the main streams of Protestant theology" as the critical study of these thrones, powers, rulers, and authorities.[2] Hendrik Berkhof's groundbreaking work, *Christ and the Powers*, first published in Dutch in 1953, helped the study of the principalities and powers establish an important theological niche in recent decades. In this small book, Berkhof describes the nature of these principalities and powers that permeate the contextual background of the New Testament. Subsequent theologians like Yoder, Wink, and Stringfellow went on to develop theories of what exactly the principalities and powers are and how they manifest themselves. Furthermore, the powers show up in the work of Karl Barth as "chthonic forces,"[3] and Stanely Grenz highlights them under the label "structures of existence."[4]

The Powers in Hendrik Berkhof

The enduring legacy of Berkhof is that he draws attention to the nine Pauline passages that make explicit use of the language of "power" (Rom 8:38f; 1 Cor 2:8; 15:24–26; Eph 1:20f.; 2:1f.; 3:10; 6:12; Col 1:16; 2:15) and establishes a theological framework for exploring the implications and nuances

---

2. Yoder, "Translator's Preface," 5.
3. Gorringe, *Karl Barth Against Hegemony*, 265.
4. Grenz, *Theology for the Community of God*, 228–35.

power has on the Christian faith. Reflecting on the diversity of power in these passages, Berkhof suggests, "We rather have the impression that Paul means to suggest broadly, by variety of expressions, the number and diversity of the Powers."[5] He goes on to argue that Paul does not create the language of the powers, but rather seeks to demythologize a concept that would have already been familiar to the people to whom he was writing. For Berkhof, the powers are the spiritual forces at work in organizing and managing the world. They exist at the ideological intersection of spiritual being and spiritual force. He states: "They are personal, spiritual beings" and that "they influence events on earth, especially events within nature."[6] The principalities and powers are "the Man behind the curtain" helping to shape and influence the unfolding of history.

The esoteric nature of the powers makes it challenging to describe them in general, but specific examples like the one from the baseball game proves helpful. The sport of baseball is bigger than any one player, manager, owner, or umpire. While each one of these individuals has an important, even vital, role in the sport, everyone acknowledges that the sport is something much bigger than their roles, even collectively. While everyone can see Joyce made a mistake in that baseball game, the majority of people appealed to something bigger than Joyce, Galarraga, the Tigers, and even than MLB itself in allowing the result to stand. Unwittingly, people conjure up the notion of sports as a spiritual power when they refer to respecting "The Game" in an abstract way.

Central to a theology of the powers is the fact that they were created by God and are therefore innately good. The New Testament nowhere gives the impression that these forces are inherently evil and opposed to the creative intentions of God, but rather they are said to play an essential role within creation (Col 3:16). The powers comprise the invisible background that is bound together and upon which the visible creation is dependent.[7] These powers are often considered as "forces" and "spiritual beings," so it is not surprising that serious theological treatment of the powers is often confined to the world of politics, economics, technology, the media, and militarism. Although each of these spheres are undoubtedly rife with corruption and flaws, they remain essential structures that help organize and determine the affairs of the world. Berkhof seeks to symbiotically combine

---

5. Berkhof, *Christ and the Powers*, 15.
6. Berkhof, *Christ and the Powers*, 17.
7. Berkhof, *Christ and the Powers*, 28.

the pre-modern, mythological understanding of supernatural forces, like angels and demons, with the modern, liberal, post-Enlightenment tendency to see these forces strictly through scientific, sociological perspectives.

This statement from the end of *Christ and the Powers* reiterates the significance of the spiritual powers: "In light of God's action Paul perceived that mankind is not composed of loose individuals, but that structures, orders, forms of existence, or whatever they be called, are given us as a part of creaturely life and that these are involved, as much as men themselves, in the history of creation, fall, preservation, reconciliation, and consummation."[8] In other words, the principalities and powers are rooted in the communality of humanity and provide a spiritual framework for understanding contemporary social sciences and the ways that human beings relate to one another. As Wink writes, "What people in the world of the Bible experienced as and called 'principalities and powers' was in fact the actual spirituality at the center of the political, economic, and cultural institutions of the day."[9] It could be said that the powers and principalities represent the socio-spirituality of civilization.

The Powers in Walter Wink

While Hendrik Berkhof helped instigate much subsequent work on the powers and principalities, it was the eccentric theologian Walter Wink who is responsible for the most significant and far-reaching contributions on the subject. His trilogy dedicated to the powers provides a unique theological contribution as it extrapolates to a much greater length the theological inquiry begun by Berkhof. Wink's trilogy provides a three-fold investigation of the powers according to tasks indicated in the title of the three volumes: *Naming the Powers*, *Unmasking the Powers*, and *Engaging the Powers*. This investigation into those powers will utilize Wink's three-fold analysis to consider sports among the powers and then explore the implications of interacting with sports as a power.

Naming the Power of Sports

In his first volume, *Naming the Powers*, Wink extends Berkhof's work by providing a more thorough textual study of the language of the powers

8. Berkhof, *Christ and the Powers*, 66.
9. Wink, *The Powers that Be*, 24.

in the New Testament. Wink's first objective is to identify what exactly is behind the language of the powers as well as what Paul means by invoking his particular choice of language. According to Wink, the New Testament conveys diversity within its power language while still evidencing patterns of similarities.[10] Wink singles out seven Greek words that manifest the different nuances of power the New Testament writers use: *archon*, *arche*, *exousia*, *dynamis*, *kyriotes*, *thronos*, and *onoma*. While these words all refer to the broader structures/powers/principalities/-isms that organize and order the world, each word also conveys a nuanced reality within these structures. In other words, none of these words encapsulate the entirety of the concept of power, nor are the words completely synonymous with one another.

Colossians 3:16 provides a helpful case study for illustrating the significance of the diversity seen in the concept of power. The thrones (*thronos*), powers (*kyriotetes*), rulers (*arche*), and authorities (*exousiai*) to which Paul refers in this verse provide a nuanced description of different earthly manifestations of power. Although it may be impossible to know for sure the exact nuance Paul may have intended for each of these different words, it seems more likely to believe that each of these words implied some unique nuance rather than that the writer was simply exercising some kind of linguistic variety for variety's sake. Wink provides a hypothetical (though completely plausible) analysis of how these nuances could have been intended. He suggests that the Greek use of *thronos* resonates with the symbolic place of power still utilized in our language today: "the county *seat*, the judge's *bench*, the *chair*person, the *oval office*."[11] This manifestation of power is different from the *kyriotetes* that might have been intended to imply the dominions over which the thrones hold power. Wink describes this aspect of power as the "'sphere of influence' which the throne possesses."[12] Additionally, the *arche* may represent the temporary wielders of this power through political office, military command, or other recognized position of authority. Furthermore, the *exousiai* may refer to the "legitimations and sanctions by which authority is maintained."[13]

Although Wink's proposal remains plausible, he is not setting out to provide a detailed and definitive hierarchy of power in this analysis (nor

10. Wink, *Naming the Powers*, 10.
11. Wink, *Naming the Powers*, 65.
12. Wink, *Naming the Powers*.
13. Wink, *Naming the Powers*, 66.

does he believe Paul does that here or anywhere else). Instead, he is making the point that there are nuances of some kind in the realities of power that make it logical that these diverse descriptions in the New Testament text do correspond to actual, existential, sociological realities. While Wink prefers phenomenological language (referring to spirits, angels, and demons) rather than scientific/metaphysical language, it does not take away from the remarkable ways these concepts resonate with contemporary understandings of social systems. Wink is arguing that these manifestations of power do exist, the biblical authors were fully aware of their existence, and they play a vital role within the unfolding events of history.

By now, you may be wondering what any of this has to do with youth sports, but I believe Wink's case study of Col 3:16 proves to be especially relevant to sports. He concludes the above discussion by stating, "With these four terms one could in principle analyze any conceivable institution or system of power 'on earth or in heaven.'"[14] With this in mind, he goes on to propose, "Every business, corporation, school denomination, bureaucracy, *sports team*—indeed, social reality in all its forms is a combination of both visible and invisible, outer and inner, physical and spiritual."[15] In other words, to view sports strictly sociologically or physiologically is to fail to consider the bigger, spiritual dynamic at play. Like all other aspects of society, sports have a soul. In his memoir on college football in the South, author Chad Gibbs's description of what football does to him conjures the soul of the sport.

> Football can take your emotions from zero to awesome in 4.2 seconds. When I'm there, in the stadium, it all feels so important, and when the big play comes, I am screaming and leaping around. I raise my arms in the air and sing with all my might. The feeling can last for weeks if the win is big enough. The flip side is the immediate despair a loss can bring, and that feeling can last for weeks as well.[16]

The powers are so big and entrenched in our social lives we find it difficult to address them. We are not surprised, then, to see Michael Novak remark, "We find it hard to express just what it is that gives sports their spirit and their power."[17] In reality, sports *are* a power.

14. Wink, *Naming the Powers*.
15. Wink, *Naming the Powers*, 4. Emphasis mine.
16. Gibbs, *God and Football*, 92.
17. Novak, *The Joy of Sports*, 31.

Elite?

Unmasking the Power of Sports

At the heart of Wink's second volume, *Unmasking the Powers*, Wink sets out to demythologize some of the Bible's most misunderstood teachings regarding the complexities of supernatural realities. One of Wink's most significant presuppositions is the fact that the modern, secular world has repressed the spiritual realm to such an extent that he says, "we no longer have ready access to it."[18] Thus, the specific powers Wink's second volume discusses—Satan, demons, angels of churches, angels of nations, gods, elements, and angels of nature—sound archaic and rather fanciful to the ears of most modern readers. Wink limits his discussion to powers specifically mentioned in the Bible, but he also acknowledges that "the list of possible candidates for examination . . . is virtually endless."[19] He proceeds to list several specific possibilities including propaganda, education, and—not surprisingly—sports.[20]

Incidentally, there may be no aspect of culture today that remains as open to the world of phenomenology as that of sports. It is commonplace in sports to talk of team *spirit*, to refer to the various *gods* overseeing the games, and it is one of the few places where superstitions, blessings, and curses are widely embraced. My wife confesses to having prayed for the Atlanta Braves to win the National League Championship game she attended in 1995. Two of my favorite professional sports team, the Cleveland Browns and Cleveland Indians, are often said to be cursed. My son's baseball team regularly has a special handshake and team cheer that accompanies the beginning and ending of their games. Many of the football players I stand beside on Friday nights refuse to wash their uniforms throughout the season out of deference for "good luck." While these traditions are often readily dismissed as juvenile, immature, or "just for fun," theologically, it is difficult not to make the case that these are phenomenological elements rarely seen in other aspects of today's society. Wink singles out the powers specifically mentioned in the Bible but, in the end, acknowledges these powers are not the likely candidates to resurrect the biblical teachings of the powers today. His point is while the manifestation and awareness of these powers evolve, their essence remains a crucial and essential part of the creation and demands reinterpretation.

18. Wink, *Unmasking the Powers*, 2.
19. Wink, *Unmasking the Powers*, 5.
20. Wink, *Unmasking the Powers*.

Sports as a Spiritual Power

Engaging the Power of Sports

In the Introduction to the concluding volume of his trilogy, Walter Wink uses an example from the world of sports (a riot at a soccer game) to illustrate a contemporary manifestation of the powers.[21] What the social sciences would label "mob mentality," Wink seeks to give spiritual vitality to, describing them as "impersonal spiritual realities at the center of institutional life."[22] Wink suggests it is impossible to transform social structures and systems without appealing to both the inner, spiritual realm as much as the outer realm. Thus, his tripartite thesis is summarized: the powers are created good; the powers are fallen; the powers must be redeemed and therefore engaged.[23] These three statements provide a practical framework by which to analyze sports as a spiritual power.

MANIFESTATIONS OF SPORTS AS A SPIRITUAL POWER

The three-part framework described above provides a starting point acknowledging sports as a gift of God, created by humanity in their free and playful existence. It avoids the shortcoming, seen in some who offer critique of sports, whose impulse is to sweepingly condemn organized sports as a competing pagan religion or as outright idolatry.[24] It is an overreaction to contemporary indulgence in sports to label them heretical (although the extent to which sports has been ignored does help make sense of the overreaction). To understand sports as a spiritual power acknowledges that sports have been created for our use and enjoyment. It helps to avoid throwing the proverbial baby out with the bathwater and brings us back to where we ended in the previous chapter: "Sports were made for humankind, not humankind for sports."

Even a cursory study of sports reveals many of its shortcomings today. To suggest sports as inherently good is not a full-fledged embrace of everything done in the name of sports. From cheating scandals to performance

---

21. Wink, *Engaging the Powers*, 9.
22. Wink, *Engaging the Powers*.
23. Wink, *Engaging the Powers*, 10.
24. For instance, Robert J. Higgs begins his book, "I will contend that sports and religion—I will mostly be thinking of Christianity—are in many ways incompatible. I would even argue that the ways in which modern sports have become entangled with religious practices constitute a (Christian) heresy." *God in the Stadium*, 1.

enhancing drugs, the cloak hiding the dark side of sports is pulled back all the time. Just last summer, I witnessed a nine-year-old boy's baseball tournament game end with a shouting match between coaches, parents, and the umpire over a disputed call that ended the game. Hardly a Friday night football game goes by when one of my fellow crew members or I do not have to enforce an unsportsmanlike conduct penalty on a player or coach. In the summer of 2014, the Little League baseball team, Jackie Robinson West from Chicago, won over the heart of the nation when they won the Little League World Series only to have their title later stripped away when it was revealed that not all their players lived within their district. We are surrounded by the dark side of sports. As Norbert Muller cautions, "Not all manifestations and developments of modern sports can find approval from a Christian point of view."[25] Understanding sports from the perspective of the spiritual powers helps reveal this dark side of sports as collateral damage and a systemic result of the Fall.[26] It also helps prevent the creation of a false dichotomy where one must choose between God and sports or between participating in church-sponsored sports and not playing sports at all. The final point, and what amounts to the impetus for this book, is that even sports themselves (as much as their organizing structures) cry out for redemption alongside all the other powers within creation.

In his systematic theology, Stanley Grenz utilizes the work of Berkhof to help construct his theology of the "structures of existence." Grenz defines the structures of existence as "Those larger, suprahuman aspects or dimensions of reality which form the inescapable context for human life and which therefore condition individual and corporate human existence."[27] While Wink tends to emphasize the supernatural aspect of the powers, Grenz emphasizes their role in organizing the social dynamics of humanity. He goes on to say, "They form the context for individual human life within the human community and for human social interaction."[28]

Grenz reiterates the same elusiveness evident in Berkhof when attempting to articulate the qualities of the powers, stating: "There always

---

25. Muller, "Concrete Pastoral Action within Sports," 224.

26. George Castle provides a poignant example of the symbiotic way the spiritual powers can work. He tells the tragic story of the Jackie Robinson West baseball team by interweaving with relative ease the political, racial, and economic powers that have long plagued the city of Chicago. Castle, *Jackie Robinson West*.

27. Grenz, *Theology for the Community of God*, 228.

28. Grenz, *Theology for the Community of God*, 230.

remains a dimension of the mysterious about them."[29] He describes them as both "quasi-independent" and "quasi-personal," highlighting their complex relationship within the human social condition. They are inextricably linked to humans while at the same time existing and working independently of them. They are partly determined by the actions and decisions of human beings, but they also take on a life of their own. While the discussion of the powers still may seem far removed from the world of sports to this point, some examples from the real world will illustrate how sports operate as a spiritual power.

The aloofness and complexity of the structures of existence is illustrated by a cable customer's vain attempt at talking with someone who can rectify his or her problems over the telephone. While passed from one customer-service representative to another, the customer realizes that the cable company is much larger than any one customer service representative. This can make it difficult when looking for someone with whom to voice the customer's frustration and help rectify his or her billing issues. I find situations like this endlessly frustrating and my impulse is to lash out at the person who has wronged me, but who is that person? How many of us have given the person on the other end of the phone a piece of our mind when we know that they are not really the one to blame? The company is certainly larger than any one customer-service employee, and it is equally larger than the company's CEO or individual stockholders. This is dramatically exemplified when the creator of a company (like Steve Jobs) is fired by the very company he or she helped create.

In sports, the elusiveness of defining the powers is seen in the way athletes and coaches often refer to "The Game," where they seemingly imply a higher, existential reality of which all who participate in "The Game" are a part. "The Game" is bigger than any one player, coach, team, and even league (football does not belong to the NFL). In 2012, Penn State University was dealt harsh penalties from the NCAA regarding a sex-abuse scandal and cover-up involving their former assistant football coach Jerry Sandusky. On July 23, 2012, NCAA President Mark Emmert announced the penalties assessed on the school. I remember listening to this press conference in the car and being amazed at the direct correlation to his statement and the language of the spiritual powers: "One of the grave dangers stemming from our love of sport is that the sports themselves can become too big to fail, indeed, too big to even challenge. The result can be an erosion of academic

29. Grenz, *Theology for the Community of God.*

values that are replaced by the value of hero worship and winning at any costs."[30] This dark page in the history of Penn State football highlights the havoc that the powers can inflict when they are not held in check.

This is the very nature of the powers that especially resonated with William Stringfellow. The powers and principalities are not only the ethereal structures themselves but the physical corporations and institutions. In other words, they are not only the -isms, but their corporal manifestations as well. Stringfellow describes the situation like this, "Human beings are reluctant to acknowledge that institutions—or any of the other principalities—as creatures having their own existence, personality, and mode of life. Yet the Bible consistently speaks of the principalities as creatures."[31] Stringfellow provides extended treatment on several particular powers,[32] and, in one instance, sweepingly lists several examples.

> The Pentagon or the Ford Motor Company or Harvard University or the Hudson Institute or Consolidated Edison or the Diners Club or the Olympics or the Methodist Church or the Teamsters Union... capitalism, Maoism, humanism, Mormonism, astrology, the Puritan work ethic, science and scientism, white supremacy, patriotism plus many, many more—sports, sex, any profession or discipline, technology, money, the family—beyond any prospect of full enumeration. The principalities and powers *are* legion.[33]

Alongside the oft-cited examples of capitalism, humanism, patriotism, and others, Stringfellow recognizes sports (not to mention one particular, corporeal manifestation of sports in the Olympics) as a spiritual power.[34]

Stringfellow was among eight panelists who had the opportunity to question the theological giant, Karl Barth, at an event at the University of Chicago on April 25–26, 1962. At this event, Stringfellow queried Barth on this topic specifically, asking, "Who are the principalities and powers today in our world?" Barth's response bears repeating.

---

30. Mark Emmert, "Press Conference Remarks," July 23, 2012.

31. Stringfellow, *An Ethic for Christians*, 79.

32. Bill Wylie Kellermann organizes Stringfellow's writing according to his specific address of the powers of the state, science and technology, medicine, law, money, race, higher education, and the church in *A Keeper of the Word*, 223–58.

33. Stringfellow, *An Ethic for Christians*, 78.

34. It is noteworthy that in his recent updating of Stringfellow's list, Bob Ekblad provides contemporary examples of many of the powers listed by Stringfellow, but overlooks the category of sports completely. His oversight further evidences the neglect of sports in contemporary theology. Eckblad, *A New Christian Manifesto*, 101.

> Everywhere that an ideology is ruling, there is such a power: a communist or anticommunist ideology; money is such a power. No need to give a description. Sport is such a power. Traditions of all kinds are such angelic powers. Fashion for men and women is also a power. What we call religion—in all kinds of expression—is also a world of powers. Angelic powers—the thing unconscious within us—that is a real power. But also what we call reason is such a power. And let us not forget sex.[35]

Considering the 1962 backdrop of this gathering, it is not surprising that Barth's mind is drawn immediately to communist and anti-communist ideologies as examples of the principalities and powers. However, it is somewhat surprising that he so quickly turns from money to sports as his next examples. With the first Super Bowl still five years in the future and with the excesses of today's sporting culture unimaginable to Barth in 1962, sports still stood ensconced enough in the culture more than fifty years ago for him to quickly acknowledge their supernatural reality and theological potency right alongside communism and money.

Although failing to provide additional commentary on this occasion, Barth does discuss sports further under the moniker of "chthonic powers" at one point in *Church Dogmatics*. Barth states that these powers "serve in and of themselves to bind man who has broken free from God, to put him under obligation, to tyrannize him, to lead him where he does not want to go, to rob him of his freedom under the pretext and appearance of granting him every kind of freedom."[36] Clearly, Barth speaks to the fallen state of the powers. He goes on to speak directly to sports: "Today what is called sport seems to have become the playground of a particular earth-spirit."[37] Barth then catalogs a long list of examples of the ways that this "spirit" or power manifests itself in sports. This "earth-spirit" lives on in the social complex of clubs, teams, leagues, divisions, and tournaments that make up the contemporary youth-sports industrial complex. It is by this youth-sports industrial complex that so many families, to use Barth's words, are bound (believing a particular sports lifestyle is their child's only hope for athletic success), led to where they don't want to go (finding it a much more consuming commitment than they ever believed possible), unwittingly robbed of their freedom (believing they have spent too much time, money, and

---

35. Barth, "Introduction to Theology, Conversation with Karl Barth," 190.
36. Barth, *CD* 4/4: 228–29.
37. Barth, *CD* 4/4: 230.

energy to let their child quit), and ultimately have their family's relationship with God negatively impacted.

THE FUNCTION OF SPORTS AS A SPIRITUAL POWER

Few social structures in contemporary culture are as powerful and affect other structures to the extent that sports does. Any discussion of power and sports must quickly make its way through the influence of economics, politics, physiology, media, medicine, and countless others. Washington and Karen edited a collection of readings highlighting sports' complex, interwoven relationships with other social institutions and practices. In, "A Note to the Reader," the authors preface the collection by stating: "We demonstrate not only the ways that the interactions with these social institutions or practices shape sport, but how sport, in part through its enormous popularity, influences those social institutions."[38] Such commentary relates directly to how sports function as a spiritual power.

Sports and Politics

Sports are often looked at as an escape from politics as much as a reprieve from work, financial stress, or family strife. Sports and politics are as formidable bedfellows as religion and politics—something we are reminded of just about any time a sports figure chooses to make a public, political statement. During the 2016 NFL season, San Francisco 49er's quarterback Colin Kapernick sparked national debate by refusing to stand during the pre-game national anthem. Often drawing the ire of many sports fans, several African-American athletes have expressed public support of the Black Lives Matter movement. Former Major League Baseball pitcher Curt Schilling lost his job as an ESPN analyst for making comments about a politically charged issue. The controversy created when politics enters the boundaries of sports provides continual storylines beyond the gymnasia and playing fields.

The disdain for allowing politics to mix with sports is a long tradition, and the loudest public outcry long has been, "Keep your politics out of my sports!" Although so many people want to view sports as apolitical or

---

38. Washington and Karen, "A Note to the Reader," xi.

neutral, Dave Zirin exposes this as myth in the introduction to his provocative book, *A People's History of Sports in the United States*. In this concise and powerful statement from the preface, Zirin highlights the extensive relationship between sports and politics that is so often ignored by participants of sports in the United States.

> In an era where the building of publicly funded stadiums has become a substitute for anything resembling an urban policy; in a time when local governments build these monuments to corporate greed on the taxpayer's dime, siphoning off millions of dollars into commercial enterprise while schools, hospitals, and bridges decay, one can hardly say that sports exists in a world separate from politics. When the sports page—with its lurid tales of steroids, Michael Vick, referee gambling, and high-profile sexual harassment suits—no longer can be contained in the sports page, then clearly we need some kind of framework to take on and separate what we love and hate about sports so we can challenge it to change.[39]

Sports, in fact, have become so intertwined with politics that it is difficult to discuss sports at all without stirring at least some areas of the political waters. Novak even accuses famed sportscaster Howard Cosell of underestimating politics' relationship to sports, suggesting "Cosell too much believes that politics is the real world, and sports an escape."[40]

Perhaps the most dramatic example of the relationship between sports and politics in America is the long-standing anti-trust exemption granted to Major League Baseball in 1922 by the federal government. The 1972 U.S. Supreme Court Case *Flood vs. Kuhn et al.*, widely known as the court case that opened up MLB to free agency, affirmed the 1922 decision while at the same time referring to it as an "aberration" and an "anomaly."[41] The judge delivering the court's ruling, Harry Blackmun—a lifelong Cubs' fan, even began the ruling with what the website baseball-reference.com describes as: "A poetic paean to the game of baseball, citing the names of dozens of famous ballplayers from the past and underlining baseball's role at the center of American culture."[42] Baseball received judicial assistance in becoming "America's pastime." Baseball, and more recently, American football, fulfills a patriotic, civic function for the United States in the way that hockey does

---

39. Zirin, *A People's History of Sports in the United States*, xii.
40. Novak, *The Joy of Sports*, 280.
41. Zimalist, "May the Best Team Win," 22.
42. Baseball Reference, "Flood v. Kuhn."

in Canada, Aussie rules football does in Australia, and soccer does in many other nations in the world.

Attempting to classify sports as a spiritual power does not negate the quasi-religious function it continues to maintain in nearly all cultures. For example, sports in the United States functions, at least in some capacity, as a civil religion. Novak's assessment provides a helpful foundational point: "At all times and in all places, sports do have a relation to politics and culture; it would be foolish to believe that sports are apolitical."[43] S. W. Pope makes the case that sports largely helped shape American identity in the early part of the twentieth century. He writes: "More than mere amusement, sport both as metaphorical activity and class drama, helped define and display uniquely American visions through public discourse and through people's actual experiences on ball fields, in gymnasiums, and on playgrounds throughout the country.[44] Religious professor Craig Forney singles out specifically football, baseball, and basketball as representative of civil religion in the United States in the following roles: "providing a religious orientation," "a worldview of far-reaching influence," and "working together in a yearly cycle, they portray key ingredients for belief system of the nation."[45]

The intermingling of the U.S. ethos and the playing of sport is embodied in the pervasive pageantry of red, white, and blue that accompanies nearly all major athletic contests in the United States. The event that best displays this patriotic confluence is the annual college football game between Army and Navy that is always one-part football spectacle, two-parts U.S. military propaganda. There is an undeniable nationalistic overtone to many games in the United States, but sports also provides regional and metropolitan solidarity as neighbors and coworkers in the same areas cheer for "their team." As David Morris and Daniel Kraker point out: "Professional teams have become an integral part of our community fabric and our emotional and civic lives."[46] In particular, the American South has seen college football further codify that region's pride in recent years through their support of the South Eastern Conference, which is the subject of Eric Bain-Selbo's interesting book *Game Day and God*.[47] Minnesotans play hockey, Californians surf, Hoosiers play basketball, high schools in Texas,

43. Novak, *The Joy of Sports*, 279.
44. Pope, *Patriotic Games*: 3.
45. Forney, *The Holy Trinity of American Sports*, 8.
46. Morris Kraker, "Rooting the Home Team," 33.
47. Bain-Selbo, *Game Day and God*.

Alabama, and Ohio fill football stadiums with tens of thousands of fans, and lacrosse is the game of choice for many in the Northeast. Sports has an undeniable influence on both nationalistic zeal and community pride that, at its best, can help bolster positive, social cohesion and reinforce the solidarity of neighborhoods.

Sports and Economics

Politics and nationalism, of course, are not the only spiritual powers to join forces with sports. To talk of sports and ignore its complex and evolving relationship with economics has become impossible. Sports economics has become its own field of study and contains endless complexities. An incident from the 1992 Summer Olympic Games in Barcelona, Spain, illustrates how the economic side of sports actually can be more powerful than political ramifications. For that year's Olympics, the United States Olympic Committee sold the sponsorship rights for the warm-up outfits the men's basketball team was to wear during the medal-receiving ceremony to Reebok. This was the first year professional basketball players were permitted to compete in the Olympics and the United States assembled the "Dream Team"—a team roster that included some of the NBA's greatest players. The problem was that several of those basketball players were already sponsored by Reebok's competitor, Nike, and so they refused to wear Reebok's outfits. Basketball player Charles Barkely said, "Nike has helped me make a whole lot of money, and I'm not about to forget it!"[48] While Nike eventually caved and the athletes wore the Reebok outfits, they did place American flags over the Reebok logo.[49]

Authors and social commentators regularly lament the abundance of money present in modern-day sports. The negative effect excessive money has on sports seems so self-evident lengthy commentary here seems unnecessary. Instead of exploring the countless examples of money's negative influence on sports, one example will suffice. In one of his few comments directly regarding sports as a spiritual power, William Stringfellow writes, "Commercial sports have a political significance in this nation markedly similar to that of circuses and athletic spectacles in Imperial Rome."[50] Having written these words in the early 1970s, one can only imagine what

---

48. Pope, *Patriotic Games*, viii.
49. Pope, *Patriotic Games*, viii.
50. Stringfellow, *An Ethic for Christians*, 90.

Stringfellow's reflections would be on today's world of sports. This comparison with the Roman circus is not lost on Indiana University professor Murray Sperber, who chose as a title for his investigation into big-time college sports, *Beer and Circus*.[51]

Sports and Higher Education

Former president of Yale University and former commissioner of MLB, Bart Giamatti, once said: "What was allowed to become a circus—college sports—threatens to become the means by which the public believes the entire enterprise [higher education] is a sideshow."[52] Increasingly, universities are known for their athletic programs and, especially, for the success of those athletic teams. Athletic programs have become the dog that wags the tail of university policy for colleges throughout the United States, and they often produce such a significant amount of revenue that it is impossible for administrators to ignore while setting their agendas. The revenue produced by the nation's largest athletic programs, for example, is staggering—the top thirteen schools each posting over $100 million of revenue in 2012.[53]

While the headlines are dominated by the biggest athletic programs, smaller private institutions (many of them Christian colleges) have also seen the allure of becoming a big-time sports university. Much like professional sports teams often are seen to increase a city's reputation and image (they are even known as a "Major League City"[54]), universities also often are enamored by the prospect of the national reputation and name recognition that success in sports can bring. To witness sports as a spiritual power, one must look no further than Jerry Falwell and his emphasis on sports at Lynchburg Baptist College (later renamed Liberty University). Baker reports Falwell "envisaged strong sports programs as a means of instant credibility, Christian witness, and financial support."[55] Only two years after founding the school, Falwell started a sports program and told a reporter from the *Washington Post*, "he wanted to field a football team that would beat Notre Dame."[56]

51. Sperber, *Beer and Circus*.
52. Giamatti, Convocation Speech at Williams College, September 12, 1987.
53. Berkowitz, "2014–2015 NCAA Finances: Top College Revenues."
54. Delaney and Eckstein, "Public Dollars, Private Stadiums, and Democracy," 13.
55. Baker, *Playing with God*, 211.
56. Hoffman, *Good Game*, 138.

Historically, Notre Dame may provide the most stunning example of the power of collegiate sports. Well before John F. Kennedy was elected President and dealt a harsh blow to anti-Catholic sentiments in the United States, Catholic bigotry was already undergoing a major attack due to the incredible success of Notre Dame's football program. Baker goes as far to say head football coach, "Knute Rockne was Notre Dame's answer to the Ku Klux Klan," and he reports that some people saw Notre Dame's football team as the "one Catholic institution immune to the bigotry."[57] Although it has diminished slightly in recent years, the popularity of Notre Dame football remains among the most popular teams in the country, and its popularity is a direct reflection of its success.

Each of these examples highlights the ineffable power of sports. From politics to economics, higher education, and even racism, there are few corners of society sport does not have an influence. However, for every university that partners with sports to expand the reach of its message and success, the fallen side of the power is not far away from wielding its evil side effects. The fundamentalist Christian university Oral Roberts seemingly made a deal with the devil as it rose to national prominence in the NCAA Men's Basketball tournament in the 1970s. The school was quickly overrun by investigations of impropriety and misconduct a few years later.[58] The only university to ever receive a "death penalty" for its football program was the private, Christian college Southern Methodist University, which was so overrun with corruption and cheating that the NCAA disbanded their football program entirely for the 1987 season. The 2010s witnessed the ascent of (Baptist) Baylor University's football team to national prominence through its success on the field. However, in separate incidents in 2014 and 2015, Baylor football players were arrested for sexual assaults, and an outside investigation would go on to expose a cover up involving coaches, athletic directors, and other administrators. (Incidentally, the athletic director at Baylor during this time was fired and then subsequently hired by another private Christian college seeking to raise the profile of its athletic program: Liberty University.) To see sports as a spiritual power acknowledges the great potential for social contribution they offer, but it also takes seriously the great harm they can perpetuate when they join forces with other, equally powerful, spiritual powers.

57. Baker, *Playing with God*, 133.
58. Ibid., 210–13.

The Christian community has so warmly embraced sports that this discussion of sports functioning as a spiritual power may seem foreign or even hyperbolic, but it is impossible to separate sports from their social structures. The moment we buy our child their first ball, we have begun to enter the world of the spiritual powers. Athletic leagues and organizations throughout the country are some of the most popular and prevalent civic groups in the community. The scope of these leagues and their impact on communities highlight their social influence and power. While many of the examples in this chapter focused on professional and collegiate athletics, the problems and obstacles seen in those examples have trickled down vociferously into sports at all levels. We have established the general neglect of sports within theological circles, but the neglect of sports at the grassroots level is even starker. For this reason, Part 1 of the book has given much attention to theological discussions involving the purpose of sports, the role of competition, and an examination of the supporting social structures in sports. Having spent a good deal of time exploring theological and philosophical questions, we now turn to youth sports, specifically, and consider how these theological foundations can help us come to terms with recent trends in youth sports that are having a dramatic influence on families in the United States.

PART 2

The Youth-Sports Industrial Complex

Sports are such a dramatic part of our culture, and we are so accustomed to their omnipresence, that it's not until we actually set out to examine them that we realize just how big they are. My church's suburban community has been one of the fastest growing areas in the country for over a decade. The district had one high school when we moved here fourteen years ago, but it has just broken ground on its fourth high school, which is set to open next school year. Once the funding measures have been approved by voters, one of the first matters of importance for each of these new high schools has been determining the nickname and mascot. Some of the first noticeable construction at each site has been the sports complexes.

Hardly a day goes by when I don't see an advertisement for another local travel team. The numerous universities and high schools in our area all host countless summer camps for a number of sports. Local news coverage is dominated by local high-school and college-sports stories and scores. There are numerous businesses within a ten minute drive from my house that sell sporting goods. New sports clinics and sports-medicine offices are being built all over the city. Just off a local highway, Ohio State University recently built a brand new, state-of-the art building that houses their sports-medicine school. Hardly a week goes by when one of our teenagers isn't gone from our Sunday services due to sports conflicts—sometimes my own children.

Whether we want to admit it or not, the massive world of youth sports has a dramatic influence on our communities. Professional sports and sports at the highest levels tend to garner the most attention, but it is grassroots sports that have the most dramatic affect on communities. While Part 1 examined some of the theological and philosophical underpinnings of sports in general, Part 2 examines the specific world of youth sports and subjects many of its current trends and practices to the theological framework established in the previous chapters. As we consider the many cultural artifacts of youth sports surrounding us, how can Christians better understand them and engage them cautiously and surreptitiously?

5

Children at Play: The Power of Youth Sports

Some of my most joyous occasions of parenthood have been watching my children play. My wife and I often lamented our youngest daughter's seeming desire to want to skip ahead a few years to match her older brother's and sister's interests. We are not the first parents who have tried to convince their children to simply enjoy being children and not to be in a hurry to grow up. My heart was always full whenever I would walk by her room and overhear her playing with dolls or whatever toy happened to be her favorite that particular day. It brought to my mind the days (already gone!) when my son would build monsters with Legos, when my older daughter would dress up in princess dresses, and it was a dramatic reminder of the fleetingness of childhood.

    Moments like those made me think of my own childhood—playing in the woods behind our house, playing soccer with my siblings, chasing our dog around the yard, playing catch with my grandpa, and swimming in our pond. We had a beautiful, natural playground just outside the door of our country home, and we spent countless hours playing, exploring, and just being kids. Equally as memorable were the days I spent playing on different kinds of playgrounds throughout my small hometown. I remember waking up early on Saturday mornings and counting down the hours before the start of my soccer game later that afternoon. I remember waking up in the middle of the night during summer evenings being haunted by a play from that night's baseball game or still excited over our win. I remember the highlight of Friday-night home football games when everyone in town seemed to show up at Fred J. Brown Stadium to cheer on the Bulldogs.

Elite?

Before traveling too far down the path critiquing today's world of youth sports, it is important to be reminded that there is still *much* good that takes place in the name of youth sports. Amid the sordid tales of scandals and cheating that tend to dominate the headlines are stories like Robert Lewis, a young man with Down Syndrome. He was the team manager for Franklin Road Academy's basketball team in Nashville, but got to suit up and play for his senior night in 2016. Incredibly, he made a game-winning three pointer and fans of both schools rushed the court and hoisted him atop their shoulders.[1] During the 400-meter semifinal race in the 1992 Olympic Games in Barcelona, England's contender, Derek Redmond, tore his hamstring mid-race and the entire stadium was moved to tears watching his father break through security to help him hobble to the finish line. If you have never watched Coach Dave Belisle's postgame speech after his Cumberland, Rhode Island, baseball team was defeated in the 2014 Little League World Series by a team from Chicago, put this book down for five minutes and go watch it. He highlights just how beautiful youth sports can be. These stories and countless others garner national attention and can move even the most calloused heart to tears.

These kinds of things take place in sports all the time. Sports provide Hollywood some of their greatest storylines: an undersized, hardworking football player who never gives up and finally gets into a game at Notre Dame (*Rudy*); a family takes in a young homeless boy who grows into a massive left tackle and makes millions of dollars in the NFL (*The Blindside*); and a high school football coach in West Virginia overcomes racial discrimination within his football team (*Remember the Titans*). The ubiquity of the experience combined with the melodramatic nature of its constructed theatrics make sports the perfect platform to display the best of humanity.

It is easy to lament the negative impact money and competition have on youth sports, and stories of excess and abuse are routinely showcased in the media. Using the language from the previous chapter, we could say sports has colluded with any and all of the spiritual powers and youth sports are no different. At their core, the spiritual powers have been created good, and it is important not to lose sight of the fact that the involvement of young people in organized sports is innately good. In addressing the current plight of youth sports, this reminder must continue to guide the way: like the rest of God's creation, the Fall has not irredeemably corrupted

---

1. Lev, "Teen with Down Syndrome Makes Perfect Final Play to Win Basketball Game."

youth sports. While tales of corruption, cheating, and excess are easy to uncover in youth sports, there are plenty of reasons to be encouraged by much of what happens when young people play sports.

YOUTH SPORTS AND THE CREATIVE INTENTIONS OF GOD

The benefits of young people's involvement in sports are so widely publicized it can appear to function as carte blanche justification for any and all aspects of youth sports. The benefits provided to young people through organized sports are immense, but sports demands the same constant spirit of discernment that engaging in any activity requires. The Catholic Church has long viewed sports as an effective way to help develop virtues within young people, as illustrated by the numerous successful Catholic-led athletic programs available in nearly every local diocese. Norbert Muller identifies the potential sports has for helping develop Christian character. "The practice ... of youth sports, offers some common ground where the values of 'sports and culture' and many gospel values intersect and can complement one another."[2] He mentions, specifically, face-to-face interaction, teamwork, and making sacrifices as counter-cultural ideals from the sports world that reinforce similar counter-cultural gospel values.[3] McNamee offers a similar sentiment, "Sports thus offers one of our best vehicles for moral education in the light of the clash of moral cultures that the present world throws up."[4] Although not written for a Christian audience, O'Sullivan's list also finds much overlap with "gospel values": physical benefits, leadership, communication, accountability, responsible risk taking, self-esteem, determination, and organizational skills."[5] Similar lists of benefits are fairly commonplace among youth-sports literature and are promoted among youth-sports organizations. Rather than reiterate a similar list here, the benefits below represent some of the most significant theological contributions that sports offer young people.

---

2. Muller, "Concrete Pastoral Action within Sport," 225.
3. Muller, "Concrete Pastoral Action within Sport."
4. McNamee, "Youth Sports and Virtues," 75.
5. O'Sullivan, *Changing the Game*, 19.

ELITE?

Sports and Play

Although I lament the loss of innocence and free play in my children as they grow older, it is not as though play disappears from their lives as they age. Considering the theological significance of play, we affirm that an important role of sports is to serve as a primary venue where young people play. We have been created to play and the places where we play are important. While my son no longer plays with Legos, he plays on the basketball court, on the baseball field, on his Xbox, and on his phone (these latter examples are topics for another book). Sports continues to be the realm where the majority of young people most dramatically and most often experience play.

Study after study and statistic after statistic illustrate the positive benefits young people reap by participating in sports. The Aspen Institute's Project Play provides a succinct summary of numerous statistically-validated physical and social benefits of playing sports. Sports help young people develop and improve cognitive skills; young athletes are more likely to attend college than non-athletes; sports can positively affect aspects of personal development among young people; and they can contribute to their career success as adults.[6] Jerry Lynch sweepingly attests, "The magic of sports can influence a significant portion of a child's physical and emotional development for years to come."[7] When experienced in a healthy manner, few things will promote the overall health of young people better than sports.

I have watched firsthand as technology has slowly taken over the lives of my children. The ease at which they maneuver from one screen to another is alarming. To be sure, screens, games, and social networking experienced through technology can be healthy, positive experiences of play and should be encouraged in moderation. Sports, however, offer an alternative that requires much-needed physical activity while also providing an important counter to *virtual* reality via actual physicality. In this regard, sports has never been as important as they are now. In light of the theological role of play, we have seen that our children are fully human when they play. Ultimately, however, play requires active mind, body, and soul. The biological responses to physical activity (increased heart rate, release of endorphins, perspiration, increased brain function) all literally help our

---

6. Project Play, "Facts: Sports Activity and Children."
7. Lynch, *Let Them Play*, 30.

children become more human. The true beauty of sports is that it symbiotically enacts mind, body, and soul through activities intended to be fun.

Sports and Transcendence

One nagging obstacle confronting many Christians in their relationship to sports is the remnant of a spiritual-physical dualism that has long plagued Christian theology. This tendency among Christians has often led to a rigid separation that divorces any spiritual realities from real-world physicality. This fallacy is often on display in many Christian authors who write about sports but focus exclusively on "spiritual lessons" seen in the games while ignoring the actual, physical play itself and the supporting institutional structures. This is not to take away from the endearing sports stories that have long provided the fodder for preachers' sermons (much like the movie storylines mentioned earlier); it simply acknowledges that this always must be secondary.

Josh Tinley's book, *Kneeling in the End Zone: Spiritual Lessons from the World of Sports*, exemplifies this approach in relating sports to theology. In chapter 2, Tinley examines what he calls "the most ubiquitous biblical narrative in sports," David and Goliath.[8] I'm not sure there is any biblical metaphor used more often in sports. Tinley discusses many specific situations in recent sports history where the consummate underdog story relates. While he advises caution in applying the metaphor to situations in sports and attempts to provide a broader perspective for using it, his conclusion is insufficient.

> Instead of using a familiar Bible story to interpret the triumphs of underdogs, we should look to the stories of these underdogs as illustrations of perseverance and faith. Surprise champions (such as the 1980 U.S. Hockey Team), contenders (such as the 2006 George Mason Patriots), and the overachiever (such as Daniel "Rudy" Ruettiger) inspire us to persevere when we face adversity and low expectations, to have faith that we can accomplish extraordinary things, and to act on that faith.[9]

First of all, we should be hesitant to reduce the story of David and Goliath to a sports metaphor because the central motif at play in the story is how

---

8. Tinley, *Kneeling in the End Zone*, 19–32.
9. Tinley, *Kneeling in the End Zone*, 31–32.

Yahweh interacts with and protects his covenant people. Central to this story is God's faithfulness to his collective people in the face of their enemies. To reduce the story of David and Goliath to an inspirational Aesop-like tale aimed at helping us overcome our own personal giants is to moralize a story that is better understood within the communal framework of the Bible's story.

More importantly for our purposes here, this kind of moralizing of Scripture shows a complete disregard for the actual physicality and social constructs involved in sports. In the words of former Fuller Seminary President Richard Mouw: "I think God takes delight in Benjamin Franklin's wit and in Tiger Woods' putts and in some well-crafted narrative paragraphs in a Salman Rushdie novel."[10] God delights in seeing his children play. There is no need to always search for some deeper meaning or spiritual truth behind the game. Guttman refers often to the transcendence that Roger Banister described feeling while he ran, and concludes, "It is actually one of the happier ironies of modern sports that we can lose ourselves in play."[11] While it is tempting to want to employ the famed story from the life of King David when facing a heavily favored opponent or personal setback, a more theologically consistent approach would be to emphasize the joy and beauty of play. It is to be reminded that winning and losing within the construct of a game is simply the outcome of a created fanciful reality.

Play can be described as *autotelic*—existing as an end in and of itself. Ellis finds a more apt description of play as *autocharatic*: "something that is *enjoyable* for its own sake."[12] One of the most powerful statements that can be made to a young athlete is: "God delights in seeing you play." It is not surprising then, after working with athletes for decades, that the youth-sports activists Bruce Brown and Rob Miller discovered that the six words young athletes most wanted to hear their parents say are, "I love to watch you play."[13] Such a perspective echoes the words of the prophet Zephaniah, "The Lord your God is with you, he is mighty to save. He will take great delight in you" (Zeph 3:17).

In many positive ways, sports embodies the pursuit of transcending mere physicality. The suspense of a closely contested game, the marvel of seemingly impossible athletic feats, and, of course, the feeling induced by

---

10. Mouw, *He Shines in All That's Fair,* 36
11. Guttmann, *From Ritual to Record,* 160.
12. Ellis, *The Games People Play,* 266.
13. Elmore, "What Parents Should Say as their Kids Perform."

the "thrill of victory," all point to experiences beyond themselves. As Ellis describes, "Sports is always reaching outward and upward and in this movement outward and upward the sportsman or woman finally reaches outward or upward to God."[14] Since ancient times, people have turned to athletics in hopes of bridging the gap between the sacred and secular. Stephen Amidon's description of the ancient Greek Olympians further highlights the transcendence often experienced in sports. "What people really came to see were the athletes . . . It was here that the athlete became a figure who bridged the gap between the sacred and secular. Godlike in his aura, he was also very earthly in his sweat and struggle."[15] Spectators of today's major sporting events certainly find resonance with this psudeo-spiritual pursuit, and we should be quick to affirm the similar pursuit in young athletes.

In a very significant way, this transcendent element of sports provides a nexus between this world and the next. Stated theologically: sports has important eschatological overtones that may be understood in its relationship to Sabbath. Referring to Jurgen Moltmann and his classic work, *Theology of Hope*, Ellis suggests: "His own views on play, and the Sabbath, suggest that sport has its part in hoping for and actualizing God's promised future."[16] Hoffman ends his book, *Good Game*, with an eschatological perspective: "Our games are but dim images of the real game that will begin when this world has been left behind."[17] For children who take a break from schoolwork in order to play their games in front of their parents (who are able to take a break from their day jobs), sports is very much an experience of a "certain day called Today" (Heb 4:7) where all are reminded of the holiness and purpose of Sabbath. Harvey goes as far to say, "Worship and sport together inform a Sabbath-shaped life."[18] Thus, a significant experience within sports for young people is their inherent longing for and experience of transcendence. As young people traverse the vicissitudes of adolescence it is important for Christians to help affirm that transcendental longing of the supernatural in a God who can be known and who has revealed himself.

14. Ellis, *The Games People Play*, 247.
15. Amidon, *Something Like the Gods*, 15.
16. Ellis, *The Games People Play*, 225.
17. Hoffman, *Good Games*, 292.
18. Harvey, *A Brief Theology of Sport*, 108.

Elite?

Sports and the Experience of Community

During middle school and high school, my social sphere largely revolved around my teammates and friends I made playing sports. My family forged relationships with other families largely from our interaction together during practices or watching our games. I have fond memories in college of playing intramural sports with friends, and attending our university's basketball games together. The tradition continues now through my own children's experiences in sports as we continue to meet new friends and introduce our children to new experiences through sports. Even sports involving individual competition like running, ice skating, and golf promote various experiences of community (thousands run together in races, ice skaters often train in small groups, golfers compete in groups of four).

In Alan Hirsch's important book on the missional church, *The Forgotten Way*, he devotes an entire chapter to the topic of *communitas*. Hirsch describes *communitas* as the "intense feeling of social togetherness and belonging brought about by having to rely on each other in order to survive."[19] Hirsch believes a sense of *communitas* is one of the most important identities of the church. Teammates rarely depend on one another for literal, physical survival, but within the socially constructed world of sports, community is experienced more intensely and there is more mutual dependence among participants than most places in society. According to Hirsch, *communitas* involves adventure and movement—both realties on display in nearly every manifestation of sports.[20] This socially constructed realm of sports allows for participants to experience a sense of *communitas* not easily replicated even within the church itself (at least the experience of the church within a free and non-oppressive nation and culture).

If Christians are honest, many (most?) have had a more authentic experience of community within the context of sports than within the holy church. Sports beckon its followers to pilgrimage together to travel tournaments, to wear sacred garments embroidered with team logos, and to join in the blessed hymns and cheers together. Nothing else regularly attracts huge throngs of people numbering over 100,000 all donned in the same colored clothing to arenas, singing the same songs, and hoping for the same result. On a smaller level, travel teams bring families together around the shared goals of success and fellowship among their children and enjoy

---

19. Hirsch, *The Forgotten Ways*, 221.
20. Hirsch, *The Forgotten Ways*.

camaraderie all season long. While it is easy to focus on the excesses in these areas, at the same time it is important to acknowledge that the experience of *communitas* among sports teams is an authentic experience and one that connects with the inherent communal nature of humankind.

In a culture driven by hyper-individualism and competition (standardized tests, chairs in band, leads in musicals, scholarships, achievement awards, etc.), sports can be a haven for young people as one of the few places where team spirit and accountability are found. John O'Sullivan observes that young people most often say their main reason for playing sports is to be part of a team and to have fun with friends.[21] Gary Warner notes that, "We all long for some form of community, and sport seems to offer a unique chance to overcome our unrelatedness."[22] While youth sports may not have 100,000 fans flocking to its events, high-school football stadiums seating tens of thousands and nationally televised high-school basketball games and Little League World Series highlight the immense opportunity for team camaraderie and *communitas*.

Teamwork elicits an important component of transcendence as well. One of former Ohio State football coach Jim Tressel's "Big Ten Fundamentals" in his *New York Times* bestselling book, *The Winners Manual*, is Team about which he writes, "*Any* endeavor is a group journey. When you play for more than just the guys on the field, you can achieve the inner satisfaction and peace of mind that comes from being part of something much larger than yourself."[23] Perhaps nothing epitomizes "being part of something much larger than yourself" in sports more than college athletics. Every college athlete knows when he puts on his uniform, he is not only playing for his teammates on the field, the school's alumni and student body, or the fans in the stadium, but also for the millions of fans in the region and all over the world whose pride and identity are tied to the success of "their" team.

To a lesser degree, at least numerically, but with every bit of the passion of college fan bases, local youth leagues and teams can evoke a similar experience of *communitas* and team spirit within small towns and communities throughout the country. One year my high school's football team won the state football championship for the first time and nearly half the city drove the three-and-a-half hours to watch the championship game. Large

---

21. O'Sullivan, *Changing the Game*, 21.
22. Warner, *Competition*, 97.
23. Tressel, *The Winner's Manual*, 213.

banners hang on the walls of the high school near where I now live, honoring the professional football players who have graduated from the school. Upon entering the city limits of small towns across the country, visitors are greeted by signs that list the state titles won by the town's high school teams in various sports throughout its history. During the Little League World Series of 2014, the power of *communitas* was on display in the Jackie Robinson West Little League team from Chicago as baseball led the way to unite a community behind a team of twelve-year-old boys playing baseball.[24] Hundreds gathered to welcome them at the airport and the city of Chicago celebrated by having a parade in their honor.

The next chapter will discuss many ways that travel teams can be detrimental to local communities, but *communitas* can be powerfully on display among teams comprised of families that travel together throughout a long sports season. They eat many meals together, sometimes share hotel rooms together, take long trips together, and share much life together during the sports season. Teams that stay intact for several years become like a large extended family. Although this type of community-on-the-road has obvious drawbacks, there is equally great potential for a powerful experience of community. Surely theological virtues like selflessness, humility, hospitality, love, and acceptance can be experienced in a real way within sports teams.

Sports and Self-Discipline

In analyzing the biblical examples of sporting metaphors, we have seen that the Bible offers little direct teaching as to how the Christian is to interact with sports. Paul's use of sports metaphors are consistent and provide some insight into another benefit provided by sports. 2 Timothy 4:7 epitomizes Paul's use of sports in this regard: "I have fought the good fight, I have finished the race, I have kept the faith." It is not insignificant that Paul turns to sports in order to emphasize the longsuffering experience of keeping the faith.

---

24. Incidentally, the Jackie Robinson West Little League team also provides a case study in how systems can betray the children participating, particularly by the adults who are in charge of these systems. On February 11, 2015, the Jackie Robinson West Little League team was forced to vacate their Little League World Series Championship due to the fact that all of their players did not live within the confines of the team's district.

Children at Play

In a culture that embraces efficiency and cherishes time-saving techniques, sports continues to promote a counter-cultural ethic of hard work and self-discipline. It was Jane Fonda who popularized the exercise slogan in the 1980s, "No pain, no gain," and the mantra continues to find its way into the world of sports. Not everything can be sped up or shortcut, and physical fitness and athletic prowess are two prime examples. Much has been made of the 10,000-hour-rule. Informed by research of elite performers, it suggests 10,000 hours of focused and repetitive training is required in order for athletes (or musicians and other performers) to achieve the highest level of performance.[25] While the actual number may have been overemphasized by the researchers, the commitment and discipline required of sports and other performers who desire to be successful are obvious.

Paul likely had such repetition and hard work in mind as he searched for an apt metaphor by which to compare the rigors of the Christian life. Richard Foster begins his classic treatment of the spiritual disciplines by acknowledging:"Superficiality is the curse of our age. The doctrine of instant gratification is a primary spiritual problem."[26] The youth of today may be prepared better for the discipline of the spiritual life by their experiences in sports than in any other. Sport is not the only experience of discipline and practice in which young people participate. Schoolwork, music, theater, dancing, and other outlets require a similar commitment to discipline. However, considering the incredible majority of youth involved in sports, sports provides one of the most important experiences of discipline within the life of the majority of young people.

Anyone who has ever trained for a marathon, shot hundreds of free throws at the end of practice, or dribbled a soccer ball around the field until her feet went numb can empathize with Paul's tiresome declaration: "I did not run or labor for nothing" (Phil 2:16). The theological connection of sports to the Sabbath is again instructive here. It can be challenging to connect a (seemingly) rigorous daily commitment of the spiritual disciplines to any sense of free-spirited worship. In the same way, the monotonous practice of routine sports drills can equally feel devoid of the meaning and fulfillment athletes experience during a game. The monotony of practice led to star NBA player Allen Iverson's famous 2002 press conference where he lamented practice: "We talkin' about practice, man. We're not even talking about the game, the actual game. When it matters. We talkin' about

---

25. O'Sullivan, *Changing the Game*, 79.
26. Foster, *Celebration of Discipline*, 1.

practice."[27] Many Christians might provide a similar response if queried about their personal prayer lives.

Discipline and practice within the Christian tradition is so significant that it has its own branch of study referred to as "spirituality" and the "spiritual disciplines." The life of the athlete is a disciplined one and can prove instructional towards a disciplined life lived in the Holy Spirit. Stories abound of athletes arriving early for practice and staying late, committing to strict diets, and adhering to rigorous workout routines. For many young people, youth sports will be their most drastic introduction to discipline. Sports provide an opportunity for the church to utilize the disciplinary emphasis of sports so many young people have been exposed to and illustrate how a similar approach to spirituality can enrich their relationship with God. Many young people who are not involved in sports simply do not have a comparable experience of discipline in their lives. Sports is a modern-day Areopagus in youth ministry, where youth leaders can stand before their young people and offer a sports-inspired rendering of Paul's speech in Acts 17: "Your discipline is admirable and your commitment commendable. However, there is meaning and a higher calling for your life that demands greater commitment."

While other significant benefits of sports could be added to this list, these contributions highlight the kinds of theological justification that resonate with Christians and affirm why we are often so drawn to sports. In any critique of youth sports, important contributions must not be thrown out with the proverbial bath water. Sports are inherently good, make many positive contributions to society, and reinforce many important theological points. However, the shortcomings of the youth-sports industrial complex have become impossible to ignore. Central to the understanding of the powers laid out in Chapter 4 is that while the powers are inherently good, they have become corrupted by sin. The next chapter will explore the dark side of the youth-sports industrial complex and consider its implications.

---

27. Allen Iverson, NBA postgame conference on May 7, 2002.

6

From Playgrounds to Hallowed Grounds: The Industrialization of Youth Sports

From the magnificent Coliseum in Rome to the modern-day, billion-dollar behemoth AT&T Stadium in Dallas, Texas, city skylines throughout the world often are distinguishable by the unique architecture of major sports stadiums and arenas. A city's stadiums are often its most recognizable landmarks. Columbus, Ohio, offers its own display of sporting might in Ohio Stadium—home of Ohio State University's football team. Towering along the banks of the Olentangy River on the city's west side, the historic stadium boasts an impressive seating capacity of 104,944 making it the fourth-largest college stadium in the country. Otherwise known as "The Horseshoe" because of its unique shape, the stadium adds a prominent and unique aspect to the skyline of Columbus. Majestic sports stadiums and arenas are significant to cities throughout the world, and they have been part of the landscape and culture of cities for centuries. Over the past few decades, however, a different kind of sport palace has begun adding new contours to city landscapes.

In the fall of 2016, former professional dual-sport-athlete Bo Jackson and his investment firm opened their second Elite Sports complex—this one in the Columbus-area suburb of Hilliard. The 110,000 square foot complex includes a full-size infield for baseball and softball, batting cages, two large multi-purpose fields, a collegiate-style weight room, a three-lane running track, a two-lane obstacle course, and a massive 42-foot climbing tower, all under 72-foot ceilings. Jackson is one of the latest professional athletes to invest in the burgeoning world of youth sports. Just north around the I-270 loop from Bo Jackson's Elite Sports Complex is a sign for Sports Ohio—another sports complex with over one hundred acres of fields dedicated to soccer, football, lacrosse, and field hockey, in addition to a golf center, an ice hockey rink, and a gymnastics center.

These two complexes are different than massive stadiums in that these facilities are dedicated specifically to youth sports and serve as stunning manifestations of just how powerful they have become in the United States. Massive sports facilities dedicated to youth sports like these are part of something larger known as "youth sports tourism." Youth-sports activist Mark Hyman describes its scope: "It's a phenomenon involving dozens of communities and some of the biggest brands in pro sports and kids' entertainment."[1] He goes on to detail the incredible investment cities like Round Rock, Texas, have made in creating a youth-sports destination for elite travel teams. Round Rock went as far as hiring a marketing agency to help sell the city's sprawling 570-acre sports complex as "The Sports Capital of Texas."[2] While Columbus may not have invested in the youth sports scene to the extent that Round Rock has (yet), its commitment to the infrastructure of youth sports is evident throughout the city. The 270 bypass provides a thoroughfare between Bo Jackson's Elite Sports complex, Sports Ohio, Dublin Coffman High School's 8,500-seat-capacity football stadium, and Lou Berliner Park—a 200-acre metro park that is described on its website as the nation's largest softball complex. These massive, commercial complexes are in addition to other athletic complexes at schools, countless parks and fields of local municipalities, and a myriad of indoor gymnasia and facilities found throughout communities.

While the stadiums, fields, and gymnasia stand as silent witnesses to countless young athletes who play there throughout the year, the deeper realities of the immense youth-sports industrial complex seldom receive serious reflection. Parents eager to get their young children involved in activities can easily get swept into the massive world of youth sports before realizing just how much sway they can hold over their family's lives. The rapid pace at which these private training facilities and for-profit leagues are being established may seem to be evidence of a healthy, growing enterprise. In a time when technology promotes sedentary habits, organized sports seem more likely to provide solutions rather than be a source for more concern in the lives of young people. While the previous chapter highlights

1. Hyman, *The Most Expensive Game in Town*, 38.
2. Hyman, *The Most Expensive Game in Town*, 36.

some of these benefits, a growing number of activists are providing a much needed critique of the quickly-expanding world of youth sports. The excesses and negative climate of youth sports has become so widespread that authors David Shields and Brenda Bredemeier assume, "We all know that there are major problems in youth sports today."[3] Couched in the spiritual language of this book, I contend that evidence of the fallen nature of youth sports is everywhere. This chapter illustrates how many current practices in youth sports may actually be working against the many benefits sports are intended to provide.

Tom Farrey writes, "Beneath that thin, shiny layer of elite spectator sports is a system that is troubled, if not failing."[4] In 2010, *The Columbus Dispatch* published an important examination of youth sports in a weeklong series entitled, "Little Leagues, Big Costs."[5] The headline of the first article in the series hints at the dark side of the youth-sports industrial complex: "Children May Be Vulnerable in $5 Billion Youth Sports Industry." It is impossible for the very nature of youth sports not to be impacted by that kind of economic swagger. Any industry that large is bound to exemplify the collusion of spiritual powers. The previous chapter highlights some of the theological benefits of youth sports, but this chapter describes a world that has become corrupted by an overemphasis on competition, polluted by exorbitant amounts of money, and that contributes to fracturing local communities in its obsession with travel teams. There is a striking similarity between the advent of the youth-sports industrial complex and the explosion of the military-industrial complex (MIC) the United States witnessed through the Cold War.

DWIGHT D. EISENHOWER AND AAU BASKETBALL

It has been over fifty years since exiting President Eisenhower urged the United States public to be suspicious of the "acquisition of unwarranted influence by the military industrial complex." Eisenhower, who served in the middle of the twentieth century, never could have imagined the complexity of the twenty-first-century MIC. A global war on terrorism, increasingly complex technological warfare, and a constantly evolving and complex international, geopolitical landscape have provided the perfect

---

3. Shields and Bredemeier, "Reclaiming Competition in Youth Sports,"129.
4. Farrey, *Game On*, 21.
5. Jones, Wagner, and Riepenhoff, "Little Leagues, Big Costs."

storm to reenergize it in recent years. Large companies who suffered great financial loss and were on the brink of bankruptcy were deemed "too big to fail" by the federal government—a euphemism often used following the financial crisis of 2008. Statistics describing these companies are nearly incomprehensible because of their scope, and yet these numbers are dwarfed in comparison to the U.S. MIC. One statistic dramatically summarizes its scope: the United States government spends more money on its military than nearly all the other nations combined in the statistics provided by the Stockholm International Peace Institute—$618 billion in 2013.[6] If these large banks were described as "too big to fail," we quickly run out of superlatives in attempting to describe the MIC of the United States.

The NFL is currently the most lucrative professional sports league in the world, but even its projected $13 billion revenue in 2016 is but a small fraction of the U.S. MIC.[7] To compare the neighborhood soccer league, or even international youth sports organizations like the AAU to the U.S. MIC may seem riddled with hyperbole. However, it requires little effort or imagination to realize how dark the deeper recesses of organized youth sports in the U.S. have become thanks to countless high-profile cases of excess and abuse. When uninvited journalists are asked to leave AAU basketball tournaments for fear of what they will uncover,[8] when parents give away legal rights of their children for the sake of their Little League baseball team,[9] when a mother agrees to let her child play basketball for a known child molester in exchange for rent,[10] and when shoe companies pay AAU coaches full-time salaries to help court middle-school basketball players to their particular brand of shoes,[11] there is ample evidence a system has taken on an antipathetic life of its own. Anecdotes like these are often dismissed as extreme, rare, or isolated, but even a brief survey of literature from the world of youth sports shows evidence of a pervasive, dark underside that is best understood as a collusion of spiritual powers.

Tim Keown's ESPN article "Where the 'Elite' Kids Shouldn't Meet" takes Eisenhower's language of the MIC and applies it to youth sports. His assessment is direct and should give all participants in the system reason

---

6. Frohlich and Alexander, "Countries Spending the Most on the Military."
7. Isidore, "NFL Revenue: Here Comes Another Record Season."
8. Farrey, *Game On*, 166.
9. Farrey, *Game On*, 282.
10. Dohrmann, *Play Their Hearts Out*, 344–47.
11. Ibid., 155.

to pause and reflect on the status quo. Referencing a recent newspaper article that celebrated a successful ten-and-under AAU basketball team from North Carolina that was planning to compete in tournaments in New York and Houston, Keown asks crassly, "What the hell are we doing? .... Is there anything dumber than holding tryouts for 9-year-olds?"[12] Comparing the governing structures of youth sports to the MIC is not so much about their size and scope, but rather their power and influence. As we saw in chapter 4, colluding spiritual powers can oppose the very purposes they are created to serve. An increasing number of voices are sounding an alarm that youth sports today are dramatically broken.

Organized Youth Sports in the US

Nearly all U.S. high school students take the Arms Services Vocational Aptitude Battery test, more popularly known by its acronym ASVAB. The government requires every male between the ages of eighteen and twenty-five to register with Selective Services. These two events are a kind of civilian rite of passage into the U.S. MIC. Another rite of passage the overwhelming majority of U.S. citizens goes through is playing sports. The "youth sports" label covers an incredible diversity: from traditional games like baseball, basketball, and football to individual sports like tennis, figure skating, and snowboarding to more niche sports like skateboarding, rugby, and field hockey. Physical education requirements continue to wane across the United States, but many students in the United States still have some exposure to sports in public schools.[13]

Certainly not all children participate in sports, but only a small percentage of children never play some kind of organized sport at some point in their childhood. According to Kelley and Carchia, between 60 percent and 80 percent of third-to-fifth-grade students are involved in at least one organized sport (percentages vary depending on gender, geographic setting, and socio-economic situation).[14] These statistics do not account for the number of children who play pickup sports with their parents and friends. According to research conducted by the Women's Sports Foundation, only

12. Keown, "Where the 'Elite' Kids Shouldn't Meet."
13. According to the 2016 "Shape of the Nation" physical education report, 44 states require physical education as part of their high-school curriculum. http://www.shapeamerica.org/advocacy/son/index.cfm.
14. Kelley and Carchia, "Hey, Data, Data—Swing."

13 percent of boys and 18 percent of girls between the ages of eight and seventeen "have never joined a team or club, had never shared the experience of getting a uniform, practicing with teammates and running onto the field or court to compete."[15] Children raised in the United States who never experience playing sports remain rare.

Opportunities for children to participate in organized youth sports in the U.S. began early in the twentieth century before exploding in later decades.[16] Pop Warner football was one of the first youth leagues to be established in 1929, but it was a few decades later before the real avalanche of youth-sports institutions began. Carl Stotz helped organize Little League Baseball in the 1930s and had its first "national tournament game" in 1947. The first PONY baseball league (which interestingly stands for Protect Our Nation's Youth), a league dedicated to older children, was formed in 1951 (the same year as the competing Babe Ruth League). The American Youth Soccer Organization started in California in 1964. These national organizations had locally run leagues throughout the United States and, almost without exception, limited the holding of regional and national tournaments to once a year (if they held them at all). Regan McMahon notes, "Up until the early 1990's, the pinnacle of many young people's sports experience was playing for their high school team."[17] The youth of a community would gather at the local parks or gyms, compete against their fellow classmates and neighbors on equally-divided teams, and play for bragging rights that were just as important (if not more so) than championships. The players who were especially talented and interested in the sport would later try out for the limited number of spots available on the local high-school teams, and then, in very rare instances, a superstar would emerge on the team who was good enough to receive a full-tuition, athletic scholarship to college. This was the typical trajectory of the youth-sports experience in most cities and towns throughout the United States until the last few decades. These grassroots youth leagues had sown the seeds of a youth-sports industrial complex that has risen to incredible power and prominence no one could have anticipated.

---

15. Kelley and Carchia, "Hey, Data, Data—Swing."

16. The list of these youth-sports institutions summarizes content in Engh, *Why Johnny Hates Sports*, 30–37.

17. McMahon, *Revolution in the Bleachers*, 32.

As McMahon writes, "That was then. Now private clubs offer the highest level, most competitive play."[18] City leagues and neighborhood competitions have given way to a new "higher level" of competition that scours the region for talent as well as potential, top-caliber opponents. Tim Keown poignantly describes the new climate of youth sports that has become familiar to any family who has dabbled in sports with their children.

> The big three terms are "elite," "select," and "travel ball." Oh, the power of those words. Waving the prospect of "travel ball" under the nose of an ambitious father of a talented 9-year-old is like wafting a steak under the nose of a sleeping dog. After all, the more you travel and the farther you go to play a sport, the better you must be at that sport, right? . . . . and if it's *"year-round* travel ball"—a red flag across the orthopedic medical community for the dangers of repetitive overuse—all the better. It's a status symbol, one promoted by parents and justified by the guy who collects tournament fees, and it's the main reason baseball in this country is becoming the province of wealthy suburbia.[19]

Bo Jackson's Elite Sports and similar facilities throughout the country have become beacons of hope and status symbols "wafting" dreams of successful children and athletic prowess to their parents. "A spot on a 'travel' team carries more prestige—and more cost—than playing in a recreational league," writes professor Ronald Bishop.[20] The industrialization of youth sports in the United States is most clearly represented in this shift from the neighborhood, recreation youth-sports leagues to the new world of "elite," "select," and "travel" teams where competition is the lingua franca and status comes by label.

THE FALLEN STATE OF YOUTH SPORTS

The world of "elite," "select," and "travel" teams has helped foster a national youth-sports climate built on unrealistic parental hopes and dreams of college scholarships—an elitist mentality that often neglects huge percentages of "ordinary" players (not to mention children with disabilities), a beckoning to regional tournaments and leagues that prove detrimental to local communities, and a culture of favoritism and celebrity where gifted

---

18. McMahon, *Revolution in the Bleachers*, 33.
19. Keown, "Where the 'Elite' Kids Shouldn't Meet."
20. Bishop, *When Play was Play*, 41.

athletes are often excused of bad behavior and given special treatment and privileges. Recently, this new experience of competition and the hyper-organized professionalization of youth sports has begun to invite criticism and critique from the highest levels. In 2013, the education and policy organization, The Aspen Institute, initiated Project Play—an initiative tasked with "Reimaging Youth Sports in America." The program struck such a chord that the participants at a town hall event included former President Bill Clinton, former NBA superstar Kobe Bryant, and was held in conjunction with ESPN and the Clinton Foundation. Policy makers, physicians, and even successful athletes themselves are beginning to question the culture that has developed in recent years. Noticeably absent during the rise of these trends in youth sports has been a clear and distinct voice of the church.

The competitive drive, so ingrained in the country's psyche, has shaped the experience of youth sports dramatically. Soccer coach and youth sports activist John O'Sullivan describes youth sports as, "a multi-billion dollar industry now, with many corporations, hotels, small businesses, and even entire cities dependent upon the youth sports industry."[21] The history of modern sports in the U.S. has developed as one sports gold rush to the next: sports leagues vying for widespread acceptance, sports-equipment companies racing to get these leagues to sign on with their products, corporations rushing to attach their company names to uniforms, stadiums, and other advertising platforms, and the telecommunications arms race where companies continue to chase the powerful trailblazer, ESPN. Sports has colluded with any and all of the spiritual powers and youth sports is no different. There are many shortcomings in today's world of youth sports, and a thorough review of them is an immense undertaking on its own. As the previous chapter limited its scope to a few of the most significant benefits of sports, we now consider some of the ways these same benefits can be undermined by the fallen nature of youth sports.

"Elite" Sports and the Betrayal of Play

Chapter 2 includes a lengthy account of two soccer games John O'Sullivan witnessed simultaneously: his six-year-old daughter's game and a nearby ten-year-old boy's game. During his daughter's game, "The parents clapped and cheered, the coaches hustled to keep the ball in play, and everyone

---

21. O'Sullivan, *Changing the Game*, 24.

doled out high fives and cries of 'great play' on both teams."[22] He describes the other game quite differently: "The parents screamed and yelled to 'get up,' 'get back,' 'pass it,' 'shoot it,' 'hustle!' The coaches screamed at the players, everyone screamed at the referee and no one was smiling. Unless, of course, there was a goal, at which point the goal scorer would glance to the sideline to see if mom or dad approved."[23] Here, exemplified on these two adjacent fields, is the representations of what youth sports is intended to be as well as what it has become. O'Sullivan asks the question that serves as an appropriate segue into an analysis of the dark side of youth sports, "When and why did we take the joy and romance out of youth sports between the ages of six and ten?"[24]

The current climate of youth sports throughout the United States has been driven by a fiercely competitive spirit that has largely abandoned the "joy of sports" Michael Novak celebrates, downplayed the *autocharatic* character of sports that Robert Ellis honors, and ignored the single-most popular reason young people play sports: to have fun. Numerous studies have shown that the vast majority of young people would rather play on a losing team than sit the bench of a winning team, and this betrayal of the purpose of sports is not lost on children. O'Sullivan reports that 70 percent of youth drop out of organized sports by age thirteen.[25]

Shields and Bredemeier propose, "The problems that plague youth sports have less to do with kids than adults. And they stem from adults precisely because we, more than our children, have embraced a model of sports based on the presuppositions of decompetition [their word for negative iterations of competition]."[26] Most people seem to acknowledge when there are problems in youth sports, youth are rarely to blame. It is the overbearing, overly competitive moms and dads who organize and coach the teams, set their children's athletic goals, structure the leagues, and maintain a hyper-competitive environment made in their image and not that of their children. Bishop darkly captures this new world: "Parents seem to feel that they can't leave their children alone to chart their own sports path—they might screw up, or change their minds, or blow their big chance, even

---

22. O'Sullivan, *Changing the Game*, 3.
23. O'Sullivan, *Changing the Game*, 4.
24. O'Sullivan, *Changing the Game*.
25. O'Sullivan, *Changing the Game*, 17.
26. Shields and Bredemeier, "Reclaiming Competition in Youth Sports," 117.

though they likely won't have one."[27] Youth leagues increasingly resemble professional leagues not because of the desires of the children playing, but because of the coaches, parents, and other adults in charge. Parents frequently are more up-to-date with their children's tournament brackets and league standings than their children.

In the cutthroat world of youth sports dominated by tryouts, specialization, and personal trainers (all from the earliest ages), one of the biggest casualties has been Sabbath. Many practices look more like military exercises than groups of children at play. The competition-obsession has brought with it additional pressure for young people already wilting under hectic schedules, standardized tests, and countless other expectations. McMahon addresses this head on when she writes, "The hardest pill to swallow, for kids and some parents, is the need for rest—rest between seasons, rest during the week and rest after an injury."[28] When attention shifts from playing to winning, rest becomes a threatening proposal. What if my opponents are working hard while I am resting? Such thinking leads to a host of unhealthy practices.

When competition overshadows play, the lives of young people are affected, often dramatically. It has become commonplace for students to miss school for out-of-town tournaments and for families to face financial strain due to the cost of sports. In her book, Regan McMahon includes "player profiles," which provide personal testimonies of the residual effect playing elite sports can have on young people and their families. Soccer player Caitlin Meyer writes in one, "I could never have birthday parties because I was always playing soccer. We never could plan vacations because I had soccer. And if you missed it, it was a really big deal and there were consequences—you didn't play."[29] She goes on to give a dramatic example, "I missed a day of a soccer tournament once, for my sister's wedding, and I had to go back to the tournament the day after, and I didn't get to start because I had missed the day before."[30] While this example may seem extreme, examples like this are becoming commonplace. Gone is "for the love of the game" having been replaced by a new mantra: "at all costs."

---

27. Bishop, *When Play Was Play*, 39.

28. McMahon, *Revolution in the Bleachers*, 77.

29. Caitlin Meyer, "Player Profile," 38–41, in McMahon, *Revolution in the Bleachers*, 38.

30. Caitlin Meyer, "Player Profile," 41.

From Playgrounds to Hallowed Grounds

"Elite" Sports and the Idolatry of Transcendence

One reason we are drawn to sports is because of its promotion of transcendence, but anything that promotes experiences of transcendence can easily be confused as the object of worship itself. Theologically, this is the sin of idolatry. Psalm 19:1 states: "The heavens declare the glory of God; the skies proclaim the work of his hands." Throughout the Psalter, the poets celebrate the transcendent aspects of nature that help draw humanity into ethereal realms that reveal God. The heavens and the beauty of nature point to a reality beyond themselves. Unfortunately, however, the denigration of nature and humanity by the Fall leads some to "exchange the truth of God for a lie, and worship and serve created things rather than the Creator" (Rom 1:25). Throughout the first chapter of Romans, Paul emphasizes that nature points to God, but nature itself was never intended to be the object of worship.

While one of the great benefits of youth sports relates to transcendence, it is important to also acknowledge, for many families, this experience of transcendence often becomes the goal. Rather than seeing sports as an opportunity for a transcendent experience of the holy, many families see the sport experience itself as holy (or the pursuit of success in sports). Many families become obsessed with the thrill of victory and pursue winning at all costs. Winning and success, more than the actual sports themselves, have become the idol countless American families spend their income, time, and energy chasing. Climbing the ladder of athletic success leads families to pursue one elite club tryout after another, one personal trainer after another, squeezing in one more elite camp after another, and purchasing every latest/greatest bat, stick, pair of shoes, or whatever sports equipment promises to improve their game.[31]

Sports are hardly unique in their promotion of transcendence and potential for promoting the "exchange of the truth for a lie." Just as people are regularly drawn to nature, drugs, alcohol, music, sex, and movies, many families with young athletes look to sports for their experience of the transcendent. Divorced from its purpose as revealer of holiness, sports

---

31. It should be noted here that the experiences described in this paragraph are reflective of the affluent middle and upper class societies in the United States further complicating an assessment of the practice of sports in this country. Many sports (perhaps even the majority of youth sports in the U.S.) are becoming "elite" in this regard. For the church, this is a matter of justice and it will be examined in more detail in chapter 9, but I thought it was important to acknowledge the limited scope of this paragraph.

become its own chief object of desire. Harvey provides theological rationale for the "thrill of victory," stating: "Life has the final word, which is to say winning wins in the end. As a result, it will always feel much better—as we all know!—to win."[32] Winning—and sports in general—is best understood eschatologically. This same tendency is seen in the Pharisees, who saw the Sabbath as the object of their desire rather than the transcendent purposes for which God had created it. "Sabbath (like sports!) was created for humankind, not humankind for Sabbath (or sports)."

Elite Sports and the Betrayal of Local Community

Although basketball was invented indoors to keep young people active in the cold winters, it also has long been a staple of outdoor playgrounds across the United States, particularly in urban settings. Installing and maintaining basketball hoops are simple and affordable, making it difficult to find a park without one. Notably, the evolution of the youth-basketball machine prompted a recent *ESPN* article to declare, "Playground Basketball is Dying." The authors purport, "High school players in search of scholarships and exposure spend May, June and July in indoor, showcase tournaments and AAU events, not parks."[33] The move from the playground to showcase tournaments provides a poignant illustration of the broader transition within youth sports that has begun to betray the local communities they once brought together.

This same trend is noted in baseball by professors Jessica Skolnikoff and Robert Engvall as they use the movie *The Sandlot* to highlight "the loss of community through specialized sports and the loss of unstructured play."[34] The neighborhood playground that served as a backdrop for the baseball posse in *The Sandlot* has become regional and national tournaments held in immense venues and in cities that are anywhere from a day's drive to a commercial flight away from home. The authors summarize the situation "back at home" poignantly: "Children who might otherwise rake leaves, mow lawns, and otherwise interact with their neighbors . . . are now far too busy with their organized sports and sports-related activities

---

32. Harvey, *A Brief Theology of Sport*, 102.

33. Medcalf and O'Neil, "Playground Basketball is Dying,"

34. Skolnikoff and Engvall, *Young Athletes, Couch Potatoes, and Helicopter Parents*, 125–36.

to find the time to engage with the neighbors."[35] Youth sports once were a staple of neighborhoods, but now they take place in palaces built exclusively for them. Bishop once again aptly captures the impact of these trends: "Today, truly meaningful, productive participation in sports (as we now define it) can only happen in facilities—often well-heeled facilities—designed solely for competition. Sports have moved almost completely out of the community."[36] Furthermore, this move toward youth-sports palaces left behind countless children who ultimately withdrew from organized sports at an early age because they failed to achieve "elite" status, lacked the resources to afford these more expensive options, were late bloomers, or simply lacked a supportive family structure that could help connect them to the elite programs.

While it may be too early for statistical data to quantify these trends, a recent move by the Kenner City Council in Louisiana to no longer offer traditional, recreational sports programming at its Butch Duhe Playground certainly suggests the way forward many local communities may soon be taking. The decision was made because participation in the local sports league hosted at that park had declined dramatically, moving the City Council to begin renting the facilities to the travel and elite teams where, seemingly, the children who previously populated the recreation leagues now play. *Forbes* author Bob Cook writes a column dedicated to youth sports and believes this incident to be "a signal that parents' desire (whether by choice or for fear of their kids being left behind) to put their children in travel sports at ever-earlier ages—and the enormous amounts of money to be made from this trend—is sucking the wind out of casual, recreational organized sports."[37] We seem to be leaving the original intent of sports further and further behind.

Project Play calls for, as one of its eight strategies, revitalizing in-town leagues. The report echoes the problematic trend of youth sports betraying local communities.

> The flight to travel (and to for-profit club) teams thins rosters and the number of teams that can be created. The kids left behind can get the message that they're not good enough, and start checking

---

35. Skolnikoff and Engvall, *Young Athletes, Couch Potatoes, and Helicopter Parents*, 29.

36. Bishop, *When Play Was Play*, 40.

37. Cook, "After Killing Pickup Games, Adults Now on Way to Killing Recreational Youth Sports."

out of sports. By the end of grade school, in some areas, in-town leagues in sports like soccer and basketball have lost enough participants that they are no longer viable. That's a major loss, especially as local play is the only affordable option for many families.[38]

Project Play argues the current state of youth sports is detrimental to the health of young people in the United States, reinforces age-old socio-economic and racial barriers, in addition to other corresponding problems. Any serious Christian ethic should be equally concerned with these trends, and we will examine the church's role in promoting matters of justice in sports in chapter 9. Furthermore, all of this should be especially troubling for anyone claiming the name Christ since central to the message of Jesus was to "love your neighbor as yourself" (Mark 12:31). This is difficult to do when the majority of families with young athletes no longer have time to know their neighbor.

"Elite" Sports and the Fine Line between Discipline and Obsession

Every youth pastor is familiar with the challenges of scheduling youth-group activities around the sports schedules of their youth group. A 2008 *Faith Communities Today* survey statistically confirmed what is nearly universally accepted among the youth pastors I know: school- and sports-related activities are the biggest obstacles to regular participation in church.[39] The challenge of the youth-sports industrial complex to the local church is immense. On one hand, if churches simply cater to the scheduling limitations of their families with young athletes, the church becomes another purveyor of a consumerist spirit. On the other hand, if churches confront the families directly about being accountable to how they are spending their time, they simply may further alienate themselves from the church.

One of the theological benefits mentioned in the previous chapter regarding youth sports is self-discipline. There are few people in today's society better disciplined than athletes, and such discipline can prove instructive to Christians (as the athletic metaphors used in the New Testament attest). However, just as the other benefits of youth sports can be denied of their contributions and manipulated into forces for evil, so too can the positive qualities of discipline when youth sports become an obsession.

---

38. Project Play, "Play Four: Revitalize In-Town Leagues."
39. Briggs, "The Final Four, Travel Teams, and Empty Pews."

Symptoms of this exploitation of discipline in youth sports manifests in many ways: the push to specialize in one sport at an early age, injuries resulting from overuse and the lack of rest, and the inability to balance the life of sports with the other aspects of being a child.

The Old Testament described a very intentional way of communal life for Israel that possessed a determinative rhythm. That rhythm was dictated by regular feasts, festivals, and sacrifices offered at specific times and coinciding with different times of the year. The Christian liturgical calendar does something similar as Advent gives way to Christmas and Lent to Easter. The rhythm of life is significant for Christians. Unfortunately, many Christians live a life that is driven more by the rhythm of their sports schedule than by a divine commitment or posture. In my congregation, one parent whose son played on a travel baseball team used to say every May, "We'll see everyone in the fall," because they would be out of town at weekend baseball tournaments all summer long.

In order to make a positive contribution towards the current climate of youth sports, it is important to move beyond the argument that sports harm Christian families only because it takes them away from church services and other church-sponsored events. This must always be part of the conversation (after all, being together as part of the assembly of the saints *is* crucial in the life of Christians according to Hebrews 10:25), but it must not limit the conversation. The concept of rhythm of life is a better alternative than simply church attendance. Too many families are caught up in a system (spiritual power) of youth sports that feels oppressive rather than liberating. Too many families are serving sports instead of allowing themselves to be served by sports. Too many Christian families claim to use their involvement in sports as a missionary outreach (a valid possibility to be sure), but in reality are more shaped by their sports community than they are by their faith community.

The repetition of practice and the seemingly mundane drills that require commitment and promote a sense of discipline can, at the same time, create an unbalanced life that overemphasizes sports. One of the most significant by-products of the industrialization of youth sports has been the tendency to specialize in a sport at an early age. This has sociological implications for neighborhoods that were mentioned above, but the most significant fallacy in this movement toward specialization is that it is not best for young athletes. O' Sullivan argues, "Participation in multiple sports leads to better overall athleticism, fewer overuse injuries, and fewer kids who burn out at a young age."[40] Hyman reports, "Each year, as many as half of all youth sports injuries are the result from overuse," and "The American Academy of Pediatrics is worried enough to have issued two policy statements on overuse injuries in three years."[41] Sports medicine facilities and rehabilitation centers are opening up all over the country. Younger and younger children often are receiving unnecessary treatment in order to speed along recoveries from sports injuries that otherwise simply need rest.

The writer of Ecclesiastes proclaims the beauty of creation in great holistic balance. "There is a time to be born and a time to die; a time to plant and a time to uproot, a time to kill and a time to heal, a time to tear down and a time to build" (Eccl 3:2–3). Life is experienced as a balance of birth and death, killing and healing, tearing down and building up, and tears and laughter. Eventually the writer concludes, "He has made everything beautiful in its time" (Eccl 3:11). Perhaps more than anything, the biblical concepts of balance and the rhythm of life need to be proclaimed to the church's families with young athletes. Although neglecting to mention a time to play, the author does mention a time to laugh and a time to dance, each counterweighted by mention of a time to cry and a time to mourn. There *is* a time to play sport, but there is also a time to rest. While play has its connection to Sabbath, play does not equate to Sabbath. There remains the necessity among all those who play to rest and to rest regularly, especially in a climate where youth sports seldom resembles its restful, playful intent.

Unfortunately, much of the play children experience is caught up within the fallen youth-sports industrial complex. Exposing the lies and deceit of any of the principalities and powers is a tall order, but it is particularly so in the context of something as beloved as sports. It requires honest narratives (like George Dohrmann's compelling story of grassroots basketball[42] and Mike Nicoll's revealing documentary *At All Costs* that explores the world of AAU basketball) and fearless prophets (like John O'Sullivan and Tom Farrey) who are willing to speak boldly, challenging the current practices of youth sports.

Although the church has largely neglected the topic of sports and has been noticeably absent in regards to the topics discussed in this chapter, one significant exception has been Christian sports ministries. These ministries

40. O'Sullivan, *Changing the Game*, 6.
41. Hyman, *Until it Hurts*, 67.
42. Dohrmann, *Play Their Hearts Out*.

often operate on the periphery of the institutional church as parachurch entities. In some ways, these ministries have become part of the larger youth-sports industrial complex, and they are the subject of the next chapter.

7

Youth Sports and Sports Ministries

The fitness website *Health Fitness Revolution* created a list of "The Top Twenty Fittest Churches in America"—mega churches offering everything from sports leagues to personal trainers and from indoor tracks to pilates.[1] Throughout the country, many communities still look to local churches to provide and organize sporting experiences for their young people. It is not unusual to find motivational posters captioned with Scripture hanging on the walls of high-school weight rooms and training facilities. Sports ministries have a presence on countless school campuses. Our church property has hosted dodgeball games, football, soccer, and basketball practices. High-profile athletes using their platform to publicly endorse their Christian faith has become a staple of the sports scene in the United States. These anecdotes highlight how successfully the church has permeated many corners of the institutional culture of youth sports in the United States.

One of the most popular endeavors in the church's efforts to infiltrate sports with the message of Christ has been frequent, public testimonies given by professional athletes. Earlier we saw how professional athletes are often paid to use their platform to sell products, and Christians also have capitalized on using the platform of celebrity athletes to sell Christianity. Forty years ago journalist, Frank Deford saw this trend emerging as part of what he termed "Sportianity" in the United States and claimed, "the use of athletes as amateur evangelists is so widespread that it might be fairly described as a growth industry."[2] Tom Krattenmaker, in his book *Onward Christian Athletes*, projects Deford's descriptions forward and claims that

1. Health Fitness Revolution,"Top 20 Fittest Churches in America."
2. Deford, "Religion in Sport."

Youth Sports and Sports Ministries

the current relationship Christianity has to sports is the result of "a quarter century of hard work by evangelical Christians to assert themselves in the public square, to grab hold of the tools of culture—television, movies, technology, media, politics, sports—and use them to spread their message and their values."[3] Ironically, as it turns out, the church has made a very intentional effort to utilize sports for the efforts of evangelism at the same time there has been a general neglect for the theological study of sports by the church. I contend this has created a culture of sports ministries that often neglect the important and rigorous work of theology and helped foster a culture of well-intended practitioners who do not always approach sports with a discerning leadership.

The 2014–2015 annual report published by the Christian sports organization Upward Sports states, during that operational year, Upward had over 400,000 youth participants in its various sports teams and events. Additionally, the parachurch sports organization collected over $28 million in revenue for that fiscal year.[4] The 2014 annual report of another leading Christian sports ministry, Athletes in Action (AIA), reports a similar $26 million budget from the 2013 fiscal year.[5] The behemoth among all Christian sports and recreation ministries, the YMCA, boasts a worldwide staff of over 100,000 and has a presence in over 100 different countries.[6] There are countless other sports ministries throughout the country and many that operate as an arm of local churches or parishes. There are sports ministries that focus on specific schools, specific teams, specific sports, and even baseball umpires have a separate sports ministry. In short, the tentacles of sports ministries reach into almost every facet of the youth-sports industrial complex.

A detailed history of the long and complex relationship between sports and the church lies beyond the scope of this book, and other authors already have provided valuable contributions to an important and emerging field of study.[7] However, a concise overview highlighting some

---

3. Krattenmaker, *Onward Christian Soldiers*, 15.
4. Upward Sports. "2014–2015 Annual Report."
5. Athletes in Action, "2014 Annual Report."
6. World YMCA, "2015 Annual Report."
7. Higgs provides a general history of the relationship between religion and sports through a critical perspective in Higgs, *God in the Stadium:*; William J. Baker provides a more sweeping examination of religion and sports (focusing mostly on Christianity) in Baker, *Playing with God*. For shorter treatments of the topic, see the first half of Shirl Hoffman's book, *Good Game*, 1–166, and the first chapter in Robert Ellis's book, *The*

of the more significant developments in sports ministries in the United States helps provide a framework for Christians seeking to faithfully engage sports. Before moving on to some practical suggestions for helping churches better engage the power of sports, this chapter provides a brief depiction of the changing attitudes Christians in the United States have had toward sports over the past two hundred years. It also describes the corresponding attempts made by the church to minister through sports and recreation outlets. U.S. history has witnessed Christians approach sports in nearly every possible way: from outright rejection, to full-sale embrace, and everything in between. The evolution described below follows the major trends in the church-sports relationship and mirrors similar trends seen within the church's approach to culture at large over the same time period. The relationship between sports and the church can be described by loosely following the well-known approaches to culture that the great Christian thinker H. Richard Neibuhr outlined in his classic book, *Christ and Culture*.

CHRIST AGAINST SPORTS: THE PURITAN DISAVOWAL OF SPORTS

H. Richard Niebuhr's first description in *Christ and Culture* states, "Whatever may be the customs of the society in which the Christian lives, and whatever the human achievement it conserves, Christ is seen as opposed to them, so that he confronts men with the challenge of an 'either-or' decision."[8] This description largely reflects the relationship early American Puritans had with what they deemed cultural amusements like sports. The Puritan antipathy towards sports prompts Christian sports historian, Brad Wesner, to harshly describe the time period between the early colonization of New England in 1620 and the end of the Civil War as "The Era of Apathy and Disgust."[9] In reality, the playing of games and sports garnered scant attention from clergy as long as it remained a fringe activity and failed to distract from God's higher calling. However, when organized sports began to emerge during this time period, the church began taking a harsher stance.

Games People Play, entitled, "Reaching for the Heavens: A (Very) Brief History of Religion and Sport," 1–34. Also worth noting is Patrick Kelly's article "Christians and Sports: An Historical and Theological Overview, 33–61, as it provides a history of the relationship to sports and Christianity from a Catholic perspective.

8. Niebuhr, *Christ and Culture*, 40.
9. Wesner, "Visions and Re-Visions," 37.

Robert Higgs challenges one of the more widely held historical stereotypes: "The simplistic idea of the Puritans as humorless detesters of idleness is no longer acceptable to historians, especially sports historians."[10] Similarly, Baker describes "the Puritan posture on sport" as "complex, ambivalent, and inconsistent."[11] Although historians have (wisely) nuanced the "avoid-pleasure-at-all-costs" stereotype of Puritan culture writ large; at the same time, this stereotype originates from a real tendency among many Puritans to eschew and demonize leisure activities. The majority of early Puritans did value hard work and discipline while mostly limiting pleasure and pleasure-giving activities to spiritual activities like prayer and worship. Although innocent children's play was mostly ignored by Christian leaders, the institutionalization of play that was just beginning to take shape was much more threatening to the religious authorities and thus garnered enhanced attention.

Puritans saw sports, and all activities that fell under the broader category of amusement, as sinful in their distraction from more important spiritual practices. As Hoffman describes, "The enjoyment found in prayer, meditation, listening to sermons, and anticipating heaven were far superior to any worldly pleasures."[12] Ellis provides a more nuanced understanding of the Puritan disavowal of sports in seeing their objections more due to the fact that the contests were often held on Sundays, accompanied by drunkenness and gambling, and prompted visceral consequences rather than seeing sports as innately evil.[13] Regardless of their reasoning, sports were largely disregarded as distractions from the spiritual walk (at best) or inherently evil (at worst) by many early Puritans.

Wesner frames this time period beginning with King James's edict (which became known as the *Book of Sports* and made games and amusements lawful on Sundays), and ending with the 1872 quadrennial conference of the Methodist Episcopal Church (who amended their institutional documents to include games and other forms of entertainment as "imprudent conduct.")[14] The 1618 mandate issued by King James (and later reissued by Charles I in 1633) was a blatant attack on Puritan prohibitions against recreation and, according to Wesner, "Much of the negative

10. Higgs, *God in the Stadium*, 22.
11. Baker, *Playing with God*, 18.
12. Hoffman, *Good Game*, 88.
13. Ellis, *The Games People Play*, 21.
14. Wesner, "Visions and Re-Visions," 41–43.

Puritan philosophy regarding recreation stemmed as a rebellion to this document."[15] Wesner designates the end of the era with the 1872 Methodist Episcopal prohibition, which he sees as a preemptive attempt to weaken sports just as they were in the infantile stages of organization, expansion, and growth. Incidentally, according to Wesner, this document helped force "proponents of recreation to state their case carefully" and wound up helping set the stage for a new era where the church would much more readily embrace the culture of sports.[16]

CHRIST OF SPORTS: MUSCULAR CHRISTIANITY'S EMBRACE OF SPORTS

While the Puritans found it difficult to celebrate pleasures outside of "spiritual" exercises, at the same time they were projecting an image of Christ that came to be described as both effeminate and ethereal. Stated theologically, the Puritan perspective of sports was far from incarnational. The image of a soft and effeminate Christ is exemplified by William Holman Hunt's famous picture of Jesus, *The Light of the World*. Michael Frost and Alan Hirsh refer to the Christ depicted in this painting, as well as the subsequently-inspired Warner Sallman painting *Head of Christ*, as the "bearded-lady Jesus."[17] Although the Puritans viewed hard work as an essential extension of their faith, their tireless emphasis on the gentle, internally-focused spiritual exercises projected an image of Christ that was bereft of the sweat, ruggedness, and physicality that came to describe much of frontier American culture. Such an aloof and feminized depiction of Jesus eventually helped prompt a counter-movement that came to embrace an austere and ascetic image of Christ that reconciled much more easily with the physicality of sports. Christians began to accept sports and physical exertion not only as permissible but as spiritually beneficial. This era in U.S. church history has become known as Muscular Christianity. History professor Clifford Puttney defines Muscular Christianity simply as, "a Christian committed to health and manliness."[18] Such a perspective was resolutely absent in any early Puritan understanding and helped serve as a kind of courtship period for the eventual marriage between Christians and sports.

15. Wesner, "Visions and Re-Visions."
16. Wesner, "Visions and Re-Visions," 43.
17. Frost and Hirsch. *ReJesus*, 92–95.
18. Putney, *Muscular Christianity*, 11.

Muscular Christianity traces some of its earliest roots to Thomas Hughes's book *Tom Brown's Schooldays*.[19] The book, which is widely known as one of Theodore Roosevelt's favorites, was one of the first Protestant books to posit the idea that sports promoted a diversity of positive attributes in young men. The Englishman Hughes, along with his friend and fellow author Charles Kingsley, would inspire many leaders in the United States who would eventually help lay the foundation of the Muscular Christianity Movement there. Early clerical leaders like Thomas Wentworth Higginson and Henry Ward Beecher became significant early voices and proved prophetic in helping promote the acceptance of sports and physicality by Christians even though it would take several generations for this widespread acceptance to blossom.[20]

Niebuhr's description of "the Christ of culture" states, "The great work of Christ may be conceived as the training of men in their present social existence for the better life to come."[21] Whereas the previous era of Christians sought to disentangle faith from their surrounding culture and all its manifestations (including sports), the Christ *of* culture approach upholds a more established continuity between Christ and culture. Niebuhr goes on to write, "Christ is identified with what men conceive to be their finest ideals, their noblest institutions, and their best philosophy."[22] For these early leaders of Muscular Christianity and those who would come after them, sports was a noble institution that was a reliable purveyor of Christian ethics and a refined training ground for life lessons.

At the turn of the century, athletes-turned-preachers, like Billy Sunday and Amos Alonzo Stagg, represented a new direction within Christianity, which was able to embrace sports as a purveyor of morality and defender of un-emasculated faith. According to Hoffman, "Sunday urged his crowds to be ready to stand and fight against an 'off-handed, flabby-cheeked, brittle-boned, weak-kneed, thin-skinned, pliable, plastic, spineless, effeminate, ossified three carat Christianity.'"[23] Far from seeing sports as opposed to the message of the gospel, evangelists like Sunday and Dwight L. Moody saw sports as a legitimate avenue by which to spread the gospel

---

19. Thomas Hughes, *Tom Brown's Schooldays*.
20. Putney, *Muscular Christianity*, 21–22.
21. Niebuhr, *Christ and Culture*, 84.
22. Niebuhr, *Christ and Culture*, 103.
23. Hoffman, *Good Games*, 130.

and eventually helped morph into a third era in the history of the church-sports relationship.

The grittiness and physicality of Muscular Christianity found much in common with the Social Gospel Movement. The Social Gospel was a significant shift in U.S. Christianity that followed a similar shift in trajectory towards culture at the onset of the twentieth century. In the preeminent work of the era, *Christianity and the Social Crisis in the 21st Century*, Walter Rauschenbusch specifically draws attention to public parks and pools, swimming, skating, gymnastics, and open-air games as significant social institutions at which the church should direct its attention.[24] It should be noted here that the thrust of Muscular Christianity's acceptance of sports was rooted not in the competitive games themselves nor in some spiritualized understanding of the games, but in an emphasis on good health and healthy bodies.[25] Thus, the YMCA, in many ways, represents the pinnacle of the Muscular Christianity Movement. If there was a biblical theme for Muscular Christians it was, "Your body is a temple of the Holy Spirit" (1 Cor 6:19). Furthermore, beyond the extolling of sports and games as conduits for building up the body, sports came to represent a chief metaphor in the struggle of the kingdom of heaven on earth.[26]

The YMCA provided the institutional organization to help spread the gospel of Muscular Christianity quickly and is largely responsible for its widespread acceptance. It is not overstating its effects to acknowledge, without the groundbreaking work and proselytizing structure of the YMCA, sports ministries today would be far less significant. Although many Christians would continue to struggle with the playing of sports on Sundays (as well as some of the other ethical concerns that had long plagued sports), the rapidly growing popularity of sports forced the church to largely accept the defeat of some of those principles. The proliferation of the relationship between sports and the church was certainly more nuanced than is presented here, but the largest trend in the early part of the twenty-first century was towards acceptance and utility. The following question from Walter Rauschenbusch illustrates the crucial turning point: "How would it affect the recreational situation if the churches took a constructive rather than a prohibitive attitude towards amusements and if they promoted the

---

24. Rauschenbusch, *Christianity and the Social Crisis in the Twenty-First Century*, 306.

25. Baker, *Playing with God*, 36.

26. Baker, *Playing with God*, 27.

sociability of the community rather than that of church groups?"[27] Although embraced by Muscular Christianity largely through a renewed theology of the body and personal health, Billy Sunday and other contemporaneous evangelists had opened the door for the church to use sports for another purpose. Sports, as it turns out, is a great way to draw a crowd, and I have yet to meet an evangelist who didn't love a crowd.

CHRIST ABOVE SPORTS: THE RISE OF THE ATHLETE EVANGELIST

Within Niebuhr's third description of the relationship between Christians and culture, he proposes three further nuances: synthesists, dualists, and conversionists.[28] While each of these three descriptions has functioned at some level in recent years, the most recent history of the church's relationship to sports resonates mostly as dualistic. Niebuhr provides the additional moniker of the dualist as "Christ and culture in paradox," and it is largely indicative of the sports ministries that emerged in the latter half of the twentieth century. According to Niebuhr, "Dualism may be the refuge of the worldly-minded persons who wish to make a slight obeisance in the direction of Christ, or of pious spiritualists who feel they owe some reverence to culture."[29] For the modern Christian athlete, the dualistic reality of a public obeisance to Christ has become commonplace via postgame testimonies, prayers in the end zones, and Bible-verse adornments.

This third attempt is supposed to be a way Christians moderate between the previous two descriptions (being anti-cultural at one extreme and cultural accommodators at the other), and this moderate approach has been manifested in various ways in the recent past. One could hardly claim that the church moved from an embrace of sports at the early part of the twentieth century towards a less accommodating posture more recently. Instead, by referring to the most recent history of the church's relationship with sports as "Christ above sports," in this third era the church began to minimize Muscular Christianity's emphasis on a spirituality seen in health and physicality and instead began to focus on sports, principally, as a medium for evangelism. As the subtitle to Krattenmaker's book *Onward Christian Athletes* describes, the church intentionally set out with the

27. Rauschenbusch, *The Social Principles of Jesus*, location 2134.
28. Niebuhr, *Christ and Culture*, 120.
29. Niebuhr, *Christ and Culture*, 184.

aim of "Turning Ballparks into Pulpits and Players into Preachers."[30] Brad Wesner's description of the modern Christian sports world reflects a similar picture as he describes it as the "Era of Promotion."[31]

The Christian book genre has become inundated with professional athletes and successful coaches who give all the credit of their success to God. Specific examples are too numerous to list, but the past two decades have seen Super-Bowl-winning quarterbacks and coaches,[32] MLB Most Valuable Players,[33] gold-medal-winning Olympians,[34] NBA lottery picks,[35] and NCAA college football national champions[36] all become the subjects of books celebrating their victories and their God. Evidence of God-fearing athletes seem to be everywhere in big-time sports and, as Krattenmaker states in the introduction to his book, "The athletes' gestures and shout-outs to God are fruits of a campaign by well-organized, well-financed evangelical sports ministries committed to leveraging sports to reach and change the broader American culture."[37] In other words, these vocal Christians in professional and big-time sports are products of the most recent era in the relationship between the church and sports. In this era Christians seek to embrace a Christ who can use those who have been given the platform of sports to preach the Gospel and make disciples. In his book dedicated to sports ministry, *Beyond the Gold*, Bryan Mason states, "In a sentence, the local church is ready-made for sports evangelism."[38] The Methodist Church and the Southern Baptist Convention both established national chairs of recreation during this timeframe.[39] In reality, however, it was the parachurch sports-ministry organizations rather than the local church that would promulgate the conflation of sports evangelism in the second half of the twenty-first century.

Two of the most significant sports ministries, FCA and AIA, were both started in the latter half of the twentieth century (1954 and 1966,

30. Krattenmaker, *Turning Ballparks into Pulpits and Players into Preachers*.
31. Wesner, "Visions and Re-Visions," 46–53.
32. Dungy, *Quiet Strength*.
33. Lamb and Ellsworth, *Pujols*.
34. Douglas and Burford, *Grace, Gold, and Glory*.
35. Lewis and Lewis, *The Admiral*.
36. Tressel, *The Winner's Manual*.
37. Krattenmaker, *Onward Christian Athletes*, 6.
38. Bryan Mason, *Beyond the Gold*, Location 216.
39. Wesner, "Vision and Re-Vision," 50.

respectively). This was the era that saw cooperative institutional efforts blossoming throughout evangelicalism: Youth for Christ in the 1940s, Young Life in 1941, Campus Crusade in 1951, Sports Ambassadors in 1952, and Billy Graham conducted his first of hundreds of crusades in Grand Rapids, Michigan in 1947. Christianity also became further entangled in the world of sports during this era through their additional institutions of Christian colleges. Hoffman writes, "Small evangelical colleges began to venture into the deeper waters of intercollegiate sports in the 1950s for the self-professed aim of evangelism."[40] Oral Roberts University found success (not to mention controversy) in their men's basketball program, and no one has epitomized the embrace of sports for the purpose of evangelism and outreach as much as the late Jerry Falwell. He once told a reporter from the *Washington Post* that he wanted to field a football team that could beat Notre Dame.[41] Falwell had witnessed how the success of Notre Dame's football team had played a significant role in promoting a rise in status for Catholics in the United States. According to Baker, *Touchdown Jesus*—a famous mural of Jesus visible from the Notre Dame football stadium—is a "majestic reminder of Notre Dame's central importance in the American saga of sport and religion."[42] Falwell had a similar vision for what a successful sports program could do for the cultural embrace of, not only his private school (now Liberty University) and his denomination (Southern Baptist), but for the broader acquiescence of all conservative evangelicals in the United States.

THE CHRISTIAN YOUTH-SPORTS INDUSTRIAL COMPLEX

The above institutions helped launch the massive world of Christian youth-sports ministries that, in the perspective of chapter 4, could be described as the *Christian* youth-sports industrial complex. In the latter part of the twenty-first century, the conservative Christian subculture emerged as a significant target market that promoted Christian "alternative" options to various cultural expressions (television, movies, music, bookstores, etc.) These are prime examples of Niebuhr's "Christ above culture" typology. The Contemporary Christian Music industry (CCM) is often viewed as the

40. Hoffman, *Good Game*, 138.
41. Hoffman, *Good Game*.
42. Baker, *Playing with God*, 128.

most successful niche within this trend, though its power and influence peaked in the late 1990s and early 2000s. CCM certainly became a powerful Christian cultural institution, but seldom has the Christian youth-sports subculture garnered similar attention. It could be argued that Christian sports ministries have actually been the most successful cultural "alternative" and there appears to be no sign that these powerful institutions have yet to reach their peak. The Christian youth-sports industrial complex is immense.

Started in 1995, Upward Sports, mentioned at the beginning of this chapter, is one of the newer institutions within the Christianized version of youth sports and already claims to be "the world's largest youth sports provider."[43] *Sports Spectrum* is a Christianized version of *Sports Illustrated* that features stories from born-again athletes and coaches at the highest levels and has a circulation of 25,000.[44] Baylor University, a Baptist institution, is one of a growing number of Christian universities offering undergraduate and graduate degrees in sports ministry and sports chaplaincy. An increasing number of mega-churches have full-time recreation pastors. As a matter of fact, the field has expanded to the point that Matthew Brian White's 2005 dissertation at Asbury Seminary is entitled "Sports Ministry in America's One Hundred Largest Churches."[45] Christian sports ministry seems to be one of the most prominent and powerful Christian institutions in the U.S. culture that no one is talking about.

Hoffman's summary of the proliferation of the embrace of sports by modern Christians provides a necessary pause. He writes, "Sport would continue to capture the imagination of the Christian community, although largely unaffected and unexamined by the ethical derivatives of any theological motif."[46] The beginning of this chapter argued that sports has become so enmeshed in the world of the Christian faith it is difficult to imagine a time when it was not this way. This chapter has provided a simplified summary of the relationship between sports and Christianity in the United States. Despite its brevity, the chapter has attempted to highlight some of the most significant ways in which the relationship between Christians and sports has been indicative of larger trends in the relationship between Christians and the culture at large.

43. Upward Sports, "About Upward Sports."
44. Hoffman, *Good Game*, 140.
45. White, "Sports Ministry in America's One Hundred Largest Churches."
46. Hoffman, *Good Game*, 128.

The Victorian antipathy towards sports has never completely been ejected from the Christian community. We see it in contemporary scholars like Robert Higgs who continues to believe that sports and Christianity "are in many ways incompatible."[47] Its vestiges have surfaced occasionally when prompted by ethical issues raised in such areas as brutality in boxing, head trauma in football, and aggression in mixed martial arts. However, those who truly hold to a "Christ against sports" position represent a small minority today. Even Christians who mostly adhere to a "Christ against culture" posture, like Mennonites, have high schools and universities across the country that field intervarsity and intercollegiate sports teams. The shortcoming in this Neibuhrian typology is, if the church were to truly withdraw from the world of sports, their withdrawal would simultaneously result in the absence of a voice to promote the good of sports highlighted in earlier chapters. Sunday as Sabbath has perhaps been the chief capitulation of the Victorian heritage. The NFL rules Sundays in the fall, and youth sports leagues have come to see Sundays as a prime time for scheduling games, tournaments, and practices. As is often the case, the pendulum has swung too far from the Victorian extreme to the one acknowledged by Hoffman where the majority of Christians offer little or no theological reflection of how they play.

In Muscular Christianity, Christians found a much-needed theological justification for sports, games, and amusements. This proved to be a corrective not just for rationalizing the playing of games, but also for unemasculating the Christ of Christianity. Through mega-church-sponsored sports leagues, gymnasiums, recreation pastors, Christian-based workout routines, and the recent commitment to better health (like Rick Warren's *The Daniel Plan*),[48] the legacy of Muscular Christianity lives on today. In many ways, it was a natural progression to see Muscular Christianity give way to the era of the athlete-evangelist. Unfortunately, this transition has witnessed a spiritualization of sports that fails to integrate a holistic understanding of sports and is often little more than a workout routine reinforced by an out-of-context Bible verse. Here, the shortcoming of Niebuhr's "Christ of culture" type is realized as it is difficult to maintain a distinct Christian identity in the midst of embracing the broader culture. The only differences for many Christian leagues is that they may offer a prayer before the game

---

47. Higgs, *God in the Stadium*, 1.
48. Warren, Amen, and Hyman, *The Daniel Plan*.

or a devotional at halftime. While this inclusion is noteworthy, it does little to address the manner or spirit of the playing of the games themselves.

The rise of the Christian youth-sports industrial complex has become so intertwined with the status quo of the larger youth-sports industrial complex that it is difficult to know where one ends and the other begins. As the industrial complex has rooted itself in contemporary culture, the theological distinctiveness Christians espouse has often been minimized (at best) or completely cast aside (at worst). The early chapters of this book provide a specific theological rationale for play and for competition. The problem with the current Christian youth-sports industrial complex can be seen by juxtaposing them next to the non-Christian alternatives and noting if they are any different from one another. In my experience as a high-school football official, I have seen little difference between the conduct or sportsmanship of Christian high-school teams and their public high-school counterparts. Save the prayer they say before the opening kickoff, every other aspect of the game tends to look identical. A Major League Baseball umpire recently told me that some of the worst behavior he has ever witnessed has been in church softball and basketball leagues. Considering the antics of MLB managers—that's saying a lot! The problem with seeing sports simply as a neutral platform by which to share the gospel is that it fails to reflect on the medium itself. The result is that Christians fail to lead the way when real ethical concerns with the medium of sports come along.

WHERE DO WE GO FROM HERE?

Amidst the quest for cultural relevance and meaningful engagement, it can be difficult to maintain an authentic and distinguished Christian identity in any cultural endeavor. The dilemma Niebuhr has drawn so much attention to continues to find itself at the heart of the public life of Christians as they wrestle with how to engage their culture. Rather than settling on one of Neibuhr's proposals, a better solution seems to be a conflation of each of his categories with an infused missional impulse to which we will turn our attention in chapter 10. There is a great deal of good in the world of today's youth sports, and much of that good can be attributed to Christianity's involvement with sports throughout different eras. While many well-intentioned Christian leaders have established sports and recreation ministries that have accomplished much of this good, it remains that many of these sports ministries have simply duplicated the same shortcomings and problems that already existed in the world of youth sports. Furthermore, the modus operandi for many Christian sports ministries reflects an attractional church model that has largely fallen out of favor among leading Christian voices.

In critiquing the current status of sports ministries, it is easy to appear unnecessarily critical. Countless athletes, coaches, and fans have been blessed and are being blessed by and through these ministries, and it is far from my intention to call for their abandonment. There is certainly nothing wrong with churches organizing softball and basketball leagues and building gymnasia to serve as community centers. Many communities throughout the country continue to rely heavily on churches to organize their neighborhood sports leagues and activities. I believe unequivocally that the sports experience in the United States is better because of the active involvement of Christians. There is no need to completely dismantle the entire Christian sports and recreation complex as it currently exists. At the same time, however, it is important to continually subject the current organizations and their practices to rigorous and critical theological review.

Without question, the rise of parachurch sports ministries has been one of the most significant developments in the most recent era of the church's relationship with sports. An unintended consequence of these parachurch organizations has been, at the local level, congregations largely have neglected any kind of critical approach to sports. Furthermore, this neglect has occurred at the same time the popularity of youth participating in sports has been at an all-time high. In other words, as the youth-sports industrial complex has begun to grow, the local church's attention to the topic has waned significantly. As a youth pastor, I constantly face the challenges that students active in baseball, softball, dancing, ice skating, football, and other sports pose to the communal bonds within our church family. The challenge facing me is the same challenge facing youth pastors throughout the United States: what to do when sports fail to attract families to the church but, instead, take families away from the church?

I am convinced that one of the most significant tasks before the local church involves a missional transformation of the church's involvement in youth sports. From my research I have determined that the missional conversation (defined it the broadest possible sense) that has been at the forefront of pastoral leadership conversations and studies for more than a decade has been almost completely absent within sports-ministry circles.

An important starting point is for the local church to be re-empowered to engage sports in their communities. Parachurch sports ministries will always have an important role for Christian athletes. However, as the theological understanding of evangelism and mission continue to evolve, it is important for the local church to consider how this affects the way Christians see sports as mission. Part 3 of this book sets forth a new vision for the church's relationship to sports as it relates to the church's role as prophet, spiritual conscience, and missionary.

PART 3

Ministering to the Youth-Sports Industrial Complex

For Christians trying to live out our faith and be "*in* the world, but not *of* the world," we find ourselves in a precarious position when it comes to addressing our culture's most popular practices. There are times when we can stand alongside our friends and neighbors and join them wholeheartedly. There are often points of convergence between the morals and principles of our communities and those of the community shaped by Jesus Christ (as we have seen in sports). These moments conjure Niebuhr's "Christ of culture" category and are the times we feel most at home in this world. For Christians participating in sports today, this appears to be the most common experience.

When cultural practices deviate from Gospel values, Christians are charged with the difficult task of speaking up, withdrawing, or working for change. Christians are often encouraged to speak out publicly about their faith in Jesus Christ, but what may be more challenging is combating the subtle and oppressive ways cultural practices negatively influence our spiritual formation. These are moments Christians are forced to swim upstream against the current of culture and embody the words of Paul, "Do not conform to the pattern of this world, but be transformed by the renewing of your mind" (Rom 12:2).

In his book, *To Change the World*, James Davison Hunter pushes Niebuhr's classic assessment of Christ and culture further with the notion of faithful presence. He concludes the ultimate role for the church in culture is to be faithfully present. The church needs this vision for engaging the culture of youth sports in the United States. Part 3 considers what it might look like for the church to be faithfully present in the youth-sports community via three essential roles: prophetic for matters of justice, pastoral for matters of identity formation, and missional for matters of community engagement.

8

Finding the Prophetic Voice of the Church in Youth Sports

One of the most famous examples of religious practice conflicting with professional sports happened in 1965 when the Dodger's ace Sandy Koufax, who was Jewish, refused to pitch in Game 1 of the World Series because it coincided with the Jewish holiday of Yom Kippur. The Dodgers went on to lose Game 1 to the Minnesota Twins 8–2, despite the fact that future Hall of Famer Don Drysdale pitched for Koufax. After sitting out Game 1, Koufax pitched in three of the remaining six games of the World Series, threw a shutout in the deciding Game 7, and was awarded the Series Most Valuable Player. Ironically, as Rabbi Shais Taub points out, "the legend of Sandy Koufax is more associated with that first game of the series that he *didn't* pitch than with any of the games that he went on to play."[1] At the time, Koufax's decision was extolled by Jews throughout the United States and has remained an indelible source of Jewish pride—"one of the best American Jewish stories we have," says one rabbi.[2]

Koufax's decision resonates a great deal with the history of the Jewish people. In Daniel 3, while the Israelites were in Babylonian exile, King Nebuchadnezzar had a massive ninety-foot golden statue erected that all people were instructed to bow down and worship whenever music was played. Three Jews, Shadrach, Meshach, and Abednego, refused, and the king was given this report concerning the three dissenters: "They neither serve your

1. Taub, "Why Sandy Koufax Sat Out the World Series on Yom Kippur."
2. Rosengren, "Myth and Fact Part of Legacy from Sandy Koufax's Yom Kippur Choice."

gods nor worship the image of gold you have set up" (Dan 3:12b). For the conquered Israelites, life under various foreign empires proved challenging, and the prophets reflect the tension they faced between settling down and making a home in the foreign land (see, for example, Jeremiah's letter to the exiles in Jeremiah 29), and weeping and longing for their homeland, never quite at home in exile (see, for example, the song of lament in Psalm 137).

A less familiar story is that of one of the most famous pitchers in the history of baseball, Cy Young, who had a contractual agreement that excused him from pitching on Sundays for the Cleveland Spiders because of his religious convictions. Like Koufax, Young's religious convictions came in direct conflict with his sports responsibilities at the highest levels of competition. At the end of the 1895 baseball season, the Cleveland Spiders were in a tight pennant race when they were scheduled to play a doubleheader on September 15. Knowing this would be especially taxing on their pitching staff (and these late-season games were crucial to their title hopes), Cy Young told his manager he would be willing to make a relief appearance if he was needed.

Young was summoned from the bullpen and even got the win in this rare and important Sunday appearance. He often referred to this religious conflict later in life. In his biography of Cy Young, Reed Browning captures the frivolity Young used in justifying his appearance in that game, "The Bible, he liked to note, stated that rescuing your neighbor's ass from the pit on the Sabbath was not a sin. 'Well boys,' he said— and I can readily imagine the smile spreading across his face—'I'll be durned if I know any bigger ass than Tedbeau [his manager] anywhere, and he was certainly in an awful hole. So I helped him out.'"[3] While Sandy Koufax steadfastly maintained his religious convictions over the demands of his sports team, Cy Young was willing to make an exception for the sake of his team.

If Koufax and Young represent two approaches to reconciling sports and personal religious conviction, it seems as though Young's philosophy has won the day, at least for Christians involved in youth sports. Koufax's approach stands out dramatically against the backdrop of today's all-consuming sports culture. Young was clearly on the side of the prophet Jeremiah who beckoned Israel to "build houses and settle down; plant gardens and eat what they produce" because they were going to be there awhile (Jer 29:5). However, even in their settling down, Israel remained God's chosen nation and, as such, was called to be different. This same message was

---

3. Thanks to Paul Putz for pointing me to this anecdote. Browning, *Cy Young*, 52.

reiterated to Christians as believers were addressed as "aliens and strangers in the world" (1 Pet 2:11). Old Testament scholar Walter Brueggemann notes, "As the Jews in the Babylonian Empire had to struggle with the seductions and insistencies of empire, so Christians in the midst of U.S. empire must struggle for peculiar identity."[4] There are few greater seductions than all that youth sports promises, and it is becoming increasingly difficult to see any peculiar identity of Christians immersed within its throes.

Marvin McMickle says prophetic preaching asks the question, "What is the role or appropriate response of our congregation, our association, and our denomination to the events that are occurring within our society and throughout the world?"[5] This seems like a central question for the church to ask regarding all that is happening with sports, but the church's lack of theological attention to sports has left it in a difficult position to begin responding. Building upon the theological framework of Part One, this chapter considers how those principles might inform a proper response to the current culture of youth sports. It has become apparent to me that countless people are wrestling with the influence sports are having on their families. Many families feel burdened, burned out, and unsure of how to balance their good intentions for their children with the overwhelming demands of their children's sports. Many parents enter youth sports with the convictions of Sandy Koufax, but somewhere along the way offer the concession of Cy Young. Unfortunately, Christians have tended to focus more on creating large sports programs and proselytizing through the platform of successful athletes than on providing a prophetic conscience amid the aspects of the youth-sports industrial complex that are especially hostile towards a more holistic Christian worldview.

WHERE HAVE ALL THE PROPHETS GONE?[6]

Much like Cy Young, Christians involved in youth sports often get so caught up in the dreams and aspirations of their sports culture they allow this part of their lives to subjugate their Christian identity. It never happens all at once, but as the demands of sports increase and responsibilities become more complex, many families adjust core values that once were non-negotiable. John Tauer illustrates how small concessions in youth sports

---

4. Brueggemann, *Out of Babylon*, 15.
5. McMickle, *Where Have all the Prophets Gone?* 2.
6. I am borrowing this title from Marvin McMickle's book of the same name.

can eventually lead families to make decisions that betray their core values: "Few parents would make an initial investment of several thousand dollars for youth sports. However, as time goes on, small investments of a few hundred dollars lead to larger ones of a few thousand dollars, and before we know it, several thousand dollars may seem reasonable, given all we've already invested."[7] Youth sports test the boundaries of every family's core values: from how much time and money they are willing to spend to how they treat umpires and coaches. David King and Margot Starbuck allocate an entire chapter to unpacking the myth: "Youth sports instills our family's values."[8] Although many people extol sports for the values and lessons they can teach young people, in reality, many of those values become negated by unintended messages that are simultaneously at work.

Furthermore, the youth-sports industrial complex operates much like the Roman poet Juvenal's famous description of Roman political strategy: bread and circus. Youth sports have become the circus for many Christians today. Rather than presenting an overt false god as an object of worship, they tend to keep families busy enough to distract them. This book grows out of my concern, not that Christians are showing too little reflection or pause in their involvement in sports, but that the vast majority seem to be showing no reflection or hesitancy at all. As families zip from one practice or game to another, squeezing in a quick meal and homework along the way, there seems little time to offer thoughtful, reflective consideration as to whether or not this whole system might actually be standing in the way of our faithfulness to God. This very suggestion seems tantamount to heresy, but also highlights how comfortable Christians have become with the status quo in youth sports. Just like the prophets became too comfortable with Israel's injustices, when Christians become too at home in this world, they become too comfortable with practices and values that are detrimental to their faith identity and too easily ignore matters of injustice. Our addiction to sports often blinds us from realizing when we are complicit with a system that maintains practices in direct opposition to Gospel values.

Voices Crying in the Wilderness

Dion Sanders famously quipped "Christianity and sports go together like peanut butter and jelly," which is reminiscent of Frank Deford's well known

---

7. Tauer, *Why Less is More for WOSPS*, 177.
8. King and Starbuck, *Overplayed*, 131–57.

Finding the Prophetic Voice of the Church

description of this marriage in the U.S. as "Sportianity." The congeniality experienced between sports and Christianity in the United States made it natural for the emergence of a very powerful and influential Christian sports ministry empire. In the previous chapter, I emphasized these leading parachurch sports ministries have accomplished much good and are not inherently problematic. However, their ascendance in power, popularity, and influence has created a blind spot for the church to some of the negative, ancillary challenges the current sports culture presents to followers of Christ. First John 2:15 states: "Do not love the world or anything in the world. If anyone loves the world, the love of the Father is not in him." While the Puritans may have taken biblical passages like this to an excessive extreme, there remains in the Bible a clear witness to be cautious in our engagements and interactions with this world. The prophets established a long tradition of standing at the periphery of culture crying out against practices that were contrary to the nature and character of God.

In 2008, Tom Farrey published the groundbreaking exposé of youth sports, *Game On*, and was subsequently chosen to lead the Aspen Institute's newly founded initiative Project Play. In 2012, John O'Sullivan founded the organization Changing the Game Project, which according to the website, has the purpose of returning "sports to our children and [putting] the 'play' back in 'play ball.'"[9] In a September 2014 TED talk, Dr. Matt Roth begins his talk by stating, "Organized youth sports in America has lots of potential for our children: be physically active, establish relationships with their peers, and build self confidence. But in its current state, it might also be one of the most dangerous epidemics in America."[10] There is a growing list of leaders speaking out against increasing concerns regarding the current practices of youth sports. Many of these concerns resonate deeply with Christian convictions of justice, health, and community. As the voices critiquing the current state of youth sports in the U.S. grow louder, the lack of outspoken Christians at the forefront of these discussions becomes more striking.

PROPHETIC CONCERN

The youth-sports industrial complex is in dire need of a prophetic message at both individual and systemic levels. We have seen many of the pressing challenges facing families who are immersed in the world of sports. Having

9. http://changingthegameproject.com/about.
10. Roth, "Rethinking Youth Sports."

considered the dramatic role the spiritual powers play in organizing and influencing this world, the challenges facing individual families are symptomatic of larger, systemic shortcomings that are equally in need of an outside prophetic voice. Because analysis of youth sports by Christians tends to be limited to conversations of parenting and individual sportsmanship, many of the broader, sociological shortcomings are often ignored. The rest of this chapter offers a brief outline of four areas in youth sports that are most in need of prophetic concern: body, Sabbath, community, and justice.

A Prophetic Message of the Body

The first time I ran a half marathon I collapsed at the finish line and required medical attention. The good news is I finished the race; the bad news is I ended up in the hospital receiving IV fluids due to heat exhaustion. Nothing like that had ever happened to me before and nothing similar has happened to me since. I trained adequately to finish the 13.1 miles, but I was fooled by the unusually warm and humid December day. I didn't drink enough water along the course and chose to tough it out in order to finish my first race by a time I set as my goal. It turns out, there's a fine line in sports between pushing yourself and pushing too hard. Fortunately, the only thing that was really harmed was my pride, and through my first trip to the emergency room I learned an important lesson: we must respect our bodies.

Ironically, while physical health most often is cited as a significant benefit of sports, it can no longer be accepted unequivocally. Active children are healthy children, to be sure; however, alongside an obesity crisis in the U.S. that is the result of inactive young people, participation in sports often leads to other health concerns. Although completely preventable, "as many as half of all youth sports injuries are the result of overuse."[11] As I ran my half marathon, it was just me pushing myself too hard, but as we shift our attention back to youth sports, we see countless examples of parents, coaches, and the very system itself pushing children too hard, too much, and too often when they are too young. When sports are robbed of the spirit of play and are transformed into a means to an end (playing time, scholarship, money, fame, winning, etc.) it turns them into something that is no longer sports.

---

11. Hyman, *Until It Hurts*, 65.

Overuse injuries are but one example of the ways that young athletes sometimes abuse their bodies. Concussions and other types of head injuries have received national attention by helping to bring sweeping changes to football and other contact sports. Anabolic steroids and other performance-enhancing drugs are a constant temptation for athletes seeking to outperform their competitors. Other sports, like wrestling, often perpetuate eating disorders as performance is directly connected to weight classes. ACL and Tommy John surgeries have become so commonplace among athletes at all levels that they have become part of everyday sports vernacular. The problem has become so widespread that during the 2015 Major League Baseball Hall of Fame inductions, former pitcher John Smoltz used his induction speech as a platform to tell parents it is not normal for fourteen and fifteen year olds to be having surgery. Yet, all of this evidence notwithstanding, more children are encouraged to specialize in one sport and play that sport year-round.

No Pain, No Gain

As my embarrassing experience in the half marathon illustrates, there is a fine line between challenging your body and punishing your body. As children play more games at earlier ages and for longer seasons all the while injuries become more and more common, Christians must be reminded of a healthy theology of the body. Contrary to the platonic dualistic philosophy that often has plagued Christianity, God created humanity *in the flesh*. Our bodies matter. God has imbued our bodies with incredible, natural indicators that tell us when the stove is too hot, a noise is too loud, or if we have been pushing it too far. If we never push our bodies beyond our levels of comfort then we will never realize our full athletic potential. "No pain, no gain," isn't just a catchy slogan; it's reality. That being said, more parents need to be considering the physical toll their child's sport is having on the bodies of their young and developing children. When perfectly healthy children have to see a doctor to deal with chronic injuries, this should be a sign that something is amiss. Parents can easily become intoxicated by the dreams and aspirations they see in their children's athletic future, all the while ignoring the real physical harm they are causing to their bodies right now.

Honor God with Your Body

Sports are at their best when they showcase physical prowess. Watching Michael Jordan soar through the air, Aroldis Chapman throw a fastball 104 mph, a gymnast land a mind-boggling, twisting vault, or Odell Beckham make a miraculous one-handed catch are the kinds of experiences that draw us to sports. The majority of us work in professions that are largely removed from the physicality that once dominated the labor force. Instead, we sit at our desks and stare, hypnotized, into our screens all day long, so it is no wonder we have a tendency to live vicariously through our children's physicality in sports. Two of the theological foundations of the Christian faith are the *imago dei* and the incarnation of Jesus Christ. Our bodies are created in the image of God and maintain an inherent and essential worth in the eyes of God. Moreover, in the incarnation, Jesus "became flesh and made his dwelling among us" (John 1:14) further displaying the inherent value of the physical realm.

N. T. Wright has critiqued the way a dualistic worldview has promoted a deficient understanding of the resurrection. He notes, "robust Jewish and Christian doctrine of the resurrection, as part of God's new creation, gives more value, not less, to the present world and to our present bodies."[12] Paul maintains this high view of the body as well by encouraging Christians to "honor God with your body" (1 Cor 6:20). The U.S. youth-sports industrial complex is in desperate need of Christian prophets to speak out against practices and tendencies that are detrimental to young and developing bodies. Christians should be leading voices advocating for the health of young people in sports. When we damage our bodies in our sports, we allow ourselves to be subservient to the sport rather than being their master. More Christians need to consider how many games their children are playing in a weekend, how long their sports seasons last, and how much violence is inherent in the games they are playing. Certainly, there are ways to honor God through the playing of sports, but it should never be at the detriment of their physical health.

A Prophetic Message of Sabbath

Youth sports has become synonymous with a busy and hectic life. No parent is adequately prepared for the drastic change of life a new child brings.

---

12. Wright, *Surprised by Hope*, 27.

As a newborn grows and eventually develops their own social life, however, parents often lament the simplicity of the early years of life. Seemingly, in the blink of an eye, parents go from changing diapers and feeding bottles, to balancing homework and driving to practices and games. In his book on the Sabbath, Dan Allender suggests, "We live in a dark day, but it is still rare for someone to publically tout his or her violation of the Ten Commandments, with one exception—our debasement with busyness. We love to tell others how much we work, how much we still have to get done, and how overwhelmed we are with the exhaustion of our labor."[13] Facebook has become a place for parents to lament how many tournament games they attended last weekend, or how far next weekend's tournament is away from home. Parents in the U.S. have become addicted to being busy in many corners of our culture, but nowhere is busyness worn as a badge of honor more than in the world of club and elite sports.

In chapter 2 I laid out the case for understanding sports as lying at the nexus of Sabbath and work. In its proper place, sports have a restful and restorative function that reconciles well with Sabbath (re-creation). As we saw above with the body, a presumed benefit of sports can be betrayed when not held in proper balance, and it seems such is the case with current practices in the youth-sports industrial complex. Sports seasons have prolonged (if they end at all), teams play more games, have more practices, and receive more specialized (and often individual) training taking up more and more of their families' lives. Laws that prohibited businesses from opening on Sundays (known as blue laws) are a distant memory in most corners of the United States, and the residual effect of their demise has been dramatic for families whose children play sports. Sundays, once revered as days for family and faith, have become the hallmark of elite sports.

Sabbath as Counter Culture

The practice of Sabbath is about remembering. Exodus 20 admonishes the people to root their memory in the creative act of Yahweh who "made the heavens and the earth, the sea, and all that is in them, but he rested on the seventh day" (Exod 20:11). Deuteronomy 5 admonishes the people to root their memory in the redemptive act of Yahweh who "brought you out of [Egypt] with a mighty hand and an outstretched arm" (Deut 5:15). Sabbath was intended as an interruption to the hectic life of work and the monotony

13. Allender, *Sabbath*, 6.

of everyday life. Sabbath provided the rhythm of life for Israel and helped ensure the nation's heart was beating in sync with the purposes of God and that they were not distracted. Sabbath was observed weekly providing a regular interruption and reminder of God's presence. Israel also observed longer stints of Sabbath in seasonal festivals and worship times. Sabbath was a dramatic intrusion into the lives of God's people to ensure they remained grounded in their identity as such.

It could be argued the dramatic intrusion into the lives of many Christians today is sports as weekends are now the haven for regional tournaments across the country. It is commonplace for teams to play as many as six games or more during a single weekend tournament, and those same teams will play in numerous tournaments over the course of a single sports season. In a society already obsessed with busyness, this often makes weekends the busiest time of the week. The great irony of all finds many parents looking forward to Monday so things can slow down! There is no place where Christians will stand out more dramatically from the status quo in youth sports than if they choose to take Sabbath seriously.

"Sabbath Was Made for Humankind, Not Humankind for Sabbath"

I have referenced this statement from Jesus in Mark 2:27 several times because I believe it captures the heart of the problem in youth sports better than any other teaching in the Bible. Just like the Sabbath, sports have been created to serve us for our pleasure and enjoyment, but just like the Pharisees in the New Testament did with the Sabbath, we have made sports into an oppressive force by which many parents feel hostage. Christians have a prophetic obligation to participate in sports in a way that is liberating and pleasurable, and such a way gets us closer to the true intention of sports.

Carl Stotz's retelling of the early days of Little League Baseball reminds us of how organized youth sports in the United States began with a Sabbath quality that largely has been neglected in its industrialized forms. Harkening back to the 1940s, Stotz describes how the early Little League games drew crowds from throughout Williamsport, Pennsylvania, who stayed after the game was over as "God Bless America" was played over the loudspeaker followed by several other marches.[14] It's quite a stark contrast from contemporary sports complexes where scores of teams matched up against each other from all over the region, battle their way through their respective

---

14. Stotz and Loss, *A Promise Kept*, 78.

tournament brackets after long car rides, hotel stays, and fast-food meals. At one level, times are starkly different than they were in the 1940s, and to mourn those bygone days is to hopelessly beckon for a time that will never return. At another level, however, contemporary practices in youth sports have become so all-consuming, all-year-round, that any family who desires to regularly honor Sabbath will be forced to carefully consider the teams they associate with and, occasionally, confront those teams, leagues, and coaches with such counter-cultural practices as skipping games, practices, or even entire tournaments.

A Prophetic Message of Community

One of the more endearing books I read in researching for this book is *A Promise Kept*—Carl Stotz's story of the beginning of Little League Baseball. The story is so compelling because of the way it pictures the entire community of Williamsport, Pennsylvania (a town that would hardly be known if it wasn't for its connection to Little League), coming together in order to provide a fun and meaningful activity for young boys during the Great Depression. From Stotz soliciting Lycoming Dairy, Jumbo Pretzel, and Lundy Lumber for sponsorship of the first three Little League teams in 1939, to volunteers helping build and care for the fields and bleachers each year, and to the volunteers who helped salvage the wooden bleachers of the early stadium after a severe flood ravaged the field in 1946, the early roots of Little League Baseball show the powerful way youth sports can help build and reinforce communities. Little League established community boundaries from the earliest years of its existence in order to reinforce local support and resources for local children.

Unfortunately, as we have seen in previous chapters, much of the way elite and club sports are organized actually can be harmful to local communities. Young people often play on teams with players who go to different schools and live in different neighborhoods. If this was so white, suburban, upper-middle class teams could play more diverse teams across town, Christians could be quick to applaud this as a prophetically-inspired act. Instead, these teams are most often traveling to play white, suburban, upper-middle class teams from other cities. These teams do provide exposure to a broader social network in general, but the long commutes that often accompany being part of these types of teams make it a challenge to find time for deep and meaningful interaction with anyone. From a prophetic perspective, though, the real concern regarding the busyness of youth sports is the way it tends to isolate people from life within their local church and disconnect them from a God-centered rhythm of life. Regularly observing Sabbath helps protect us from overwork and busyness within our individual lives, but it also ensures that we are connected to the worshipful rhythm of life promoted by our church.

Our Connection to the Local Church Matters

The story of Sandy Koufax's refusal to pitch in Game 1 of the World Series stands in stark contrast to the countless Christian families who abandon their commitment to a local church because of their sports commitments. As a youth pastor, I know the challenge of working around families' sports schedules, and as a parent, I know firsthand the challenges of *having* those sports schedules. I have argued elsewhere that this is not about making sure our families sacrifice everything to be at the church building every time the doors are open. Our son sometimes plays baseball games on Sundays, and my wife often takes him to the game or we make arrangements for another parent to bring him. To this point, he has never missed a game on a Sunday.

Because our coach knows that Sundays are important to us (and probably because he knows I am a pastor) before he schedules the games, he often checks with me to see if my son would be able to play on some Sundays. It is baseball season as I am writing these words, and I confess that this is a challenging topic and it is not getting easier. There are families who attend church every Sunday, but who are not immersed in the rhythm of their community of faith. There are also families who miss church frequently for sports or other commitments, but who find a way to be immersed in the rhythm of life in their community. Most churches are made up of people from across a fairly broad geographical area and the Sunday morning gathering is one of the few times most of the church is assembled. If a family is not going to regularly be a part of that time together, it is going to take a great effort to maintain a connection to that community of faith. I offer no list of bullet points of how to do this because I believe every situation and family is different, but the point must be made that it takes a great deal of effort. As travel and elite sports teams participate in more tournaments and out-of-town games, the more difficulty families will have in maintaining a vibrant relationship with their local church body.

At the heart of the Christian faith is the belief that Christ brings about a fundamental change in identity to the life of a believer. This idea was crucial in the writing of Paul. "You are not your own; you were bought at a price" (1 Cor 6:19–20). "I have been crucified with Christ and I no longer live, but Christ lives in me" (Gal 2:20). The reason the local church is so fundamental to Christians is it provides connection to brothers and sisters who share in that identity. The church is what keeps us grounded and rooted in our identity in Christ. John Nugent is unabashed about how crucial our relationships with fellow believers are. "If we don't take the time to truly share our lives with fellow believers, then our root problem is faith. If we don't take time to truly love and prioritize one another in devoted Christian fellowship, we don't believe that we have been raised to newness of life together."[15] We are not automatically at odds with the Christian faith when our sports commitments take us away from the church's gatherings, but we must find a way to compensate in our relationship to the church that truly loves our fellow believers and remains devoted to Christian fellowship.

A Youth Sports Testimony

Pastors Jay Pathak and Dave Runyon set out to take seriously Jesus's commandment to "Love your neighbor as yourself" in their Denver, Colorado, neighborhoods. In becoming intentional about knowing and loving their neighbors, the authors are more honest than most Christians are about the obstacle sports can be to Christian ministry. "By far, the biggest sacrifice that families need to make for their kids to succeed in sports is time."[16] Runyon writes about the challenges their children's sports schedules created.

> Where we live, there is a high-level baseball program that requires kids to practice three times a week and play forty-plus games a year . . . But Lauren and I knew that if we went down that route, our schedules would have to revolve around baseball for six months a year, leaving little time for much else, particularly for being present in our own lives and neighborhood. The good news is that there is also a youth recreational league nearby . . . it was clear which league Ethan would join, even if it meant that it would impact his development as a baseball player. This decision was not

---

15. Nugent, *Endangered Gospel*, 142.
16. Pathak and Runyon, *The Art of Neighboring*, 48.

easy, but it became clear that it was necessary if we were to take the Great Commandment literally.[17]

The life Christ calls his people to does not have room for split allegiance. One of the underlying motivations for writing this book is to help us wrestle with how we can participate in sports while maintaining our faithfulness exclusively to God. Jesus's beckoning is a serious one: "If anyone would come after me he must deny himself and take up his cross and follow me" (Matt 16:24). It may seem overly staid to apply this kind of language within the context of something as frivolous as sports, but—and here is the crux of the matter—there are few things that families take as seriously as sports. Runyon's commitment to the work of Christ over his son's baseball ability is refreshing and a story that needs replicating among faithful Christians throughout the country.

A Prophetic Message of Justice in Youth Sports

While these trends are troubling enough, one area of concern in youth sports relates even more directly to the Old Testament prophets than the others. In the 2016 "State of Play" report by the Aspen Institute, the organization reported that 38 percent of children from homes with incomes less than $25,000 a year played team sports, compared with 67 percent of children from homes with incomes more than $100,000 a year.[18] Such a disparity is jarring and highlights a systemic injustice that is largely overlooked. The simple fact is the elite and travel-team culture that has come to dominate the landscape of youth sports require a significant amount of money for team fees and additional expenses for out-of-town tournaments and personalized equipment and uniforms. At the same time, with affluent families rushing to sign their children up for elite teams, there are fewer options for lower-income families to participate in more affordable recreation leagues. African Americans, in particular, have become so disassociated from the sport of baseball (a sport that has especially become dominated by affluent, white, suburban culture) that the majority of historically black universities have had mostly white baseball teams for several years.[19]

17. Pathak and Runyon, *The Art of Neighboring*, 48.
18. Project Play, "State of Play."
19. Powell, "The New Face of Baseball."

FINDING THE PROPHETIC VOICE OF THE CHURCH

What is even more disheartening is the way that urban centers mobilize tax money to cater to professional sports teams (again benefitting more affluent citizens) at the expense of local recreational sports leagues and community centers. A specific example reported by Tom Farrey highlights the hypocrisy of the situation in many cities. The Baltimore Ravens paid quarterback Steve McNair $12 million in 2006, the same amount as the city spent on recreation and athletic needs for the city's 20,000 children.[20] Although the city did not pay McNair's salary, they did fund the building of the stadium in which he would earn all that money. For all the time and attention parachurch ministries have given to sports, it is alarming how much they have neglected the weightier matters of justice.

A Prophetic Imagination in Sports

In identifying sports as a spiritual power we recognize it as a wielder of power. Throughout this book we have seen many significant ways that sports wields its power—both for good and for evil. In all exercises of power, God's people should be especially concerned with those who are vulnerable under or fall victim to those in power, and the world of sports is no different. The theology of sports laid out in the first part of this book contains no qualifications. God has created a space for sports and play beneficial for everyone. The benefits and joy that accompany the playing of sports should be accessible and enjoyable by all people regardless of gender, race, socioeconomic status, or physical disability. As Christians, we don't expect to hold the rest of the world to our standards, but our identity in Christ that sees "neither Jew nor Greek, slave nor free, male nor female" (Gal 3:28), beckons us to work for justice when we see injustice.

Parents can become so focused on their child's athletic success and future path that they allow the youth-sports industrial complex to dictate their values more than the gospel. Imagine how dramatically the world of youth sports would change if Christian families began dedicating all of the resources they currently pour into elite sports, and instead began supporting inner-city sports programs and sports programs for children with disabilities. Addressing the injustices perpetuated by current youth sports practices is going to require out-of-the-box thinking and what Walter Brueggeman so poetically describes as a "prophetic imagination." Perhaps the first thing most of us need to do to address the injustices in youth sports

20. Farrey, *Game On*, 245.

is to repent for our complete and utter disregard and oversight of the forgotten children.

Seeing Sports through God's Eyes

In 2016 I attended the Inaugural Global Congress on Sports and Christianity at York St. John's University in England. One of the keynote speakers, John Swinton, presented a lecture entitled "Running for Jesus! The Virtues and the Vices of Disability in Sport." Swinton is an ordained minister in the Presbyterian Church, theology professor in Aberdeen, Scotland, and has published extensively on the theology of disability. Of the many keynote presentations, admittedly Swinton's was one that I was least interested in attending, but I left his session convicted, realizing how much (and how easily) I neglect the very people for which God calls his people to minister. He reminded me of my friend Jason who lost both of his legs from an explosion in Afghanistan and who found an outlet for his spirit of play in a local sled hockey league. I realized how little attention or care I pay to the Special Olympics, and how blind I truly am to those who are neglected by larger power players of this world. This realization was in addition to confronting remnants of my neglect of racial, gender, and other barriers that remain in youth sports.

For all the time and attention Christian parachurch ministries have given to sports, it is disappointing to see such a lack of attention for the same populations that are overlooked by the rest of the sporting world. With so many Christians actively involved in sports teams and in sports leagues throughout the country, we might expect to see a more vibrant prophetic word that speaks out against practices and policies that oppress, neglect, and (most often) ignore. The tentacles of injustice reach far and wide in our fallen world, and a worthy treatment of the many areas of society they reach is a much larger topic than can be laid out in this book. This discussion remains an important and pressing one for the church, and my hope is we are not far from a growing number of voices providing dutiful attention to justice in youth sports.

When I attended Dr. Swinton's lecture, I began to see the sports world through a different perspective. I began to see the people who are neglected and ignored by the current structures of elite youth sports. Christians have the opportunity to be the voice that speaks out against injustice, but first we must awaken ourselves to it. Whether it is girls, who continue to have less access to organized sports than boys,[21] poor children in urban and rural settings, or the many immigrant families who are looking to become a part of local communities, sports can provide a wonderful common language to help bring us together. Unfortunately, too many Christian families are too busy driving their kids all over town to their elite-sports practices to consider another way. Christians have a higher calling than to make our children athletically successful, and it is well past time for the church in the United States to be reminded of that.

---

21. Kelley and Carchia, "Hey, Data Data—Swing!"

9

"I Want to Be Like Mike": Sports and Identity Formation in Young People

Tom Emanski's fundamentals of baseball instructional tapes were staples of television advertising during the 1990s. Fox Sports journalist Erik Malinowski captures the extensive influence of Emanksi's commercials: "Tens of thousands of times over a decade, people watching sports on TV could usually expect to see one familiar name pop up during a commercial break: *Emanski*."[1] Emanksi was an MLB scout turned youth baseball coach who perfected (both technically and commercially) a series of training videos for young players that have maintained an important place in baseball lore. His commercials were so prevalent and his video series so successful that Emanksi became synonymous with the fundamentals of baseball. In his review of Game 3 of the 2002 National League Championship Series, ESPN columnist Jayson Stark conjures up Emanski in his titled description of an especially sloppy game: "Cards Win, But Tom Emanski Covers His Eyes."[2] The satirical website, *The Onion*, reported in 2006 that the woeful Kansas City Royals (who had won only twelve of their first thirty-nine games that season) had hired Emanski to teach them the fundamentals.[3]

While Emanski may not have been the first person to capitalize on young athletes' desires to improve their skills, he was one of the first to embody the perfect combination of credentials and endorsements that have come to virtually guarantee business success in the youth sports industry.

1. Malinowski, "Pitchman."
2. Stark, "Cards Win, But Tom Emanski Covers His Eyes."
3. "Royals Hire Tom Emanski to Teach Them Fundamentals," *The Onion*.

The short commercials include a personal and full endorsement by longtime MLB player, Fred McGriff. The commercials also include the claim that Emanski's techniques "produced AAU's back-to-back-to-back championships." What more validation could a parent of a young baseball player want than to know the techniques helped win national championships and are endorsed by players from the highest levels? Such claims arouse the deepest longings and whet the fiercest of appetites within the parents of young athletes, and Emanski turned out to be one of the first to strike gold in the youth-sports gold rush.

Young fans are more than spectators cheering on their favorite teams; they are alive with hopes, dreams, and aspirations about their future. Young people look up to famous athletes not simply because they want to play like them—they want to *be* like them. The famous Gatorade commercial that debuted on August 8, 1991, and became a pop-culture sensation throughout the 1990s wasn't, "I want to play basketball like Mike," but instead, "I want to *be* like Mike." Michael Jordan became a billionaire because young people not only wanted to play basketball like him, but they wanted to drink his sports drink and wear his shoes. He famously wore the number twenty-three while playing for the Chicago Bulls, and not surprisingly, his heir apparent, LeBron James, also wears twenty-three because he too wants to "be like Mike." While Babe Ruth had his own candy bar and Tom Emanski and Fred McGriff sold techniques that claimed to help young people play like a pro, Michael Jordan capitalized on a deeper reality at work within sports and sports culture: identity.

There are few social structures within a society that affect a person's identity as deeply as sports. Patriotism provides a deep component of many people's identity (*the* fundamental identity for some), and the military helps invoke an even deeper sense of nationalistic identity within soldiers. Beyond the scope of national allegiance, however, one is hard-pressed to find structures that provide more significant identity-forming realities in people's lives than sports. Sports apparel varies by region of the country as each community represents "their team." Each team has its own color scheme, history, licensed apparel, mascots, cheers, and traditions. Fans at the University of Arkansas use a hog call, "Woo pig Sooie," fans of Texas A&M say "Gig 'em Aggies," and fans of the University of Southern California chant, "Fight on!" Perhaps one of the most telling traditions is when, during home football games at Penn State University, fans in attendance often cheer in unison, "We are—Penn State." In a very palpable way, our sports can be an integral part of our identity.

The work of famed psychologist Erik Erickson centered on identity development within the human psyche. His 1968 collection of essays entitled *Identity: Youth and Crisis* explores the process of identity formation within adolescence related to the concept of "identity crisis" (a phrase he coined).[4] An in-depth analysis of adolescent identity formation is a complex, interdisciplinary study that lies beyond the scope of this book. The role that sports plays in the identity formation of young people is, nevertheless, an important topic within youth sports—particularly when undertaking a Christian analysis of youth sports. After all, one of the primary obligations of the local church is the spiritual (and identity) formation of its young people. Every family involved in youth sports must seriously consider the role their life of sports is having in the spiritual, moral, and faith development of their entire family. Sports enthusiasts often champion the positive ways sports contribute to moral and social development in young people, but this chapter will argue that few Christians have taken seriously the extent to which they can also become an idolatrous threat to the spiritual formation of young people.

YOU ARE WHAT YOU PLAY

On February 8, 1936, the NFL held its very first draft. A halfback from the University of Chicago named Jay Berwanger was drafted first overall by the Philadelphia Eagles. The rights to Berwanger were later traded to the Chicago Bears, the two sides could never agree on a contract, and the very first pick in the very first NFL draft never played a single down of professional football. That original draft pales in comparison to the 2017 NFL draft that took place in Philadelphia over three days, and the first overall pick, Myles Garrett, signed a contract with the Cleveland Browns worth over $30 million. The great pre-draft showcase event, known as the NFL Combine, has taken on a life of its own in recent years as potential draft picks run through a barrage of obstacles and skills challenges hoping to impress NFL scouts. During the 2017 NFL Combine, John Ross set a new combine record in the 40-yard dash at 4.22 seconds. He had recently signed a shoe contract with Nike and so was wearing Nike shoes in his record-breaking performance.

---

4. Erickson, *Identity*.

Had he been wearing Adidas shoes, Adidas would have awarded him with his own private island.[5]

The NFL Combine is where analytics meets athleticism. The combines are a series of speed and strength tests in addition to other tests of agility and dexterity. Sports commentators often refer to the combine as a meat market. Scouts and analysts consider the collegiate performances of these athletes, their combine performances, the specifications of their body type, cognitive capacities, and interpersonal skills before assigning players a ranking. In the end, the process reduces the players to a name and a number. The NFL is not the only professional league that has such practices, but its draft is by far the most popular.

We have seen throughout this book that youth sports has a tendency to mimic professional sports in many different ways. Leagues are often structured like professionals, training and practice methods are modeled after them, and the way the sports are played more times than not resemble the pros. We are not surprised, then, to see this commodification of athletes creeping its way into the youngest of sports leagues. Consider these postings from a baseball travel-league website of parents in search of new teams for their sons.

- "He pitches, short, centerfield...great hitter and quick around the bases." (twelve years old)
- "He has played for the YMCA for years but we are looking for something more competitive and where he can better himself. He is a big boy with a monster swing." (nine years old)
- "He has played for rec leagues since he was 3 and has a great arm! He's made AllStar twice as a leftie who loves playing shortstop and 1st base. He also played in the sectionals for PHR and earned 3rd place for his age group. We are looking for a more experience level than our rec ball group has offered." (eight years old)
- "He has an amazing arm and swing! He would like something more competitive than Rec league again. He has been playing since he was 5 yrs old and just LOVES baseball." (seven years old)

Incredibly, players as young as seven and eight years old are already being identified by their physical traits and abilities. On the surface, this may

---

5. Martinelli, "How John Ross Cost Himself an Island When He Broke the NFL Combine's 40-Yard Dash Record."

seem like an overreaction to well-intentioned parents, but there is something unsettling about parents acting as a kind of agent for their seven-year-olds. On the other side, there are teams holding tryouts for children in the same age groups who are looking for a left-handed bat in the lineup, a fast leadoff hitter, or a hefty cleanup hitter. Could it be that the parents and coaches of these youth leagues are receiving a bigger thrill by putting these teams together like a general manager than the children who simply want to play the game?

Most parents who post these kinds of descriptions of their children likely have the very best of intentions. They are spending their free time providing opportunities for their children to be challenged and helping them have a successful start to their baseball careers. At the same time, the very notion of young people even having a "sports career" or thinking of their sports involvement in this way gets us far away from the concept of play. I have no doubt these parents want what is best for their children. Most also would assure me that their children have many other gifts, talents, and qualities beyond athletics that make their children unique. After all, each of us possesses an identity that is a complex and integral mix of our personality and interests, and we each have many different components that make us who we are. Sports, though, seems to have a power that can easily and surreptitiously grab hold of us and become our primary lens of identification. Particularly, adolescents who are forging through a notoriously difficult time in their lives seem susceptible to the effects of allowing sports to become their core identity.

IDENTITY FORMATION IN ADOLESCENTS

Our concern here is not that we have these different and often competing roles, but it is which of these roles functions as the primary and unifying core of our identity. Chap Clark helpfully summarizes the primary identity-forming crisis adolescents undergo in three questions: Who am I? Do I matter? How do I relate to others?[6] Clark goes on to connect these formational questions to the role of youth ministry: "youth ministry must continually and consistently reinforce this theological truth ['I am the uniquely created, redeemed child of the living God.'] in everything we do and to every student we encounter."[7] For many adolescents, sports provides alternative

---

6. Cark, "The Changing Face of Adolescence," 54–55.
7. Cark, "The Changing Face of Adolescence," 56.

"I Want to Be Like Mike"

answers to these crucial questions and can drown out the spiritual tenets that are so crucial to the spiritual formation of young people. The question at the heart of this book is whether or not sports has usurped that core theological truth for another: I am uniquely gifted to play this sport, and my fulfillment is directly tied to the level of competition I achieve and my overall success within that sport.

To describe a seven-year-old boy as having an "amazing arm" is hardly evidence of idolatry. It is, rather, the deeper meaning that sports often provides for adolescents and their families that raises questions. I have heard countless families remark, "We don't know what to do with ourselves now that [fill in the blank—baseball/football/soccer/volleyball] season has come to an end." Youth sports can be an all-consuming bubble that dominates schedules, finances, dreams and aspirations to such an extent it is difficult to remember what life is like outside. Robert Ellis makes the point that regardless of whether or not sports is a religion, it often functions as one and "[allows] human persons and communities to express and experience significant and necessary aspects of what it means to be human."[8] As we saw in chapter 2, sports can represent an important outlet in the human experience as *homo ludens* (beings that play). We experience something fundamentally human when we play, but we have also seen that social systems and structures can so entangle and enslave us that fundamental purposes can be lost. An analysis of many expressions of youth sports might determine they actually resemble many of the tenets of a religious cult.

James Fowler, in his classic treatment of faith development, provides an illustration that relates to the challenge sports present to the identity of young people.

> The top-flight surgeon, always in heavy demand, allowed himself to let down one day in a chance, hospital corridor meeting with his minister. He talked of the pressures in his life, the professional burdens he carried, and the family strains he lived with. After a time, his clergyman [sic] put to him a frank question.
>
> "Doctor," he said, "who are you when you're not an M.D.?"
>
> Stunned, but only for a moment, the surgeon replied, "By God, I'm always an M.D.!"
>
> "Yeah, and that's just the problem," the minister responded.[9]

---

8. Ellis, *The Games People Play*, 104–5.
9. Fowler, *Stages of Faith*, 20.

Young people identify themselves in varying degrees through their experiences in sports. The most obvious is the reinforced identity through their team uniform, the decal on the back window of their family's minivan, the picture button on Mom's shirt, and the poster above the garage. Sports identities have become much more complicated than this, however. Beyond their teams, young athletes are identified by the level of competition (select, travel, elite—or "only" rec?), the position they play, their local or national ranking, and their resume. More young people need to be asked the question, "Who are you when you're *not* an athlete?"

Everybody Wants to Be the Quarterback

The intertwining of identity and sports is exemplified dramatically in the United States in the archetypal role of quarterback. The quarterback has a long history of mystique entrenched in the cultural mores of movies, music, and television shows. As their high NFL salaries attest, the starting quarterback is largely seen to be the most important player on a football team, but the identity of "quarterback" looms much larger than their passing efficiencies, interception ratios, and quarterback ratings. The NFL frequently uses quarterbacks as the face of its league. In recent decades, the names Brady, Manning, Brees, Favre, Rogers, Elway, Marino, Montana, and Young have been synonymous with American football. Shawn Duncan aptly captures their cultural significance when he writes that the quarterback "has become the quintessential cool kid that every guy wants to be and every girl wants to be with."[10] A high-school's starting quarterback is more than a leader on a football team, he is a prestigious status symbol within the local community.

While every team has only one starting quarterback, the role of quarterback provides a dramatic example of how the identities sports create within young people often permeate beyond the realm of sports. A quarterback doesn't stop being a quarterback when he takes off his pads. Consider how a quarterback might navigate the identity-forming process of adolescence with Chap Clark's tripartite summary as a guide.

- Who am I? "I am the starting quarterback for Local High School."
- Do I matter? "When I step onto the field on Friday nights before thousands of cheering fans it is easy to believe that I matter."

10. Duncan, "Sports as Compensatory Identity," 29.

- How do I relate to others? "The better I perform on the field, the more people look up to me."

The starting quarterback of a high-school football team is usually sixteen or seventeen years old and at the pinnacle of their youth sports career, but the identity-forming seeds were sown long before.

The examples of baseball parents in search of teams for their children show how, at very early ages, children are adopted into an environment that emphasizes their abilities and physical attributes as athletes. Sports are all, at some level, meritocratic, but the current system of elite and travel sports leagues can be cruelly so. Parents' competitive hunger drives a system that often provides special treatment for star athletes and creates celebrity-athletes out of children before they are old enough to drive. In his book, *Play Their Hearts Out*, journalist George Dohrmann provides a dramatic example of how the celebrity culture pervades the grassroots basketball scene in Southern California. The group Dohrmann followed went to Portland, Arizona, Baltimore, Las Vegas, and Newport News, Virginia all in one calendar year—quite an impressive itinerary for a group of inner-city twelve year olds.[11] This kind of star treatment shown to adolescents helps cultivate a culture of entitlement, special treatment, and celebrity in young people playing the highest levels of youth sports. Imagine the dramatic effect that traveling around the country to play in basketball tournaments has on the identity formation of twelve year olds.

Unfortunately, it has become commonplace to hear stories of athletes who have had their bad behavior excused or, even worse, ignored. The stories that garner the most national attention usually involve college or professional teams, but there are countless other stories that involve high-school athletes and younger. Many of these stories are as heinous as the stories from the college and professional ranks.

Author Tom Farrey recounts the story of a star high-school running back from Florida named Antwain Easterling. In September 2006, during his senior year, he had sex with a freshman in a school bathroom. Easterling was almost nineteen years old at the time, while the girl had just turned fourteen, making it a third-degree felony according to Florida law. While these kinds of sexual escapades are hardly limited to high-school athletes, the ensuing cover-up dramatically illustrates how powerful sports identities are even in high school. Upon learning of this crime that happened

---

11. Dohrmann, *Play Their Hearts Out*, 90.

on school grounds, the principal and twenty other officials did not report anything for the next two months (two months that not-so-coincidently overlapped with the football season). Farrey's description of how the principal went about allowing Easterling to play in the state championship game poignantly illustrates the power of a sports identity.

> In trying to make up his mind about whether to suspend Easterling for that game, principal Dwight Bernard was torn. Easterling had been kicked out of Northwestern previously after a knife was found in his book bag, only to return in time for his junior season. Knowing that Easterling was eligible to sign with a college program in a couple of months, Bernard asked [school administrator] Davis, "Will we be ruining his career?" The same question was not being asked about the girl, who, in her own way, had arrived at Northwestern as a rough-hewn gem with a sparkling potential: She was an honors student, classified as gifted, with a sensitivity for the pain of others that was reflected in her writing.[12]

The prestige of successful athletes can create a social caste often blinding adults and the institutions they serve to the plight of victims and prompting a litany of excuses for immoral and illegal behavior. At the college level, athletes involved in alleged sexual assaults, grade inflation, and course-records falsification all leave the impression that the status of athletes is the single most important element of the campus environment.

While this story may be an extreme example, identity formation is taking place within sports experiences at all levels and is largely driven by meritocracy and perpetuated by celebrity culture. As a high-school football official, I have seen firsthand the aura that a highly successful player brings to the field on a Friday night. There are often more news cameras, the player receives more attention on the sidelines, people in the stands and on the sidelines are pointing, and there is a general buzz in the air regarding these kinds of players. For young athletes who were baptized into youth sports at an early age, sports provides one of the earliest answers to their question of, "Who am I?"

Youth League Prestige

The age of elite, select, club, and travel teams has helped create a new dynamic within the identity-formation process in young athletes. Although

---

12. Farrey, *Game On*, 310–11.

young people still dramatically identify themselves with the particular sport or position they play, a more important qualifier has emerged. A fellow dad from my son's baseball team recently shared an experience they had in scouting out new potential teams for his son to play on the following season. He had been in contact with several different coaches, and he said that whenever he brought up his son's pitching statistics they would dismiss them because of the league in which he played. His son's friends often told him he doesn't play "real" baseball because he doesn't play in the most popular travel league.

Sports were largely the creation of people coming together and sharing their leisure time through organized, active games. Sports activities remain some of the most popular youth activities in every community. However, the advent of specialized, competitive leagues have begun to have the opposite effect. Instead of bringing communities together, the very selective nature of these types of leagues create additional divisions within communities. King and Starbuck write, "Too often the special bonds of friendship that have developed in neighborhoods and churches, through years of going to school and playing together, are dropped for the individualism of travel team culture."[13] Recreation and neighborhood leagues encouraged diversity and inclusivity while elite and travel leagues do the exact opposite.

Local recreation teams sometimes have to vie for time on local athletic fields in their own communities because there is so much demand by regional and selective competitive teams that bring together players from a broad geographic area. With the exception of the most naïve parent, most parents realize talent is but one element helping create this separation—and it could be argued, maybe not even the chief element. Beyond the talent of individual young people, elite sports teams are often determined by which families can afford to pay the excessive yearly fees (often exceeding thousands of dollars); which families have the flexibility to shuttle their children to all the practices throughout the week (often across town when playing for regional teams); which families are willing to coordinate their family vacations with their children's out-of-town tournaments; and which families aren't having to divide their attention between more than one athletically-inclined child.

Select, elite, club, and travel sports have become the lingua franca of the suburbs. Small towns throughout the United States contribute to these kinds of leagues as well, but I'm not sure they embody the same cultural

---

13. King and Starbuck, *Overplayed*, 133.

swagger they do within suburban America. The elite decal on the back of a family's minivan has become one of the most recognizable status symbols in some communities. I recently heard of a seventh-grade girl from my neighborhood who didn't want to play in the local recreational soccer league because she was afraid her friends (who played for elite clubs) would make fun of her. Now the competitive level a child plays at has become yet another extension of his or her identity.

THIS IS OUR TEAM: IDENTITY FORMATION IN PARENTS

Before we are too hard on young people for allowing their identities to be so closely tied to sports, the reality is for many families, parents are just as susceptible to allowing sports to shape their identity as their children are. Have you ever noticed how many parents refer to their children's sports experience in the first person? "*We* haven't played them very well," or "*We* are really looking good tonight." In many ways, having an athletic child involved in sports takes a commitment from parents as much as it does for the children. Undoubtedly, a parent who spends countless hours chauffeuring children from one practice to another, sits on the sideline for numerous games, and washes ludicrous amounts of sports-stained laundry is going to feel a certain level of commitment to their child's teams. Most families involved in sports would count their time together at these sporting events as quality family time.[14] We saw in chapter 5 that one of the greatest things we can tell our children is, "We love to watch you play," but it is possible for parents to become over-involved in their children's sports. Parents must constantly be reminded whose team, whose game, and whose experience youth sports are.

There are many children who, unfortunately, do not receive the kind of support and encouragement that drive many parents to sign their children up for elite, select, and club sports. However, there is also a time and a place for allowing children to have their own space, experience, and identity that doesn't involve their parents. Few things provide the kind of boost to the ego as having a gifted athlete for a child and far too many parents allow that to become the chief identity of their family. "We are a soccer family," many

---

14. Though more families may want to consider the merit of this idea. King and Starbuck suggest, "If we're honest, it's 'sit in a van and sit on bleachers to watch one person perform' time." *Overplayed*, 140.

proud parents declare. "Parents bask in the reflected glory of the superstar, even on the smallest scale. If my kid's a hero, I'm a hero, too."[15] You don't have to attend very many sporting events before being exposed to a parent who has over-indentified herself or himself with their child athlete. They can be heard yelling and screaming from the sidelines at the officials and, more times than not, at their own children.

Perhaps the greatest evidence of over-identification with their children's sports is the length that many parents go to attend each and every game. Parents should consider more seriously the message they are giving their children when they champion the fact that they have never missed a single game. King's and Starbuck's words hit close to home for many well-intentioned parents, "While parents complain about being so busy, many of them are still at every game their child plays, and most of the practices. These parents have heard the message from somewhere, loud and clear, that being a good parent requires attending every single one of your child's athletic events."[16] Our children need to know, beyond a shadow of a doubt, that they are loved, that we care about them, and that we love to watch them play. There are ways to communicate this message and still not be at every game. A more rewarding experience may be for parents to skip a game to prepare dinner so the family can sit down over a home-cooked meal and allow the young athlete to recount the game through his or her eyes.

In order for children to see their identity beyond the sports they play, it is crucial for their parents to model their own identity beyond their role as sports mom and sports dad. Sports will always be an important aspect of an athlete's identity, but a chief duty of parents is to help their children put that into the larger perspective of their lives—to see sports as a *part* of life and not its goal. Nearly all parents would agree with this statement, but often our actions are saying something else (and often saying it much more loudly). In bringing this important chapter to a conclusion, it seems prudent to be reminded of our identity in Christ and what it might look like to maintain that identity at the core of our being.

BEING LIKE JESUS

The first word my son ever said was, "Ball," although it sounded more like he was trying to name the Old Testament fertility god, "Baal." He has been

15. McMahon, *Revolution in the Bleachers*, 194.
16. King and Starbuck, *Overplayed*, 163.

drawn to sports and sports equipment since before he could walk. T-shirts that were popular a few years ago that said, "Sports is life, the rest is just details" resonate with him. John Tauer remembers when this phrase was especially popular. "Before long, the shirts were available for virtually any sport a child might play. Whether it was soccer, football, softball or even cheerleading, these shirts promoted the idea that it is entirely acceptable for sports to be the focus of one's life."[17] Many families in the United States have become so immersed in the world of youth sports that this mantra accurately captures the way they have ordered their lives: "Sports is life, the rest is just details."

In the Gospel of John, Jesus taught, "I have come that they may have life and have it to the full" (John 10:10). For many families, sports have taken the place of the full life Jesus has promised. It has become all too common for Christian families to be more enmeshed within the culture of their sports teams than within their local church. Dave King aptly captures the disheartening situation that Christian families increasingly face.

> Parents who have driven their children from tournament to tournament, weekend after weekend, year after year, become distraught when their child goes to college and leaves faith behind. Yet for years the parents have been communicating to a child that their faith community, communal worship, and church life aren't important. Parents rarely intend to communicate that, and following Christ might be very important to the parents themselves. Regardless, they have sent a clear message to their children that their faith community is not more important than their athletic schedule.[18]

In other words, these parents are raising their children with an identity primarily formed by their experiences as athletes instead of as faithful Christian disciples. Jesus tells his disciples, "It is easier for a camel to go through the eye of a needle, than for someone who is rich to enter the kingdom of heaven" (Matt 19:24). For Christians involved in sports, it may not be as difficult as that to enter the kingdom of heaven, but it may be like a camel trying to fit through the front door of a house. Jesus goes on to assure the disciples (as well as us), "With man this is impossible, but with God all things are possible" (Matt 19: 26). We have not taken seriously enough the

---

17. Tauer, *Why Less is More for WOSPS*, 139.
18. King and Starbuck, *Overplayed*, 134.

"I Want to Be Like Mike"

many challenges youth sports present to the identity formation of young people during their very formative adolescent years.

A Christian approach to sports has often been reduced to being a good sport, abiding by the rules and spirit of the game, and not taking the sport too seriously. As with all participants in sports, Christians would do well to follow this advice. Such an approach, however, fails to consider some of the deeper implications that the actual social structures (those pesky powers again) have on participants of the sports. The amount of time, money, and attention Christian families dedicate to sports are just as important as playing the games fairly and keeping them in the proper perspective. It is easy for parents to feel caught up in a complex, bureaucratic web of travel teams and leagues that can make them feel powerless and with few options. These powerful entities are immensely influential in helping shape the sports experiences for families, and seldom are subjected to serious consideration for the way they are shaping the identities of those participating in them.

Christian parents would be well served to bring along a copy of Dietrich Bonhoeffer's spiritual classic, *The Cost of Discipleship*, to their child's next sporting event. Reading it in the midst of your child's game is sure to be convicting, particularly when he writes, "The first Christ-suffering which every man must experience is the call to abandon the attachments of this world."[19] For parents so entrenched in youth sports, this is one "attachment" that must be seriously considered. First John 2:15 charges Christians, "Do not love the world or anything in the world." For many years this and other similar verses led Christians to denounce sports as contrary to the Christian life. More recently, however, the pendulum has swung in the opposite direction to the point where even the suggestion that sports could be detrimental to one's spiritual identity is dismissed as ridiculous.

As we have seen in earlier chapters, one of the great benefits of sport is that it teaches children discipline. Christians often champion this as one of the most easily reconcilable characteristics of both faith and sports. The question is, how many families actually integrate the discipline learned from sports with intentional, spiritual practices? Young athletes spend endless hours each week perfecting their curve balls, learning proper tackling techniques, and practicing bending their soccer shots, but what fraction of all those hours are dedicated to learning to pray more intensely, meditate more regularly, or generally cultivate the deep people that Richard Foster

---

19. Bonehoeffer, *The Cost of Discipleship*, 99.

claims the world is in such desperate need of?[20] Sports offer many great attributes that can help shape young people into noble adults, but their identity-forming potential still falls far short of the amazing identity that all Christians claim in wearing the name of Christ. It is essential that all families involved in youth sports make a concerted effort to regularly assess the identity-forming power sports is having on all members of their family.

---

20. Foster, *Celebration of Discipline*, 1.

10

Youth Sports as Missional Frontier

Much of this book has critiqued the current state of youth sports in the United States, but it would be irresponsible to ignore the countless positive contributions that youth sports continues to provide to communities, families, and individuals throughout the country. On autumnal, Friday nights, high-school football stadiums serve as a central gathering place for neighbors throughout the local community. It is not unusual to see local high-school sports schedules hanging in local restaurants, and homecoming parades still elicit a strong sense of community pride. My family has met many families in our community through our children's involvement in sports, and I have great friendships with my fellow football officials. These positive social attributes of sports reinforce the idea that, if Christians intend to engage in ministry within local communities, they must take sports seriously.

Parachurch sports ministries formed in the middle of the twentieth century largely were modeled after the arena-based Billy Graham Crusades and capitalized on the crowd-producing nature of sports in hopes of proselytizing unbelievers. Although these ministries have evolved throughout their history, they have maintained an evangelizing emphasis above all else, thus falling victim to the theological blind spots described in chapter 8. Christian ministry during the twentieth century (particularly from among conservative Evangelicals) largely was predicated on the assumption people who needed Jesus would come to them through their programs. This philosophy was not unique to sports ministries but was representative of the church's chief understanding of evangelism. The underlying motivation of this model was to build platforms and programs to make the message of the gospel as attractive and compelling as possible. This approach to Christian mission and evangelism has undergone a shift in recent decades, and this shift dramatically calls into question the ways Christians have traditionally approached sports and sports ministry. While the discussion of this shift is complex and nuanced, a simple description is that Christians have broadened their understanding of reaching others from an evangelistic focus to a mission/kingdom focus.

EVANGELISM AND THE MISSION OF THE CHURCH

Admittedly, the descriptors "evangelistic" and "missional" have been so broadly and loosely used in church contexts over recent decades they have been robbed of nearly any distinctive meaning. Scholars and practitioners alike seem to recognize a significant shift has taken place within culture and the church, and the shift has garnered a wide range of descriptions: modern/postmodern, Christendom/post-Christendom, institutional/non-institutional, and evangelistic/missional.[1] The language used to describe these changes varies across the theological spectrum and the implications are equally diverse, but most people seem to agree that some kind of monumental paradigm shift has taken place or is taking place in Christian churches and denominations throughout Western Christianity.[2] Each pairing listed above represents a different nuance within these shifting paradigms.

For our purposes here, the evangelistic/missional distinction illustrates an important transition that has taken place in many parts of the church but appears to remain largely unchanged within sports ministries. In his book, *The Road to Missional*, Michael Frost dedicates the entire first chapter to "seeing mission as bigger than evangelism."[3] With sports ministries focused on providing large platforms from which to broadcast their

---

1. There have been an abundance of resources dedicated to this topic since 2000. Rather than providing an exhaustive list, I want to mention a few of the works that have most profoundly impacted my understanding of mission. If you are unfamiliar with this ongoing discussion in ministry circles, I would recommend these titles: Frost and Hirsch, *The Shaping of Things to Come*; Hirsch, *The Forgotten Ways*; Roxburgh and Boren, *Introducing the Missional Church*; Scot McKnight, *Kingdom Conspiracy*.

2. Phyllis Tickle provides a helpful overview of some of the most important tenets of this transition which she terms: *Emergence Christianity*.

3. Frost, "The Missio Dei," 23–39.

message (through successful athletes like Tim Tebow and successful teams like the ones fielded by Athletes in Action and Christian universities), the focus has been almost exclusively on evangelism.

In 2003, John Garner published a collection of essays that, in many ways, serves as the pinnacle publication of the athlete-as-evangelist movement in American Evangelicalism. Since its publication, this book, entitled *Recreation and Sports Ministry*, has served as a seminal textbook for many of those pursuing the emerging profession of recreation and sports ministry at parachurches and megachurches across the country. The authors of the textbook's essays address many of the issues I have raised such as the biblical foundations of sports ministry,[4] the history of the church and sports,[5] and theological reflections on competition.[6] The authors are all practitioners serving in various sports and recreational ministry roles and write from many years of experience. While their commitment to reaching non-Christians through sports is undeniable and their passion for sports ministry is indisputable, the paradigm from which these authors work is evangelism-centered and contains many shortcomings.

Numerous examples could be cited from Garner's book, but the following quotation from Greg Linville provides an example of how these essays adhere to such a ministry model for using sports to attract crowds for the purpose of evangelism.

> Churches in the know realize that the nonchurched, dechurched, and other-churched person won't come to a church just because it is architecturally appealing. (In fact, if it is built to look like a church, it might even be an obstacle to their attending.) Yet these same churches know that properly programmed athletic facilities will be an *attractive* entry point for people to get involved in church. Strategically placing ball fields and walking tracks in full view of passersby is a way of *attracting* people to a church. Facilities and proper programming are tools to *attract* this leisure-oriented, competition-driven unseeded culture to the abundant life in Christ.[7]

The difference between Linville's attractional approach to ministry and the missional approach proposed by Michael Frost and Alan Hirsch is

4. Oswald, "Biblical Foundations for Sports Ministry."
5. Wesner, "Visions and Re-Visions."
6. Greg Linville, "Ethic of Competition in a Church Setting,"
7. Linville, "Ethic of Competition in a Church Setting," 158, emphasis added.

highlighted in juxtaposing Linville's quote with the rhetorical question: "How much of the traditional church's energy goes into adjusting their programs and their public meetings to cater to an unseen constituency?"[8] Frost and Hirsch are critiquing an "If-you-build-it-they-will-come" philosophy, and it seems to represent the fundamental paradigm by which most sports ministries continue to operate. This philosophy of ministry loosely follows sequential logic: first, Christians have been compelled by the Great Commission to preach the gospel; second, the more people who are exposed to the gospel message increases the number of people who will give their lives to Christ; third, planning and organizing events that bring the largest crowds increases the number of people who can hear the Gospel; fourth, sports is one of the most popular activities in today's culture; therefore, planning sports events and activities is one of the most effective ways for people to hear the gospel today.

Another way of understanding this paradigm is by reflecting upon the way Garner himself discusses opportunities for sports ministries. In his essay, "Organization of Recreation and Sports Ministry," he suggests taking a survey of the community to determine the recreation and sports opportunities that exist for ministry. He proposes that bowling alleys could "host a church bowling league," "craft shops can be used to host craft classes," "schools often let churches use or rent their facilities," cities often host "church softball leagues," and "some campgrounds have adventure recreation and ropes courses available for church use."[9] While there is nothing innately wrong with any of these suggestions and no doubt churches throughout the country take part in these and related endeavors every day, each of these suggestions from Garner presupposes an institutional, "Come-To-Us" stance that Frost and Hirsch view as counter-missional.

As opposed to Garner's approach, Frost and Hirsch believe, "The missional church recognizes that it does not hold a place of honor in its host community and that its missional imperative compels it to move out from itself into that host community as salt and light."[10] For Frost and Hirsch, the emphasis should not be bringing people to church or church-sponsored events by using sports, but rather, releasing Christians into the world of sports that already exists outside of the church and living as salt and light in those contexts. Two other Christian missional leaders write, "Being mis-

8. Frost and Hirsch, *The Shaping of Things to Come*, 19.
9. Garner, "Organization of Recreation and Sports Ministry," 85.
10. Frost and Hirsch, *The Shaping of Things to Come*, 19.

sional means we join this heritage, entering a journey without any roadmaps to discover what God is up to in our neighborhoods and communities."[11] I contend that a missional approach to sports does not seek to build a robust sports ministry inside the walls of existing churches (although that may be the way to serve some communities), but rather sends its members into leagues and teams that already exist in the community to help be a blessing to all those who participate.

SPORTS AND THE MISSION OF THE LOCAL CHURCH

In his book *Sidewalks in the Kingdom*, pastor Eric Jacobsen explores various implications of a missional vision for cities. He defines public spaces as domains "not controlled by an individual or a corporation, but [open] for everyone to use," and he laments the lack of such spaces in many cities and, especially, suburbs.[12] There are more of these public spaces devoted to sports than any other activity in most cities. However, as was highlighted in previous chapters, the institutionalization of youth sports has often limited the use of these venues to pre-scheduled and pre-organized teams that tend to be exclusivist. While the emphasis sports and recreation ministries often have had on organizing their own teams and leagues has its place, it is equally important for churches to find ways to integrate its members into the lifeblood of their local communities by using public spaces and programs that already exist. The most prominent organizations in many local communities are the local sports leagues and teams (many of which are barely surviving the onslaught of competing travel and club leagues). My daughter's softball league was begging for volunteer coaches and concession workers to begin the year. A missional approach to sports imagines how powerfully a church can serve its community by providing a robust volunteer base for the local sports league. A missional approach to sports teaches church members to consider volunteering in concessions stands and as coaches as a key part of their walk with Jesus.

Unfortunately, in their conformance to the world of travel leagues and elite sports, many Christian families have blindly supported a system that has been detrimental to many local neighborhoods and communities. Rather than investing in the local recreation teams made up of neighboring

11. Roxburgh and Boren, *Introducing the Missional Church*, 15–16.
12. Jacobsen, *Sidewalks in the Kingdom*, 79.

families, many people become more enamored by the pursuit of "elite" status for their child and, instead, participate in tournaments hundreds of miles away from home. Not only does this commitment deny friendships and interaction with a broader swath of neighbors, but it also requires an increased time commitment further limiting the amount of time they are available to interact with people closer to home. In order to maintain a missional posture of ministry, Christians must consider all the implications their children playing in select and travel league sports has.

OPPORTUNITIES FOR MISSIONAL ENGAGEMENT

Having described the difference between evangelism-centered and mission-centered approaches to ministry, what exactly does it look like for Christians to participate in youth sports missionally? Imagine how youth sports could be positively affected if Christians took the theological principles laid out in the earlier chapters of this book and allowed them to inform their approach to sports in their communities. The backbone of the youth-sports industrial complex is comprised of the thousands of adult coaches, administrators, game officials, and others who volunteer countless hours and personal resources to fuel leagues and organizations. Youth sports often stand out as some of the great achievements of a local community. Reflecting upon his interaction with recreation professionals and academics, Carl Stotz observed they "never understood or appreciated volunteers."[13] Adults most often serve in these roles selflessly, are dedicated to serving children, and possess an honest love for the sport. The selflessness that motivates many adults to these roles is, in itself, a missional touch point that Christians can affirm and even champion.

The fact that these volunteers are often carving out free time from an already over-scheduled life in order to serve in these roles means they often have little additional time or energy to challenge systemic shortcomings. It is always easier to uphold the status quo instead of asking questions and challenging current practices. Therefore, Christians need to commit themselves to redeeming the power of youth sports by volunteering through various outlets in order to encourage attitudes and practices that are often counter to the current culture of youth sports. For Christians to faithfully engage the power of youth sports in any of the following roles, they must have a steadfast commitment to spiritual discipline and an intimate faith

13. Stotz, *A Promise Kept*, 148.

community who can help maintain accountability. As has been reinforced throughout this book, the consortium of powers at work in youth sports are as deceitful as they are powerful, and Christians should proceed with caution as they seek to enact change within these environments.

Christians as Youth Sports Coaches

John O'Sullivan calls coaching one of "the most beautiful, powerful, and influential positions a person could ever have."[14] He even refers to coaching in the very Christian language of a "calling." While it is easy to project a coach's "calling" onto the most popular and successful coaches, coaches at all levels of athletics require the same characteristics and sense of calling. To refer to coaching as a calling helps reinforce the position with its high purpose and hints at the missional opportunities it offers. Few people are more influential in the lives of young people than their coaches, and volunteering to coach offers the most dramatic way for Christians to promote and purvey a distinctive approach to sports that is God-honoring and a healthy corrective to many contemporary practices.

Muller suggests that the opportunities offered in youth sports today make it a modern-day Areopagus,[15] and there are few places that parallel Paul's experience in Acts 17 as dramatically as coaching a youth sports team. According to Muller, subverting the powers at work within the youth-sports complex begins with emphasizing "common ground where the values of the 'sports culture' and many Gospel values intersect and can complement each other."[16] Highlighting the dark side of youth sports should never overshadow the positive attributes seen in playing sports, and a Christian serving as a youth sports coach has the opportunity to highlight these attributes in the lives of his young players.

The coach is the tone-setter and largely cultivates the culture of the team. Krattenmaker's principle, "Christian ministry in sports must challenge the worship of winning and all that follows it," represents an essential principle for all Christians called to coaching. With apologies to Vince Lombardi and Herman Edwards, winning can never be the "only thing" for a Christian coach, nor can it be the most important. As the tone-setter

---

14. Changing the Game Project, "Youth Sport Coaching: Not a Job, but a Calling!"
15. Mueller, "Concrete Action within Sport," 227.
16. Mueller, "Concrete Action within Sport," 225.

for the team, the Christian coach can affirm from the beginning larger and more important goals for the team than winning.

A coach who emphasizes having fun rather than winning, equal playing time over success, and the significance and need for rest is destined to stand out among the current culture promoted by the youth-sports machine. Coaches wishing to promote these values in sports could seek out Christian-based sports ministries for whom to volunteer their time, or they could choose to intentionally take part in community leagues where these kinds of philosophies often reign supreme. While all roles within the youth-sports industrial complex are significant, no other role offers the platform to initiate the changes discussed in this book more directly with young people than the coach does.

Christian Youth-Sports Parents

Susan B. Casey may have first coined the phrase "soccer mom" when she used as her slogan, "A Soccer Mom for City Council," in her bid for a Denver city council seat in 1995.[17] During the Presidential election of the following year, the "soccer mom" moniker was catapulted to a bona fide socially recognized status—at least for the sake of political polls. Sarah Palin used a similar reference in the 2008 Presidential election campaign that became a significant talking point throughout the campaign via her self-description as a "hockey mom." Although these phrases have been used mainly to represent political demographics, they can be seen to represent a sizeable percentage of the population who spend an inordinate amount of time dedicated to their children's sporting experience. These hockey and soccer moms (and dads) are easily identified by the buttons with pictures of their children's faces on them they wear pinned on their jackets, their sports utility vehicles always packed with sports equipment and emblazoned with their team emblem, and their matching team apparel.

No one has been more susceptible to the lies and deception of youth sports than parents. Whether they are enamored with the prestige and financial reward of professional sports, the benefit and opportunities presented by a big-time athletic scholarship, the status of elite clubs, or just the overall emotional high that competition in sports can elicit, parents have been at the wheel driving the youth-sports industrial complex for a long time. The pursuit of athletic success and the goal of winning often draws

17. MacFarquhar, "What's a Soccer Mom Anyway?"

out the worst of parents. According to youth-sports activist Bob Bigelow: "Read any U.S. newspaper, watch any television newscast for a week, and most likely you'll see at least one instance of over-the-top parents at a youth sports event. It's worse than you may think."[18] It is time for Christian parents to take intentional efforts at helping redeem their role in the broken system.

It has become commonplace for parents to berate officials, coaches, opponents, teammates, and even their own children in the name of sports. Parents became such a problem in Canadian youth-hockey leagues that in 2002, Canada's national governing body of hockey released a public service campaign entitled, "Relax, It's Just a Game." The campaign produced a series of humorous public service announcements that show children using the same kind of vocal criticism their parents often use of them as they attempt to sink a putt or deal with a police officer who has pulled them over.[19] The PSA ends by asking, "What if kids pressured us the way we pressure them?" and tells the audience, "Relax, it's just a game." Founder of the National Alliance for Youth Sport, Fred Engh, reinforces the double standard of parental ethics evidenced in sports: "It's ironic that nobody yells at a child who forgets some lines during a play, who misspells a word during a spelling bee, or who hits the wrong key during a piano recital. But when it comes to sports, if a youngster drops a ball, misses a tackle, or allows the opposing team to score, look out, because that child will hear about it from the parents!"[20] How many youth pastors have been embarrassed by the actions of their teens' parents while attending their sporting events?

Christians who come to view sports according to the perspective laid out in this book should resonate with the Canadian hockey league's message—it is just a game. Just like their children, sports has a tendency to bring out the worst qualities in their parents. Bigelow writes, "Even parents who enroll their children in programs with the best of intentions can be easily pulled in by the intensity of other parents in the stands and on the sidelines."[21] Above all, it is incumbent upon parents to help their children keep sports in their proper place. Many parents teach their children that there are countless things more important than sports, but their sideline

---

18. Bigelow, Moroney, and Hall, *Just Let the Kids Play*, 67.

19. These are available online, and worth looking up. They use humor to convey a very important message.

20. Engh, *Why Johnny Hates Sports*, 47.

21. Bigelow, Moroney, and Hall, *Just Let the Kids Play*, 71.

antics, tense postgame assessments, and hovering-helicopter involvement often give a completely different message.

Unfortunately, it is not unusual for parents to be more vested in their children's sports leagues and teams than the children themselves. It has become a widespread phenomenon, especially in the suburbs, for parents to wear their busy schedules as some kind of status symbol. Journalist Tom Moroney describes the phenomenon: "It used to be green lawns and shiny new cars. The new status symbol is the weekend schedule."[22] Parents often commit to never missing a game, but seldom consider the message that sends to their child. If parents move heaven and earth to attend all of their children's sporting events and arrange their dinner plans around them every night, how is a child supposed to fathom the idea that any of these things could be more important than sports? Some parents, especially those with less flexible jobs and lower incomes have difficulty making any of their children's sporting events. They are busy working in order to support their children's endeavors. There are many ways parents can support their children beyond watching every sporting in person.

There are countless ways parents can support their young athletic children, but they are summarized by two chief principles. First, young athletes want to know their parents enjoy watching them play. As the Fuller Youth Institute entitled a recent blog posting, the only six words parents need to say to their kid about sports is, "I love to watch you play."[23] Parental enjoyment should never be tied to success, winning, or achievement, but rather in the simple opportunity of being able to watch their child play. If parents are willing to abide by this one principle, it will successfully disarm nearly all of the petulance that often pours out of the sidelines and bleachers at youth sporting events while also helping remove external pressures a child may feel from his or her parents.

The second principle is, perhaps, even more countercultural to the suburban world of youth sports than the first. Bigelow proposes what may sound like heresy to the ears of many parents of young athletes.

> Watching your child play, being there to support them, can be a wonderful experience for both you and for them. You should do it right, but you needn't do it every time. Consider balance in your life. Put things in perspective. There are ways in which you can purposely turn down the intensity and involvement you have in

22. Quoted in Bigelow, Moroney, and Hall, *Just Let the Kids Play*, 79.
23. Griffin, "The Only Six Words Parents Need to Say to their Kid about Sports."

your children's games. Skip a game now and then, go home and cook dinner or have the take-out all ready so there's time to relax at the family table after the game. Every now and then, isn't that worth as much as being able to say you saw your child play?[24]

The two-fold challenge for parents is being able to ensure beyond any figment of doubt in their child's mind they are loved and supported while, at the same time, conveying the message that their life in sports is not the most important part of life. In bringing up the topic of balance, Bigelow highlights one of the most neglected realities for families involved in the youth-sports industrial complex. Families with children in sports need to be reminded: "There is a time for everything, and a season for every activity under heaven" (Eccl 3:1). An updated take on this timeless teaching would affirm there is a time to play sports, and there is a time to rest from playing sports; there is a time to watch your child play sports, and there is a time to go home early, cook dinner, and let him or her tell you about the game.

Christian Youth Sports Game Officials

Of all of the opportunities for participation offered in sports, one outlet that seems most obviously consistent with the Christian calling is that of game official. I have been a high school football official for fourteen years and that role has given me access to other officials, players, coaches, administrators, and spectators. Although being a game official does not provide the same level of influence on players being a coach or parent does, it does allow for direct access into helping control and manage the game itself. As competition escalates the emotions of coaches and players, being a game official provides the unique opportunity to navigate and manage those moments with shrewdness, dignity, and, ideally, Christlikeness. Officiating sporting events is the perfect training ground for many Christian disciplines in the same way that it provides training for athletes. In administrative posts, game officials also can become involved in interpreting rules and proposing rule changes that reinforce principles like play and community that can influence sports dramatically.

While coaches and parents will inevitably become frustrated at certain calls made in the midst of a game, they also will notice officials who always treat players, coaches, and spectators respectfully and with dignity.

---

24. Bigelow, Moroney, and Hall, *Just Let the Kids Play*, 94.

A coach has the opportunity to help shape the culture of a particular team, but referees and umpires have a unique opportunity to shape the culture of a particular game and even an entire sport. Pregame meetings with coaches and players provide the officials with the opportunity to remind the participants of the purposes of the game. Game management is a crucial responsibility for all officials and is another outlet for a Christian official to embody Christlikeness in the midst of a heated, competitive game. Sometimes it provides the opportunity to express humility when mistakes are made. Anytime I miss a blatant call in the first half of a football game, I always try to find the head coach before the start of the second half, admit my mistake, and commit to working harder in the second half. While officials work hard to remain in the backdrop of a contest, there are significant opportunities for them to help infiltrate every game or match with a Christlike presence.

Christian Youth-Sports Administrators

In addition to coaches, teams and leagues also need administrators to help organize youth sports. The role is so crucial that most high schools have full-time athletic directors. All sports leagues have to deal with legal concerns, scheduling procedures, establishing policies, managing equipment and facilities, and countless other, often overlooked essential responsibilities. Engh describes the administrators as the "key to it all."[25] In many organizations, these responsibilities are held strictly by volunteers, while other organizations hire full-time staff in order to accomplish the administration. In establishing their own entities, sports ministries have maintained their own, separate administration for their unique leagues and teams. However, a more missional approach to youth sports would consider becoming involved in the administrative levels of existing leagues. Instead of creating an alternative league, Christians can work side-by-side with community members seeking the best policies and procedures for a particular community and reinvigorating existing programs.[26]

Youth-sports administration varies largely depending on the sport and the level of competition. The influence sports administration has on sports can be seen in the major changes that have taken place in collegiate

---

25. Engh, *Why Johnny Hates Sports*, 97–121.

26. Incidentally, Project Play includes the revitalization of in-town leagues as one of their strategies for improving youth leagues in the United States. Imagine what could happen if a church made this part of their local mission.

Youth Sports as Missional Frontier

athletics in recent years. In 2014, college football administrators helped organize the first ever college football playoff for the largest football programs in the country. The recruiting business of young athletes has become a major factor in youth sports, and legislating recruiting policies has to be driven by administrators. Concerns of exploitation have trickled down to younger and younger athletes. In February 2015, the most popular college football recruiting website, Rivals.com, announced that they had begun adding sixth graders to their website.[27] That same month, NBA superstar LeBron James, publically rebuked the colleges that had already offered his ten-year-old son a scholarship.[28] It is easy to decry these instances of overt exploitation, but the only way to combat further excesses is for administrators to lead the way toward alternate practices. More youth leagues are shaping their administrative policies to look like collegiate and big-time sports making grassroots administrators as important as ever.

The administrative side of youth sports offers interested parents or other adults a platform where theologically informed proposals can be suggested and explored, and it also represents a significant front-lines battlefield where the spiritual battle for the soul of youth sports takes place. Administrators can establish policies that reduce the exposure young athletes have to media, minimize or prohibit traveling long distances to participate in tournaments, and create programmatic approaches to reinforcing the playful side of sports. When I helped coach my son's baseball team one summer, one of the most memorable nights of the entire season was when we played a parents versus sons baseball game. The children smiled and laughed more that night than at any other point in the season. A league administrator could ensure that events like these take place for every team, every season. They can explore how the league can keep winning in its proper place, broaden its expectation for involving as many children as possible, and maintain the proper balance of sports with the rest of the lives of children.

OPENING OUR EYES

Perhaps the biggest obstacle for Christians when it comes to the many challenges presented by youth sports is our lack of imagination. Our ability to imagine is directly tied to our ability to play. As youth sports have

27. Williams, "Athletes Emerge at NextGen."
28. Medcalf, "LeBron."

institutionalized and become hyper-organized and hyper-structured, many Christians seem to have lost their ability to see beyond the structures currently in place. Rather than being inspired to create new games like James Naismith did or convicted to dream of how games can reach the less fortunate and disenfranchised, too many Christians seem caught up in the systems that are already in place and are content to ascend existing competitive ladders. When we begin to open our eyes to God's purposes for sports we will breathe new life into our communities and into our young people—something the church is uniquely positioned to help lead.

11

Redeeming Youth Sports

For all the critique I've offered against elite sports, my son plays on a travel baseball team, my family spends more money on dance classes than I'm always comfortable with, I skip out on my family almost every Friday night in the fall for high-school football games, and I feel like my children's sports schedules have a tendency to pull our family away from the rhythm of our church's life. This must make me seem pretty inconsistent, but I think it points to how challenging it is to find balance in our children's involvement in sports. In this book, I don't claim to offer a definitive answer because I'm not sure there is one. I set out to write this book, not because I felt as though I had many answers, but because I found myself stumbling through the beginning stages of my children's involvement in organized sports and was at a loss to find resources aimed at helping Christian parents and church leaders. I think this book raises many questions that Christians and churches need to seriously begin discussing.

Every child is unique, and every family is different. Each sport has its own unique set of challenges and the organizing bodies of each league face obstacles unique to them. To suggest sweeping, universal proposals for all Christians involved in youth sports is to ignore these unique personalities, circumstances, communities, and traditions. However, as we come to the end of this book, one sweeping principle I do believe needs to be upheld is that families need to be more intentional and honest about how sports affects them. Too many Christians simply jump fully into sports culture with no reluctance or discernment at all. As the pastor of a local church, I believe the church plays a crucial role here as part of their mission of discipleship and spiritual formation. Few activities are having a larger role in the faith development of families and yet there seems to be hardly any churches taking a critical look at sports. In this concluding chapter, I want to challenge church leaders to consider ways they can play a more integral role in re-imagining their mission as it pertains to youth sports.

Because every church is different and each scenario is unique, the first step for most congregations is simply to pause and take an honest assessment of its current climate of youth sports. For many congregations, this simple step may be especially eye-opening as most Christians have probably never seriously considered the deeper theological implications of their involvement with sports. Below is an overview of a three-pronged approach for helping local congregations begin confronting the cultural status quo of contemporary youth sports through congregational self-assessment, educational programs, and a relational paradigm that takes athletic interest and ability into consideration.

ASSESSING YOUR CONGREGATION

Driven by a missional impulse, each congregation must address the situation and the needs of its own unique setting. Some congregations may have several elite athletes participating at the highest levels of competition while others may need to contend with the high percentages of inactive and unhealthy youth. Some congregations may be in underprivileged areas where financial hardships are a significant hindrance to participation in youth sports while others may be witnessing excessive amounts of money spent on travel, training, and equipment. The message in each of these settings will vary, but in whatever setting a local church may find itself, it must constantly seek ways to bring the theological significance of sports to bear in its own unique cultural context. Participating in a congregation that sees teenagers and their families routinely absent from the rhythms and routines of congregational life for the sake of the ball diamond or the gymnasium makes confronting these powers head-on a pastoral priority.

In order to determine the message most needed in a particular context, church leaders must provide an honest assessment of the congregation's general feeling towards youth sports. The first characteristic that must be determined is the extent to which congregational families currently are immersed in the youth-sports industrial complex. Most congregations will include a mixture of families who are fully immersed in the youth-sports machine, other families who do not participate in any physical activities on a regular basis, and many other who are somewhere in between. Knowing the makeup of a congregation in this regard will help direct the message most needed concerning sports.

Furthermore, once the families that are most infused in the youth-sports culture are identified, it is then important to determine the context of their involvement. Is their involvement limited to local leagues and tournaments, or do they travel great distances to play? Do they play for Christian-sponsored leagues and teams, community-organized teams, or select and elite teams? An important pastoral concern is the amount of time and money these families dedicate to sports, and a congregational assessment will attempt to gauge families' commitment levels along these lines. Beyond specifics of their sports involvement, pastoral emphasis should be on the underlying motivations families have. Why are these families playing on elite teams? As with all our motivational factors, there is not a simple, straightforward answer, but sports families within the church should be pressed on these questions to honestly assess their justification. My wife and I constantly have conversations about the merits of our children playing on the teams they do and at the level they do.

The second part of an assessment must consider the intentional efforts taken by the congregation both to incorporate a healthy theology of play into its lifeblood as well as to minister to its families who are involved in sports. In assessing how a congregation promotes a healthy theology of play, church leaders should ask questions like: What specific sports and recreational ministries does the congregation support? Is there a disconnect between the community's sports offerings and those that members of the congregation support? How does the congregation use sports and recreation in its rhythm of life (softball leagues, fellowship gatherings, or youth-group games)? How does the pastor utilize sports illustrations in his or her sermons? Maybe the most telling question a congregation can ask of itself is: How often do we laugh when we are together? If God has created us to play, church should be a prime example of godly play.

Beyond promoting a positive theology of play within the congregation, church leaders must be committed to ministering specifically to the needs of families with young athletes. Whether a congregation regularly offers classes and sermons aimed at helping families navigate the unique challenges brought about by youth sports speaks volumes as to how seriously a congregation takes sports. Church leaders must consider how they recognize success in their young athletes and whether or not it equally recognizes success in non-sports activities. For instance, does the congregation honor good students and successful artists as often as it does successful athletes? For that matter, does the congregation have a penchant for recognizing success in its members while ignoring those who do not "succeed" in various endeavors? Does the congregation encourage mentoring from among older families whose children have already traversed youth sports?

Numerous other questions could be added in helping reveal the role sports and competition have in the life of a congregation, but these highlight some of the most pressing. The purpose of assessing the congregation is to help leaders be honest about the role sports play in the lives of its members. Sports remain such a culturally ubiquitous practice that attempting to identify characteristics or tendencies that may be antagonistic towards a Christ-centered life proves to be a difficult task. While many conservative Christians have long wrestled with the morality of consuming alcohol, the content of movies, television, and music, and frequenting bars and clubs for fear of their "questionable moral content," rarely have similar calls of discernment been made to the panoply of youth sports. For most congregations, the first step is simply to start asking the most basic of questions.

PROGRAMMATIC OFFERINGS

For many congregations, the most common outlets of communication and teaching remain weekly sermons, classes, and infrequent seminars and retreats. Addressing the culture of sports within congregations makes utilizing these outlets essential. One of the biggest obstacles of these formats is that the families most needing to hear the church's message of sports are often most frequently gone due to their family's sports commitments. For those able to be a part of traditional Bible classes, though, churches seem to talk about everything but sports. Ted Kluck writes, "With all the books teaching us how to worship with our marriages, our money, our 'quiet times,' and our sex lives, little is written about the subject that drives most of our banter with each other and around which much of our free times revolves. Sports."[1] Congregations have opportunities to minister to the families of young athletes by offering classes to parents trying to navigate the vastly complex world of youth sports and preaching sermons to help athletes wrestle with the ethical challenges of sports. While each congregation must cater its offerings to its own unique audiences, some specific

1. Kluck, *The Reason for Sports*, 15.

areas of emphasis seem especially prudent for helping address the world of youth sports.

Young Families

In his groundbreaking work, *Game On*, Farrey chronicles how "the race to make champions of our children" has become a "race to the bottom" as parents strive to get their children on the fast track of athletic success at younger and younger ages.[2] He writes, "Now, we're effectively holding our varsity tryouts in the grade school years."[3] Churches fail to provide outlets to promote critical thinking about how the youth-sports industrial complex will affect the lives and faith of young athletes and their families until they are already a part of the system. Families can be encouraged to establish faith-inspired boundaries regarding their involvement in sports before they ever sign their child up for a league. Once a family becomes involved in organized sports, it is much easier for families who have not already established their boundaries to allow sports to dictate their lives (bowing down before the spiritual power). If we are making plans for our children's high school careers when they are ten years old, it is a pretty good sign that we're getting sucked into the thinking prevalent in the system and allowing the tail to wag the dog. Christians should be much more concerned with the faith development of their children during these formative years than whether they will make the high-school team.

Particularly, when athletes have children, they become eager parents, and they are excited to have their children become involved in sports as soon as possible. By providing parents of newborns and toddlers instructive classes regarding the purpose of play and the significance of free play, churches can help address the deficiencies on display in many youth leagues. Hopefully, it will help encourage young parents to be patient and allow their children to enjoy their time of free play instead of feeling the pressure to baptize them into the youth-sports industrial complex. Many parents simply need the assurance that their children are not going to get behind because they fail to enroll them in the gym at two years old. Parents whose older children are busy in sports leagues can tell younger parents to be patient, enjoy the early years of their children's lives, and not to be eager to rush into the world of organized sports.

2. Farrey, *Game On*, 11–23.
3. Farrey, *Game On*, 15.

Competition

Competition is among the most significant and neglected topics in the church today. Offering a sermon series dedicated to the topic of competition could provide a helpful introduction for helping members begin to wrestle with the implications of a principle that they probably most often take for granted. At the heart of the travel, elite, and select movement in youth sports has been the desire for "better competition." Helping families navigate the youth-sports complex by providing them with a framework within which to think through how competition affects their youth-sports experiences is essential. Some of the more pressing issues are: whether a more competitive team or league is worth the time commitment and the truncated relationships; whether the "heat of competition" creates an environment where it is more difficult to live out faith; how the spiritual disciplines are related to the discipline that comes through participating in sports; and the quintessential question of how Jesus would approach competition. Many young athletes and their families may have never asked themselves these basic questions regarding sports even though sports remains one of the most prominent aspects of their lives.

If churches are going to be serious about their ministry to those involved in sports, they must work towards a more theological understanding of competition. Having a regular class where parents can talk about and confess times when they have become too emotionally involved in their children's sports team could provide opportunities that are especially redemptive. The temptations of avarice and greed are ever present in the competitive environment, and the church should provide opportunities for Christians to speak openly about ways they are tempted. In fulfilling the Bible's teaching, "Confess your sins to each other and pray for each other so that you may be healed" (Jas 5:16), it seems tantamount that churches provide this opportunity of accountability especially for those susceptible to sin due to their involvement in sports. The church is often quick to celebrate the good that sports offer, but seldom takes seriously the temptations that they also create.

Sports and Youth Ministry

The most surprising aspect of my research has been the lack of critical attention sports receive by the professional wing of youth ministry. This reinforces my belief that the existence of parachurch sports ministries helped outsource the focus of sports and minimized attention within the local congregational setting. As we have seen, no other activities boast a higher participation rate among young people than sports. Youth ministry has long used games and fun activities but seldom has considered the deeper questions of why these games are so important. Youth ministry's neglect of critical study of sports is symptomatic of the church's avoidance at-large. While there are a handful of exceptions to this neglect, it seems clear that youth ministry must become more intentional about helping churches think through youth sports.

Chap Clarks asks, "Where would our youth ministry programming be without basketball or soccer tournaments?"[4] Sports and games have long had a central place in youth-ministry programming, but youth-ministry leaders must begin asking themselves important questions. What values and ethics from the world of sports are blindly embraced by the games used in youth ministry? Does competition function any differently within youth ministry than it does in the rest of the world? How well do sports and games used in youth ministry function redemptively by undermining cultural assumptions? How does youth ministry celebrate diversity and creativity in its games? It may well be the case that youth-ministry games have remained a staple of youth ministry for generations because they are one of the few places in the lives of teenagers where they still feel like they get to play.

Relational Intentionality

The above proposals in no way are meant to suggest that ministry to young athletes and their families is best accomplished through programs. The programmatic outlets of sermons, classes, and seminars are helpful ways to direct the conversations toward a critical examination of the role sports play in youth culture, but the most effective approach to ministering to young athletes is interpersonally. One of the biggest challenges for Christians attempting to navigate the difficult world of youth sports is that they most often socialize with like-minded peers whose mode of thinking most often reinforces their own. It seems unlikely that one of the other travel soccer moms is the best person to talk to in order to get an honest assessment of the virtues and vices of their current team. There's always a certain

4. Clark, "The Rules of the Game," 1.

homogeneity within peer groups as they are related to one's life setting; however, the voice of those in different life stages can provide an essential outsider's view. The church must find creative ways to integrate the perspectives of a diversity of people in order to respond faithfully to youth sports.

When it comes to sports, balance is essential, and it is important to maintain the balance of relentless and unconditional love for young athletes with a love and appreciation of sports. This same principle is necessary for wider, congregational support of athletes. Christians can show their love and support for the youth in their congregation by attending their sporting events. Not only does this promote a simple cross-generational, Christ-like congeniality, it also helps affirm the meaningfulness of the students' games. When young athletes see the support of fellow church members at their baseball games and volleyball matches it helps them see the totality of their lives matters to God and to their church family—not simply some carved-out portion labeled their "spiritual lives." It is a tangible way to convey the important message described earlier, "God delights in seeing you play."

Labels like "elite" and "select" have been used so broadly in recent years it has created the paradox of "elite" having become "common." Nevertheless, some young people are truly gifted with elite athletic abilities. These athletes are not labeled as such by their participation on a certain team or league, but rather possess a God-given talent that greatly separates them from their peers. The elite athletes are the ones that model the transcendence that draws so many people to sports in the first place. Congregations must recognize if they have members who are truly elite athletes and minister to the unique challenges they face. Had LeBron James been active in a high-school youth group while he attended Akron St. Vincent St. Mary High school, he would have had a different set of spiritual needs than I did as an average varsity soccer player. Churches must recognize the unique spiritual needs of elite athletes and work diligently to minister to them. (Incidentally, many parachurch sports ministries have spent a good deal of time focusing their work on elite athletes. Athletes who are truly "elite" will find much benefit in these ministries.)

When seeking advice on how to become a better coach, sports parent, or sports official, it is worth considering how many Christians think of the church as having a significant role. It is much more common for people to turn to the "professionals" in one of countless books, instructional videos, and other resources that promote good sportsmanship and a winning attitude. Churches are the perfect environment to promote conversation among former coaches and parents of young athletes and younger, aspiring coaches and parents. Perhaps churches can take a proactive role in pairing an experienced, Christian coach with a first-year coach. They could talk about coaching philosophy and specific tactics, but they could also engage in critical dialogue about how best to coach and play as a Christian leader. Nearly everyone has had at least some experience with sports, so it makes sense to use those experiences to help foster a faithful community that integrates the real world experiences of sports with the broader Christian walk. At the same time, Christians who have no interest in sports provide an equally crucial role in helping Christian athletes keep their sports in perspective.

THE REDEMPTIVE ROLE OF DODGEBALL

In the end, there can be little doubt that sports provide one of the richest environments for Christians to live life alongside fellow neighbors and citizens. Christians should be just as deliberate in participating in sports programming as they are in doing their jobs, watching movies, writing music, and hiking in the woods. Christians must find a way to reinvigorate their love and passion for sports in a way that reinforces a freshly discovered theology of playfulness and see sports as an opportunity to perform before God. The only way to confront the industrial complex that has built up around sports is for Christians to maintain the "faithful presence" that James Davison Hunter describes in *To Change the World*. His conclusions regarding this approach to culture resonate with the approach described in this book and are appropriate to quote at length in these closing words.

> I would suggest that a theology of faithful presence first calls Christians to attend to the people and places that they experience directly . . . . In our tasks, the call of faithful presence implies a certain modesty that gives priority to substance over style; the enduring over the ephemeral, depth over breadth, and quality, skill, and excellence over slick packaging or "high production value" . . . When our various tasks are done in ways that acknowledge God, God is present and he is glorified. Such tasks may not be redeeming, but they can provide a foretaste of the coming kingdom.[5]

Sports, when played the way they were intended to be played, can be this "foretaste of the coming kingdom."

5. Hunter, *To Change the World*, 253.

Elite?

On the edge of the Pleasant Hill Lake shoreline at Camp Nuhop, a youth camp in Perrysville, Ohio, stands a strange-looking, octagonal pit with three long pieces of lumber on each side. The boards are stacked horizontally and form each of the eight sides that stand twenty-eight inches high. The pit is the playing area for a game known as GaGa ball. The game kept children and adults of all ages occupied for hours during a recent week of church camp. "GaGa" derives its name from the Hebrew for "touch touch," and the game is believed to have been an Israeli import from camp counselors into the United States sometime in the 1970s.[6] The game is a variation of dodge ball, but minimizes size and age differences by requiring that anyone who gets "out" to be hit below the knees, meaning that everyone plays the game bent over at the waist.

I was introduced to GaGa ball as I was writing this book, and there are several things about it that highlight much of what I am trying to communicate. First of all, the game is incredibly simple. The website GaGaBallPit.com lists eleven very simple rules.[7] The rules are simple enough for any child to pick up within a few minutes of playing.

Second, the game finds a way to minimize age differences and athletic abilities more than any game I have ever seen. The website GaGaBallPit.com attests to this benefit of the game: "One of the main advantages of GaGa ball is that all children, regardless of their athletic skill level, have the ability to participate and even win."[8] The camp I attended had campers ranging in age from seven years old to college students, in addition to the older camp counselors. GaGa ball succeeded at bringing campers together from all ages to participate better than any other activity we did during that week. What a joy it was to see elementary school boys and girls taking on high-school-age students and seeing the younger children win just as often as the older children.

Third, at the completion of each game, the last child standing was crowned the winner. The games were, indeed, quite competitive with everyone playing to win, but the games moved at such a fast pace it was very rare to see anyone upset or frustrated about losing for more than a few seconds because, by the time they mustered any frustration, another game had begun. In addition to being fast paced, the game also manages to keep those who have gotten "out" involved with the promise of getting back into

---

6. GaGaBallPit.com, "History of the Gaga Ball Game in the US."
7. GaGaBallPit.com, "Sample Gaga Ball Rules."
8. GaGaBallPit.com, "GaGa Ball, Easy, Fun, Fast Moving Game."

the game if they are able to catch a ball that flies out of the pit. The game promotes physicality as everyone who plays sweats; communality as alliances were often unofficially formed between younger children to "out" the older children; and true joy with constant laughter and smiles on the faces of all of the players.

Finally, it seemed to be the only activity we participated in all week that the children knew more about than the adults. Throughout the week, it was a regular occasion to witness children teaching their parents and camp counselors the rules of GaGa ball. Again, the website mentions this as a significant appeal of GaGa ball: "Instead of children learning the game from adults, children are spreading the news about GaGa Ball and are actually teaching their parents and fellow playground participants about the game."[9] My three children loved the game so much they were able to (quite on their own) transplant an amended version of GaGa ball to the trampoline in our backyard, and they have even taught their parents how to play their version of the game.

I am not convinced that the world is about to be overrun with GaGa ball tournaments, but there seems something quite significant in having witnessed this weeklong phenomenon in rural north-central Ohio. Every bit of research I came across in writing this book confirms the number one reason children play sports is to have fun. While there is a natural progression to competition, it is important to be reminded often that people play games, first and foremost, to have fun. Throughout my years of ministry, the most popular sporting event for nearly every teenager has remained different variations of dodgeball. There are always teenagers who enjoy playing catch with a football or a baseball and kickball games have been frequent occurrences, but no other activity has been able to match the popularity that dodge ball has maintained throughout my nearly two decades of ministry. It is purely conjecture as to why this has remained the case, but in light of the arguments I've made in this book, it just might be that dodgeball remains one of the very few activities that has failed to be compromised by the youth-sports industrial complex (yet). Upon further reflection, it turns out that dodgeball and those old, cheesy youth-ministry games might actually have a more redemptive purpose than anyone ever realized.

---

9. GaGaBallPit.com, "History of the Gaga Ball Game in the US."

Epilogue

As I write the closing words of this book, the daffodil, tulip, and hyacinth bulbs I planted in the fall have poked through the soil and their colorful flowers have brightened up the front of our house with dazzling primary colors. The temperature is finally getting warmer, the days are getting longer, and as my wife and I welcome the improving weather conditions we can't help but also notice signs of the impending youth-sports whirlwind awaiting our family. Last week our youngest daughter began soccer practice. Our son's first baseball game is only a week away, and we will soon be racing our older daughter between dance classes and softball practices. Before we know it, we will be thrust into their summer swimming schedules and off we go into the busyness and craziness about which I have spent so much time reading, researching, writing, and warning. We have had to color code our calendar in order to keep up with which direction we will be headed each night and how we can divide and conquer our children's busy schedules. Having spent nearly two decades in youth ministry, this is a life stage I have watched countless other families navigate for years, and it is somewhat surreal for it to be our turn.

I have written this book not as an aloof, ivory-tower academic or disengaged outside observer, but as a father of three busy children and a pastor to other families who are just as busy. If this book does not speak to the practical matters families like ours face day in and day out, I have failed to accomplish what I set out to do. One of the questions at the heart of this book is, "What are Christian families to do with youth sports?" My wife and I know firsthand the challenges facing families who take their Christian faith seriously when it comes to sports. We have asked and continue to ask the same questions millions of other parents ask: How much money should we spend on sports? At what point does too much become too much? How many sports should I encourage my children to play and at what ages? How do we balance our time and focus between our athletically inclined child and our non-athletically inclined one? What do we do when we feel like we have no other options and are forced to choose between the lesser of two evils? And foundationally for Christians: How do we know when we have supplanted our identity in Christ with our identity in sports? Many reflective parents can resonate with John Tauer's affirmation: "the complex culture of youth sports creates a powerful situation that makes it difficult for parents to remain true to their values."[1] This book has attempted to help think through some of these questions and offer some practical advice for helping Christians remain true to their values.

At the beginning of this book, we saw how God's intention from the very beginning of creation was for his children to play. People are as passionate about their sports as they are about almost any other part of their lives. In many ways, this book has been aimed at calling out the golden calves erected in the lives of many Christians. Inevitably, such an objective is wont to disturb and unsettle. If you've taken seriously these words, it has probably made for some uncomfortable moments. I had them even as I wrote. Many of the things this book proposes cut at the heart of life in the suburbs of the United States today. I believe passionately in the message of this book, but I also want to be quick to keep that message in perspective. God has called us to play, and the very act of writing, thinking, and imagining God's will for our lives is an act of play. It's not as though any of us have this all figured out . . . we just hope to be getting a little closer each and every day. I present this book as my own playful musings on play. I hope they have challenged you and encouraged you to ask new questions, but before any of us become too serious about these matters, we should be reminded that God loves to watch his children play.

1. Tauer, *Why Less is More for WOSPs*, 41.

Bibliography

Allender, Dan. *Sabbath*. The Ancient Practices Series. Nashville: Thomas Nelson, 2010.
Amidon, Stephen. *Something Like the Gods: A Cultural History of the Athlete from Achilles to LeBron*. New York: Rodale, 2012.
Athletes in Action. "2014 Annual Report." http://goaia.org/media/default/about/annual-reports/Annual%20Report%202014.Web.pdf.
Bado-Fralick, Nikki and Rebecca Sachs Norris. *Toying with God: The World of Religious Games and Dolls*. Waco, TX: Baylor University Press, 2010.
Bain-Selbo, Eric. *Game Day and God: Football, Faith, and Politics in the American South*. Macon, GA: Mercer University Press, 2009.
Baker, William J. *Playing with God: Religion and Modern Sport*. Cambridge, MA: Harvard University Press, 2007.
Barth, Karl. *The Christian Life: Church Dogmatics IV, Part 4: Lecture Fragments*. Translated by Geoffrey W. Bromiley. New York: T. & T. International, 2004.
———. "Introduction to Theology, Conversation with Karl Barth." In *A Keeper of the Word: Selected Writings of William Stringfellow*, edited by Bill Wylie Kellerman, 187–90. Grand Rapids, MI: Eerdmans, 1994.
Baseball Reference. "Flood v. Kuhn," http://www.baseball-reference.com/bullpen/Flood_v._Kuhn.
Berkhof, Hendrik. *Christ and the Powers*. 2nd ed. Translated by John Howard Yoder. Scottdale, PA: Herald, 1977.
Berkowitz, Steve, et. al. "2014–2015 NCAA Finances: Top College Revenues," *USA Today*. http://www.usatoday.com/sports/college/schools/finances.
Bigelow, Bob, Tom Moroney, and Linda Hall. *Just Let the Kids Play: How to Stop Other Adults from Ruining Your Child's Fun and Success in Youth Sports*. Deerbeach, FL: Health Communications Incorporated, 2001.
Bishop, Ronald. *When Play was Play: Why Pick-up Games Matter*. Albany, NY: State University of New York Press, 2009.
Bonhoeffer, Dietrich. *The Cost of Discipleship*. New York: Collier, 1963.
Briggs, David. "The Final Four, Travel Teams, and Empty Pews: Who is Winning the Competition Between Sports and Religion?" *Huffington Post*. (April 3, 2013). http://www.huffingtonpost.com/david-briggs/final-four-travel-teams-and-empty-pews-who-is-winning-the-competition-between-sports-and-religion_b_3006988.html.
Brown, Jim. "Foreward." In *The Games do Count: America's Best and Brightest on the Power of Sports*," edited by Brian Kilmeade, vii–x. New York: Regan, 2004.

Bibliography

Brown, Maury. "Baseball Is Dying? TV Ratings for 2016 World Series Through the Roof." *Forbes*. (November 3, 2016) http://www.forbes.com/sites/maurybrown/2016/11/03/baseball-is-dying-tv-ratings-for-2016-world-series-through-the-roof/#3da3bcc1496e.

Browning, Reed. *Cy Young: A Life in Baseball*. Amherst, MA: University of Massachusetts Press, 2000.

Brueggemann, Walter. *Genesis*. Interpretation Bible Commentary for Preaching and Teaching. Atlanta: John Knox, 1982.

———. *Out of Babylon*. Nashville: Abingdon, 2010.

Caillois, Roger. *Man, Play, and Games*. Translated by Meyer Badrash. New York: Free, 1961.

Castle, George. *Jackie Robinson West: The Triumph and Tragedy of America's Favorite Little League Team*. Guilford, CT: Lyons, 2016.

Clark, Chap. "The Changing Face of Adolescence: A Theological View of Human Development." In *Starting Right: Thinking Theologically about Youth Ministry*, edited by Kendra Creasy Dean, Chap Clark, and Dave Rahm, 41–61. Grand Rapids, MI: Zondervan, 2001.

———. *Hurt 2.0: Inside the World of Today's Teenager*. Grand Rapids, MI: Baker Academic, 2011.

———. "The Rules of the Game." *Youthworker Journal*. January/February 2007.

Colgate, Bob, ed. *2016 NFHS Football Rules Book*. Indianapolis, IN: NFHS, 2016.

Cook, Bob. "After Killing Pickup Games, Adults Now on Way to Killing Recreational Youth Sports." *Forbes*. (March 5, 2016). http://www.forbes.com/sites/bobcook/2016/03/05/after-killing-pickup-games-adults-now-on-way-to-killing-recreational-youth-sports/#24c05c083045.

———. "Tennessee Law First To Address Sports Parents' Desires To Sit Kids For Religious And School Holidays." *Forbes*. (May 13, 2017). https://www.forbes.com/sites/bobcook/2017/05/13/tennessee-law-first-to-address-sports-parents-desires-to-sit-kids-for-religious-and-school-holidays/#5a745b2c5a87.

Deford, Frank. "Religion in Sport." *Sports Illustrated*. (April 19, 1976). http://www.si.com/vault/1976/04/19/614818/religion-in-sport.

Delaney, Kevin J. and Rick Eckstein. "Public Dollars, Private Stadiums, and Democracy." In *Sport, Power, and Society: Institutions and Practices*, edited by Robert E. Washington and David Karen, 5–19. Boulder, CO: Westview, 2010.

Dohrmann, George. *Play Their Hearts Out: A Coach, His Star Recruit, and the Youth Basketball Machine*. New York: Ballatine, 2012.

Douglas, Gabrielle, and Michelle Burford. *Grace, Gold, and Glory: My Leap of Faith*. Grand Rapids, MI: Zonderkidz, 2013.

Duina, Francesco. *Winning: Reflections on an American Obsession*. Princeton, NJ: Princeton University Press, 2011.

Duncan, Shawn. "Sports as Compensatory Identity: Getting at One of the Roots of Ethical Dilemma of Sports." *Journal of Faith and the Academy*. VI 2, Fall 2013, 24–32.

Dungy, Tony. *Quiet Strength: Ten Principles, Practices, and Priorities of a Winning Life*. Carol Stream, IL: Tyndale, 2007.

Eckblad, Bob. *A New Christian Manifesto: Pledging Allegiance to the Kingdom of God* Louisville: Westminster John Knox, 2008.

Edwards, Herman. "NFL Postgame Press Conference." October 30, 2002.

Bibliography

Elkind, David. *The Power of Play: How Spontaneous, Imaginative Activities Lead to Happier, Healthier Children*. Boston: Da Capo, 2007.

Ellis, Robert. *The Games People Play: Theology, Religion, and Sport*. Eugene, OR: Wipf and Stock, 2014.

Elmore, Tim. "What Parents Should Say as their Kids Perform." *Growing Leaders*. (August 16, 2013). http://growingleaders.com/blog/what-parents-should-say-as-their-kids-perform.

Emmert, Mark. "Press Conference Remarks." (July 23, 2012). http://www.ncaa.org/about/resources/media-center/news/penn-state-press-conference-remarks.

Engh, Fred. *Why Johnny Hates sports: Why Organized Youth Sports are Failing our Children and What We Can Do About It*. Garden City Park, NY: Square One, 2002.

Erickson, Erik. *Identity: Youth and Crisis*. New York: W. W. Norton, 1968.

Evans Jr., James H. *Playing*. Christians Explorations of Daily Living Series. Minneapolis: Fortress, 2010.

Faris, Stephen. "Why America Doesn't Like Soccer, and How that Can Be Changed." *Time*. (June 12, 2014). http://time.com/2864483/world-cup-2014-soccer-brazil-america.

Farrey, Tom. *Game On: The All-American Race to Make Champions out of our Children*. New York: ESPN, 2008.

Ferguson, Everett. *Backgrounds of Early Christians*. 2nd ed. Grand Rapids, MI: Eerdmans, 1993.

Forney, Craig A. *The Holy Trinity of American Sports: Civil Religion in Football, Baseball, and Basketball*. Macon, GA: Mercer University Press, 2010.

Foster, Richard. *Celebration of Discipline: The Path to Spiritual Growth*, 2nd ed. San Francisco: Harper Collins, 1988.

Fowler, James W. *Stages of Faith: The Psychology of Human Development and the Quest for Meaning*. San Francisco: Harper One, 1981.

Frohlich, Thomas C., and Kent Alexander. "Countries Spending the Most on the Military," *USA Today* (July 12, 2014). http://www.usatoday.com/story/money/business/2014/07/12/countries-spending-most-on-military/12491639.

Frost, Michael. "The Missio Dei: Seeing Mission as Bigger Than Evangelism." In *The Road to Missional: Journey to the Center of the Church*, 23–39. Grand Rapids, MI: Baker, 2012.

Frost, Michael, and Alan Hirsch. *ReJesus: A Wild Messiah for a Missional Church*. Peabody, MA: Hendrickson, 2009.

———. *The Shaping of Things to Come: Innovation and Mission for the 21st Century Church*, 2nd ed. Peabody, MA: Hendrickson, 2007.

Gagaballpit.com. "History of the Gaga Ball Game in the US," http://www.gagaballpit.com/history-of-gaga-ball-game.html.

———. "Sample Gaga Ball Rules." http://www.gagaballpit.com/gaga-ball-game-rules.html.

———. "GaGa Ball, Easy, Fun, Fast Moving Game That Everyone Can Play with Our GaGa Ball Pits.(October 7, 2014). http://www.gagaballpit.com.

Garner, John. "Organization of Recreation and Sports Ministry." In *Recreation and Sports Ministry: Impacting Postmodern Culture*. Edited by John Garner, 69–90. Nashville: Broadman and Holman, 2003.

Garvey, Catherine. *Play*. Developing Child Series. Cambridge, MA: Harvard University Press, 1977.

Bibliography

Giamatti, Bart. "Convocation Speech." Williams College, Williamstown, MA. September 12, 1987.

Gibbs, Chad. *God and Football: Faith and Fanaticism in the SEC*. Grand Rapids: Zondervan, 2010.

Google. "Our Culture." https://www.google.com/about/company/facts/culture.

Gorringe, Timothy J. *Karl Barth Against Hegemony*. New York: Oxford University Press, 1999.

Grenz, Stanley J. *Theology for the Community of God*, 2nd ed. Grand Rapids: Eerdmans, 2000.

Griffin, Brad M. "The Only Six Words Parents Need to Say to their Kid about Sports." *Fuller Youth Institute*. (February 4, 2014). http://fulleryouthinstitute.org/blog/the-only-six-words-parents-need-to-say-to-their-kids-about-sportsor-any-per.

Guttmann, Allen. *From Ritual to Record: The Nature of Modern Sports*. 2nd ed. New York: Columbia University Press, 1978.

Harvey, Lincoln. *A Brief Theology of Sport*. London: SCM, 2014.

Health Fitness Revolution, "Top 20 Fittest Churches in America." *Health Fitness Revolution*. (June 12, 2014). http://healthfitnessrevolution.com/top-20-fittest-churches-america.

Higgs, Robert J. *God in the Stadium: Sports and Religion in America*. Lexington, KY: University of Kentucky Press, 1995.

Higgs, Robert J., and Michael C. Braswell. *An Unholy Alliance: The Sacred and Modern Sports*. Macon, GA: Mercer University Press, 2004.

Hirsch, Alan, *The Forgotten Ways: Reactivating the Missional Church*, 6th ed. Grand Rapids: Brazos, 2006.

Hiscott, Rebecca. "13 Playful Work Environments that Reinvent Office Space." *Mashable*. (January 9, 2014). http://mashable.com/2014/01/09/playful-work spaces/#ddQYpLejSkq.

Hoffman, Shirl James. *Good Game: Christianity and the Culture of Sports*. Waco, TX: Baylor University Press, 2010.

Hughes, Thomas. *Tom Brown's Schooldays*. Reprint. New York: Oxford University Press, 1989.

Huizinga, Johan. *Homo Ludens: A Study of the Play Element in Culture*. Boston: Beacon, 1968.

Hunter, James Davison. *To Change the World: The Irony, Tragedy, and Possibility of Christianity in the Late Modern World*. New York: Oxford University Press, 2010.

Hyman, Mark. *The Most Expensive Game in Town: The Rising Cost of Youth Sports and the Toll on Today's Families*. Boston: Beacon, 2012.

———. *Until it Hurts: America's Obsession with Youth Sports and How it Harms our Kids*. Boston: Beacon, 2009.

Isidore, Chris. "NFL Revenue: Here Comes Another Record Season." *CNN Money*. (September 10, 2015). http://money.cnn.com/2015/09/10/news/companies/nfl-rev enue-profits.

Iverson, Allen. "NBA Postgame Press Conference." May 7, 2002.

Jacobsen, Eric O. *Sidewalks in the Kingdom: New Urbanism and the Christian Faith*. Grand Rapids: Brazos, 2003.

Johnson, Sharon G., and Galen Smith. "Perspectives on Competition—Christian and Otherwise." Paper presented at the Christian Business Faulty Association National Conference. San Diego, 2005. http://www.cbfa.org/Johnson_Smith.pdf.

Johnston, Robert K. *The Christian at Play*. Eugene, OR: Wipf and Stock, 1997.

Bibliography

Jones, Todd, Mike Wagner, and Jill Riepenhoff. "Little Leagues, Big Costs." *The Columbus Dispatch*. Sunday, August 29, 2010–Thursday, September 2, 2010.

Keller, Timothy. *Every Good Endeavor: Connecting Your Work to God's Work*. New York: Dutton, 2012.

Kellerman, Bill Wylie, ed. *A Keeper of the Word: Selected Writings of William Stringfellow*. Grand Rapids: Eerdmans, 1994.

Kelly, Patrick. "Christians and Sports: An Historical and Theological Overview." In *Youth Sport and Spirituality*, edited by Patrick Kelly, 33–61. Notre Dame, IN: University of Notre Dame Press, 2015.

Kelley, Bruce, and Carl Carchia. "Hey, Data, Data—Swing!" *ESPN*. (July 11, 2013). http://www.espn.com/espn/story/_/id/9469252/hidden-demographics-youth-sports-espn-magazine.

Keown, Tim. "Where the 'Elite' Kids Shouldn't Meet: Travel Teams, 'Elite' Leagues, Select Players . . . They Skewer Our Sports Perspective." *ESPN*. (August 24, 2011). http://espn.go.com/espn/commentary/story/_/page/keown-110823/elite-travel-baseball-basketball-teams-make-youth-sports-industrial-complex.

King, David, and Margot Starubuck. *Overplayed: A Parent's Guide to Sanity in the World of Youth Sports*. Harrisonburg, VA: Herald, 2016.

Kliever, Lonnie D. "God and Games in Modern Culture." In *From Season to Season: Sports as American Religion*, edited by Joseph Price, 39–48. Macon, GA: Mercer University Press, 2001.

Kluck, Ted. *The Reason for Sports: A Christian Fanifesto*. Chicago: Moody, 2009.

Kluwe, Chris. "There Can Be Only One: What It's Like to Battle for your NFL Life and Stay Human." *The MMQB*. (September 9, 2013). http://mmqb.si.com/2013/08/09/chris-kluwe-marquette-king-competition.

Krattenmaker, Tom. *Onward Christian Athletes: Turning Ballparks into Pulpits and Players into Preachers*. Lantham, MD: Rowman and Littlefield, 2010.

Koch Alois. "Biblical and Patristic Foundations for Sport." In *Sport and Christianity: A Sign of the Times in the Light of Faith*, edited by Kevin Lixey et al., 81–103. Washington DC: Catholic University Press, 2012.

Lamb, Scott, and Tim Ellsworth. *Pujols: More Than a Game*. Nashville: Thomas Nelson, 2011.

Lev, Elianna. "Teen with Down Syndrome Makes Perfect Final Play to Win Basketball Game." *Yahoo News*. (February 17, 2016). https://sg.news.yahoo.com/blogs/good-news/teen-with-down-syndrome-makes-perfect-final-play-160702724.html?nhp=1.

Lewis, C. S. *Mere Christianity*. New York: MacMillan, 1970.

Lewis, Gregg, and Deborah Shaw Lewis. *The Admiral: The David Robinson Story*. Grand Rapids, MI: Zonderkidz, 2012.

Linville, Greg. *Christmanship: A Theology of Competition and Sport*. Canton, OH: Oliver, 2014.

———. "Ethic of Competition in a Church Setting." In *Recreation and Sports Ministry: Impacting Postmodern Culture*, edited by John Garner, 161–80. Nashville: Broadman and Holman, 2003.

Lynch, Jerry. *Let Them Play: The Power and Joy of Mindful Sports Parenting*. Novato, CA: New World Library, 2016.

Bibliography

MacFarquhar, Neil. "What's a Soccer Mom Anyway?" *New York Times*. (October 20, 1996) http://www.nytimes.com/1996/10/20/weekinreview/what-s-a-soccer-mom-anyway.html.

Maier, Bernhard. "Sport as Pastoral Opportunity." In *Sport and Christianity: A Sign of the Times in the Light of Faith*, edited by Kevin Lixey, et al., 206–22. Washington DC: Catholic University Press, 2012.

Major League Eating. "Eating Contests." http://majorleagueeating.com/records.php.

Malinowski, Erik. "Pitchman: How Tom Emanski Forever Changed the Sport of Baseball—and Then Disappeared," *Fox Sports*. (July 17, 2014). http://www.foxsports.com/mlb/just-a-bit-outside/story/pitchman-tom-emanski-profile-071714.

Manfred, Tony. "Here are the Odds your Kid Becomes a Professional Athlete (Hint: They're Small)." *Business Insider*. (Feb. 10, 2012). http://www.businessinsider.com/odds-college-athletes-become-professionals-2012-2?op=1/#seball-116-of-college-players-play-professionally-06-of-high-school-players-do-1.

Martinelli, Michelle R. "How John Ross Cost Himself an Island When He Broke the NFL Combine's 40-Yard Dash Record," *For the Win*. (March 4, 2017). http://ftw.usatoday.com/2017/03/john-ross-nfl-combine-40-yard-dash-record-breaking-adidas-island-nike-cleats.

Mason, Bryan. *Beyond the Gold: What Every Church Needs to Know about Sports Ministry*. Milton Keynes, UK: Authentic Media, 2011.

McKenna, Dave. "How Red Klotz, 14,000-Time Loser, Beat the Harlem Globetrotters." *Deadspin*. (July 15, 2014). http://deadspin.com/how-red-klotz-14-000-time-loser-beat-the-harlem-globe-1605235415.

McKnight, Scot. *Kingdom Conspiracy: Returning to the Radical Mission of the Local Church* Grand Rapids: Brazos, 2014.

McMahon, Regan. *Revolution in the Bleachers*. New York: Gotham, 2007.

McMickle, Marvin. *Where Have all the Prophets Gone?* Pilgrim, 2006.

McNamee, Mike. "Youth Sports and Virtues." In *Youth Sport and Spirituality: Catholic Perspectives*, edited by Patrick Kelly, 74–87. Notre Dame, IN: University of Notre Dame Press, 2015.

Medcalf, Myron. "LeBron: Stop Recruiting LeBron Jr." *ESPN* (updated Feb. 26, 2015). http://espn.go.com/nba/story/_/id/12381552/lebron-james-does-not-colleges-attempts-recruit-10-year-old-son-lebron-james-jr.

Medcalf, Myron, and Dana O'Neil. "Playground Basketball is Dying." *ESPN*. (July 23, 2014). http://espn.go.com/espn/feature/story/_/id/11216972/playground-basketball-dying.

Merica, Dan. "Bill Clinton Relives Athletic Glory Days." *CNN*. (January 22, 2015). http://www.cnn.com/2015/01/22/politics/bill-clinton-sports-glory-days/index.html.

Miller, David L. *God and Games: Towards a Theology of Play*. New York: The World, 1970.

Morris, David and Daniel Kraker. "Rooting the Home Team: Why the Packers Won't Leave—and Why the Browns Did." In *Sport, Power, and Society: Institutions and Practices*, edited by Robert E. Washington and David Karen, 26–33. Boulder, CO: Westview, 2010.

Mouw, Richard J. *He Shines in All That's Fair: Culture and Common Grace*, 2nd ed. Grand Rapids: Eerdmans, 2002.

Muller, Norbert. "Concrete Pastoral Action within Sport." In *Sport and Christianity: A Sign of the Times in the Light of Faith*, edited by Kevin Lixey, et al., 223–33. Washington DC: Catholic University Press, 2012.

Bibliography

Niebuhr, H. Richard. *Christ and Culture*. New York: Harper and Row, 1951.

Norris, David Z. "How Computers Made Humans Better at Chess." *Fortune* (November 27, 2016). http://fortune.com/2016/11/27/computers-humans-chess.

Norworth, Jack. "Take Me Out to the Ball Game." York Music, 1908.

Novak, Michael. *The Joy of Sports: Endzones, Bases, Baskets, and the Consecration of American Spirit*. New York: Basic, 1976.

Nugent, John C. *The Endangered Gospel: How Fixing the World is Killing the Church*. Eugene, OR: Cascade, 2016.

Oppenheimer, Mark. "In the Fields of the Lord," *Sports Illustrated*. (February 4, 2013). http://www.si.com/vault/2013/02/04/106280215/in-the-fields-of-the-lord.

O'Shaughnessey, Lynn. "8 Things You Should Know about Sports Scholarships." *CBS News*. (September 20, 2012). http://www.cbsnews.com/news/8-things-you-should-know-about-sports-scholarships.

O'Sullivan, John. "The Adultification of Youth Sports." *Changing the Game Project*. (March 17, 2015). http://changingthegameproject.com/the-adultification-of-youth-sports.

———. *Changing the Game: The Parent's Guide to Raising Happy, High-Performing Athletes and Giving Youth Sports Back to Our Kids*. New York: Morgan James, 2014.

———. "Why Kids Quit Sports," *Changing the Game Project*. (May 5, 2015). http://changingthegameproject.com/why-kids-quit-sports.

———. "Youth Sport Coaching: Not a Job, but a Calling!" *Changing the Game Project*. (October 15, 2014). http://changingthegameproject.com/youth-sports-coaching-not-a-job-but-a-calling.

Oswald, Rodger. "Biblical Foundations for Sports Ministry: Defining the Phenomenon." In *Recreation and Sports Ministry: Impacting Postmodern Culture* edited by John Garner, 25–36. Nashville: Broadman and Holman, 2003.

Overman, Steven J. *The Protestant Ethic and the Spirit of Sport: How Calvinism and Capitalism Shaped America's Games*. Macon, GA: Mercer University Press, 2011.

———. "Winning Isn't Everything. It's the Only Thing!: The Origins, Attributions, and Influence of a Famous Football Quote." *Football Studies* 2 No. 2 (October 1999) 77–99. http://library.la84.org/SportsLibrary/FootballStudies/1999/FS0202h.pdf.

Pathak, Jay and Dave Runyon. *The Art of Neighboring*. Grand Rapids, MI: Baker, 2012.

Peterson, Eugene. *Christ Plays in a Thousand Places: A Conversation in Spiritual Theology* Grand Rapids, MI: Eerdmans, 2005.

Pope, S. W. *Patriotic Games: Sporting Traditions in the American Imagination 1876-1926*. New York: Oxford University Press, 1997.

Posnaski, Joe. "Loser's Lament: After Decades of Defeat, the Washington Generals Have Lost for the Last Time." *NBC Sports*. http://sportsworld.nbcsports.com/washington-generals-folding-harlem-globetrotters.

Powell, Shaun. "The New Face of Baseball." *Sports on Earth*. (April 15, 2014). http://www.sportsonearth.com/article/72021954/white-players-making-up-majority-of-historically-black-college-baseball-teams.

Price, Joseph L. "The Final Four as Final Judgment: The Cultural Significance of the NCAA Basketball Championship." In *From Season to Season*, edited by Joseph L. Price, 171–81. Macon: GA: Mercer University Press, 2004.

Project Play. "Facts: Sports Activity and Children." http://www.aspenprojectplay.org/the-facts.

———. "The State of Play." http://www.aspenprojectplay.org/sites/default/files/StateofPlay_2016_FINAL.pdf.

Bibliography

———. "Play Four: Revitalize In-Town Leagues." http://youthreport.projectplay.us/the-8-plays/revitalize-in-town-leagues.

Putney, Clifford. *Muscular Christianity: Manhood and Sports in Protestant America, 1880–1920*. Cambridge, MA: Harvard University Press, 2001.

Rauschenbusch, Walter. *Christianity and the Social Crisis in the Twenty-First Century: The Classic that Woke Up the Church*, edited by Paul Raushenbush. San Francisco: Harper One, 2007.

———. *The Social Principles of Jesus*. New York: Woman's, 1917. Kindle Electronic Edition.

Reich, Frank. "Competition and Creation." *Reformed Perspective Magazine*, 4, No.6 (February 11–February 17, 2002). http://thirdmill.org/newfiles/fra_reich/TH.Reich.Competition.html.

Reuters. "Team Repeatedly Scores Own Goals to Protest Refs." *ESPN*. (November 2, 2002). http://www.espn.com/soccer/news/2002/1102/1454712.html.

Rosengren, John. "Myth and Fact Part of Legacy from Sandy Koufax's Yom Kippur Choice." *Sports Illustrated*. (Sep. 23, 2015). https://www.si.com/mlb/2015/09/23/sandy-koufax-yom-kippur-1965-world-series.

Roth, Matt. "Rethinking Youth Sports." *TED Talk*, (September, 2014), Toledo, OH.

Roxburgh, Alan J., and M. Scott Boren. *Introducing the Missional Church: What it is, Why it Matters, How to Become One*. Grand Rapids, MI: Baker, 2009.

"Royals Hire Tom Emanski to Teach Them Fundamentals." *The Onion*. (June 1, 2006). http://www.theonion.com/article/royals-hire-tom-emanski-to-teach-them-fundamentals-1974.

Sanguin, Bruce. *Darwin, Divinity, and the Dance of the Cosmos*. Kelowna, BC: CopperHouse, 2007.

Shape of the Nation Report. 2016. http://www.shapeamerica.org/advocacy/son/index.cfm.

Shields, David Light, and Brenda Light Bredemeier. "Reclaiming Competition in Youth Sports: Catholic Perspectives." In *Youth Sports and Spirituality*, edited by Patrick Kelly, 111–32. South Bend, IN: University of Notre Dame Press, 2015.

Skolnikoff, Jessica, and Robert Engvall. *Young Athletes, Couch Potatoes, and Helicopter Parents: The Productivity of Play*. Lanham, MD: Rowan and Littlefield, 2014.

Smith, Yvonne S., Sharon G. Johnson, and Erik H. Hiller. "God of the Games: Towards a Theology of Competition." Paper presented at the national Christian Business Faculty Administration National Conference. San Antonio, October, 2004. http://www.cbfa.org/Smith-Johnson-Hiller.pdf.

Sperber, Murray. *Beer and Circus: How Big-Time College Sports is Crippling Undergraduate Education*. New York: Holt, 2000.

Stark, Jayson. "Cards Win, But Tom Emanski Covers His Eyes." *ESPN*. (October 12, 2002). http://static.espn.go.com/mlb/columns/stark_jayson/1445188.html.

Stotz, Carl E., and Kenneth D. Loss. *A Promise Kept: The Story of the Founding of Little League Baseball*. Jersey Shore, PA: Zebrowski Historical Services, 1992.

Stringfellow, William. *An Ethic for Christians and Other Aliens in a Strange Land*. Reprint. Eugene, OR: Wipf and Stock, 2004.

Sutton-Smith, Brian. *The Ambiguity of Play*. Cambridge, MA: Harvard University Press, 2001.

Taub, Shais. "Why Sandy Koufax Sat Out the World Series on Yom Kippur." *Huffington Post*. (October 6, 2011). http://www.huffingtonpost.com/rabbi-shais-taub/sand-koufax-yom-kippur_b_996111.html.

Bibliography

Tauer, John M. *Why Less is More for WOSPS (Well-Intentioned, Overinvolved, Sports Parents): How to Be the Best Sports Parent You Can Be.* Edina, MN: Beavers Pond, 2015.

Tickle, Phyllis. *Emergence Christianity: What it is, Where it is Going, and Why it Matters.* Grand Rapids: Baker, 2012.

Tinley, Josh. *Kneeling in the End Zone: Spiritual Lessons from the World of Sports.* Cleveland, OH: Pilgrim, 2009.

Tressel, Jim. *The Winner's Manual: For the Game of Life.* Carol Stream, IL: Tyndale, 2008.

Upward Sports. "2014-2015 Annual Report." https://upward.blob.core.windows.net/media/Default/docs/About/14-15-Annual-Report.pdf.

———. "About Upward Sports." http://www.upward.org/about/about-upward-sports.

Volf, Miroslav. *Work in the Spirit: Toward a Theology of Work.* Eugene, OR: Wipf and Stock, 1991.

Warner, Gary. *Competition.* Elgin, IL: David C. Cook, 1980.

Warren, Rick, Daniel Amen, and Mark Hyman. *The Daniel Plan: 40 Days to a Healthier Life.* Grand Rapids: Zondervan, 2013.

Washington, Robert E., and David Karen. "A Note to the Reader." In *Sport, Power, and Society: Institutions and Practices*, edited by. Robert E. Washington and David Karen, xi. Boulder, CO: Westview, 2010.

Wesner, Brad. "Visions and Re-Visions: A History of the Modern Church Recreation and Sports Movement in the United State." In *Recreation and Sports Ministry: Impacting Postmodern Culture*, edited by John Garner, 37–54. Nashville: Broadman and Holman, 2003.

White, Matthew Brian. "Sports Ministry in America's One Hundred Largest Churches," DMin diss., Asbury Theological Seminary, September 14, 2005. http://place.asburyseminary.edu/cgi/viewcontent.cgi?article=1276&context=ecommonsatsdissertations.

Williams, Brent. "Athletes Emerge at NextGen." *Rivals.* (Feb. 13, 201). https://footballrecruiting.rivals.com/content.asp?CID=1736635.

Wink, Walter. *Engaging the Powers: Discernment and Resistance in a World of Domination.* Minneapolis: Fortress, 1992.

———. *Naming the Powers: The Language of Power in the New Testament.* Minneapolis: Fortress, 1984.

———. *The Powers that Be: Theology for a New Millennium.* New York: Galilee, 1998.

———. *Unmasking the Powers: The Invisible Forces that Determine Human Existence.* Minneapolis: Fortress, 1986.

World YMCA. "2015 Annual Report." http://www.ymca.int/resources/annual-report-2015.

Wright, N. T. *Surprised by Hope.* San Francisco: HarperOne, 2008.

Yoder, John Howard. "Translators Preface." In Hendrik Berkhof, *Christ and the Powers.* Translated by John Howard Yoder, 2nd ed. Scottsdale, PA: Herald, 1977.

Zimalist, Andrew. "May the Best Team Win." In *Sport, Power, and Society*, edited by. Robert E. Washington and David Karen, 20–25. Boulder, CO: Westview, 2010.

Zirin, Dave. *A People's History of Sports in the United States: 250 Years of Politics, Protests, People, and Play.* New York: New, 2008.

Scripture Index

OLD TESTAMENT

Genesis
2	45
2:2	24
2:5	24
2:15	23
3:15	46
3:23	24
4:4–5	46
21:8–10	46
27	46
37:3	46

Exodus
20:11	24, 133

Deuteronomy
5:15	24, 133

1 Kings
18	51
18:16–46	46

Psalms
19:1	101
137	126

Proverbs
27:17	54

Ecclesiastes
3:1	167
3:2–3	106
3:11	106

Jeremiah
29	126
29:5	126

Daniel
3	125
3:12b	125–26

Zephaniah
3:17	84

NEW TESTAMENT

Matthew
5:29–30	53
16:24	138
19:24	154

Scripture Index

19:26	154
20:16	36, 47

Mark
2:27	56
12:31	104

John
1:14	132
10:10	154

Acts
17	90, 163

Romans
1:25	101
7:7–25	54
8:38f.	59
12:2	123

1 Corinthians
2:8	59
6:19	114
6:19–20	137
9:24–27	25–26
15:24–26	59

Galatians
2:2	26
2:20	137
3:22–23	49
3:28	139
5:7	26
6:20	132

Ephesians
1:20f	59
2:1f	59
3:10	59
5:23	36
6:12	59

Philippians
2:16	26, 89

Colossians
1:16	59
2:15	59
3:16	60, 62, 63

2 Timothy
2:5	26
4:7	26, 88

Hebrews
4:7	85
10:25	105

James
5:16	176

1 Peter
2:11	127

1 John
2:15	129, 155

Name/Subject Index

10,000-hour-rule, 89

Adidas, 145
Allender, Dan, 133
Amateur Athletic League (AAU), 42, 94, 95, 102, 106, 143
American Youth Soccer Organization (AYSO), 96
Amidon, Stephen, 85
Army-Navy college football game, 72
At All Costs, 106
athletes, 85
Athletes in Action (AIA), 9, 109, 116
Atlanta Braves, 64
attractional church model, 121, 159–60
autocharatic, 6, 7, 84, 99
autotelic, 6, 7, 84

Bain-Selbo, Eric, 72
Baker, William, 109n7, 111, 117
Banister, Roger, 84
Barkley, Charles, 73
Barth, Karl, 59, 68–69
Baylor University, 49n40, 75, 118
"bearded-lady-Jesus," 112
Beckham, Odell, 132
Beecher, Henry Ward, 113
Belisle, Dave, 80
Berkhof, Hendrik, 59–61
Berwanger, Jay, 144
Bible
    competition and, 44–48
    moralizing sports, 83–84
    sports metaphors in, 15, 25–26, 88–90
    teachings on spiritual powers, 59–65
Bigelow, Bob, 165–67
Bishop, Ronald, 21, 97, 99–100, 103
Black Lives Matter, 70
Blackmun, Harry, 71
The Blindside, 80
blue laws, 133
body as temple, 114–15, 130–32
Bonhoeffer, Dietrich, 155
Book of Sports, 111
Boren, Scott, 158n, 161n11
Braswell, Michael, 37
bread and circus, 128
Bredemeier, Brenda, 93, 99
Brown, Bruce, 84
Brown, Jim, 7
Brueggemann, Walter, 45, 127, 139
Bryant, Kobe, 98

Callois, Roger, 20, 28–29, 39
Campus Crusade, 117
Carchia, Carlos, 10, 95
Carlos, John, 5
Casey, Susan B., 164
Catholic Church, 81
Chapman, Aroldis, 132
cheating, 5, 36, 65, 150
chess, 54
Chicago Cubs, 3, 34n1, 71

Name/Subject Index

childhood, 79
Christ and Culture, 110–17.
Christian colleges and universities, sports programs of, 74, 117
Christian calendar, 105
Chronic Traumatic Encephalopathy (CTE), 9, 119, 131
chthonic forces, 59, 69
church sports leagues, 2, 33, 120, 121, 161
Clark, Chap, 31, 146, 177
Cleveland Browns, 7, 17, 64, 144
Cleveland Indians, 34n1, 58–59, 64
Clinton, Bill, 2, 33, 98
coaches, 163–64, 179
communitas, 86–88
competition, 18, 34, 176
    Calvinism [also Reformed] and, 51–52
    capitalism and, 51
    definition of, 38
    dehumanizing opponents, 47, 55
    evolution and, 44
    play and, 39
    power and, 55–56
    sports and, 37
    theological neglect of, 36
    US culture and, 34–36
concussions. *See* CTE
contemporary Christian music (CCM), 118
Cook, Bob, 103
Cosell, Howard, 71
creation, 24, 184

The Daniel Plan, 119
David and Goliath, 83
de Coubertin, Pierre, 18
Deford, Frank, 31, 108, 128
Detroit Tigers, 58–59, 60
dodgeball, 181
Dohrmann, George, 42n24, 106, 148
Dream Team, 73
Duina, Francesco, 37
Duncan, Shawn, 148

Easterling, Antwain, 149–50

Edwards, Herman, 17, 30, 163
Ekblad, Bob, 68n34
Elijah on Mt. Carmel, 51
Ellis, Robert, 6, 20, 21, 24, 85, 99, 109n7, 111, 147
Elkind, David, 30
Emanski, Tom, 142
Emmert, Mark, 67–68
Engh, Fred, 165, 168
Engvall, Robert, 102–3
Erickson, Erik, 144
ESPN, 34, 70, 98
Evans, James Jr., 26

the Fall, 23, 33, 56, 66, 80–81, 101
Fallwell, Jerry, 74, 117
Farrey, Tom, 6, 10, 41, 93, 106, 129, 139, 149–50, 175
Fellowship of Christian Athletes (FCA), 9, 35, 116
Ferguson, Everett, 26
Final Four, 51
Fonda, Jane, 89
Foster, Richard, 89, 155
Forney, Craig, 72
Fowler, James, 147–48
Friday Night Lights, 7
Frost, Michael, 112, 158n1, 158–61
Fuller Youth Institute, 166

Gaga ball, 180–81
Galarraga, Armando, 58–59, 60
Garner, John, 159–61
Garvey, Catherine, 29
Gatorade, 143
Giamatti, Bart, 74
Gibbs, Chad, 63
gladiatorial games, 26
Google, 27
Graham, Billy, 117, 157
Grenz, Stanley, 59, 66–67
Guttmann, Allen, 39, 84

Harlem Globetrotters, 19
Harvey, Lincoln, 6, 43, 44, 54–55, 102
head injuries. *See* CTE

Name/Subject Index

Head of Christ, 112
Hicks, John Mark, 44n35
Higgs, Robert, 8, 37, 46, 49, 65n24, 109n7, 111, 119
Higginson, Thomas Wentworth, 113
Hiller, Erik, 35, 36, 44
Hirsch, Alan, 86, 112, 158n1, 158–61
high school football, 10, 15, 18
Hoffman, Shirl, 8, 26, 37, 43, 44, 85, 109n7, 111, 113, 117, 118
homo ludens, 27, 147
Hughes, Thomas, 113
Huizinga, Johan, 25, 27
Hunt, William Holman, 112
Hunter, James Davison 124, 179
Hyman, Mark, 91, 106

imago dei, 132
incarnation, 132
Iverson, Allen, 89–90

Jackie Robinson West Little League baseball team, 66, 88
Jackson, Bo, 91
Jacobsen, Eric, 161
James, LeBron, 143, 169, 178
Jobs, Steve, 67
Johnson, Sharon G., 35, 36, 37, 44, 51
Johnston, Robert, 23
Jordan, Michael, 132, 143
Joyce, Jim, 58–59, 60

Kansas City Royals, 142
Kapernick, Colin, 70
Kasparov, Gary, 54
Keller, Tim, 24
Kellerman, Bill Wylie, 68n32
Kelley, Bruce, 10, 95
Kelly, Patrick, 110n7
Keown, Tim, 94–95, 97
Kilmeade, Brian, 7
King, David, 128, 151, 152n14, 153, 154
King James, 111
Kingsley, Charles, 113
Kliever, Lonnie, 30

Kluk, Ted, 174
kneeling in end zones, 52
Koch, Alois, 26
Koufax, Sandy, 125–27
Kraker, Daniel, 72
Krattenmaker, Tom, 48, 108–9, 115–16, 163

Lewis, C. S., 50, 55
Lewis, Robert, 80
Liberty University, 74, 75, 117
The Light of the World, 112
Linville, Greg, 43, 159–60
Little League Baseball, 10, 15, 66, 80, 87, 88, 96, 134–35
"liturgy of contingency," 54
Lombardi, Vince, 17, 163
losing, 19, 48, 54
Lynch, Jerry, 31, 32, 82

Maier, Bernhard, 50
Major League Baseball (MLB), 58–60, 71, 74
 anti-trust exemption, 71
Malinowski, Erik, 142
Mason, Bryan, 116
McGriff, Fred, 143
McKnight, Scot, 158n1
McMahon, Regan, 96–97, 100
McMickle, Marvin, 127
McNair, Steve, 139
McNamee, Mike, 81
Mennonites, 119
The Mighty Ducks, 7
Miller, David, 27
Miller, Rob, 84
missional approach to ministry, 121, 158f.
mob mentality, 65
Moltmann, Jurgen, 85
money, 5
Moody, Dwight L., 113
Moroney, Tom, 166
Morris, David, 72
Mosaic Law, 23
Mouw, Richard, 84
Muller, Norbert, 66, 81, 163

Name/Subject Index

Muscular Christianity, 112–15, 119

Naismith, James, 170
Nathan's Hotdog Eating Championship, 34
natural revelation, 48, 54, 101
NCAA basketball tournament, 5, 34, 51, 52, 75
NFL combine and draft, 144–45
Neibuhr, H. Richard, 110f.
Nike, 73, 144
Norworth, Jack, 28
Notre Dame football, 74–75, 117
Novak, Michael, 3, 31, 63, 71, 72, 99
Nugent, John, 137

officiating, 5, 11, 33, 55, 66, 71, 109, 120, 150, 167–68
Olympics, 5, 18, 42, 68, 73, 79
Oppenheimer, Mark, 48
Oral Roberts University, 75, 117
O'Sullivan, John, 21–22, 42, 81, 87, 98–99, 105–6, 129, 163
Overman, Steven, 40–41, 51–52
overuse injuries, 130

Palin, Sarah, 164
parents, 3–4, 41–42, 69–70, 79, 98–100, 145–46, 151, 152–53, 164–67, 175
Paterno, Joe, 49n40
Pathak, Jay, 137–38
Penn State University football, 49n40, 67–68, 143–44
performance enhancing drugs (PEDs), 5–6, 44, 65–66, 71, 131
Peterson, Eugene, 24–25
phenomenology, 63, 64
physical activity, 82–83
physical education, 95
play, 6, 20–21, 26–27, 106, 146, 173
    competition and, 37, 51
    definition of, 28, 29–30
    delight of God and, 84
    essentiality of, 30–31, 130
    evolution of, 33, 38–40, 42–43
    free play, 20
    fun and, 18, 20, 22, 29, 31, 32, 163
    quantification of, 39
playgrounds, 28, 102–4, 114
politics, 5
PONY league baseball, 96
Pop Warner Football, 96
Pope, S. W., 72
Posnaski, Joe, 19
Price, Joseph, 51
pride, 50, 53–54, 55
"Progressive Intensity Levels of Competition," 43
Project Play, 82, 98, 103–4
prophetic voice of the church, 128–41
prosperity gospel, 49
Puritans, 8, 110–12, 129
Putney, Clifford, 112

quarterback, 148–49

rankings, 41
Rauschenbusch, Walter, 114–15
Redmond, Derek, 80
Reebok, 73
Reich, Frank, 44
"Relax, It's Just a Game" PSA, 165
Remember the Titans, 80
rest. *See* Sabbath
rhythm of life, 105–6, 134, 136
Rockne, Knute, 75
Roosevelt, Theodore, 113
Ross, John, 144
Roth, Matt, 129
Roxburgh, Alan, 158n1, 161n11
Rudy, 80
Runyon, Dave, 137–38
Ruth, Babe, 143

Sabbath, 24, 100, 106, 119, 125–27, 132–35
Sallman, Warner, 112
Sanders, Dion, 128
Sanders, Red, 17
The Sandlot, 7, 102–3

Name/Subject Index

Sandusky, Jerry, 67
Sanguin, Bruce, 44
Schilling, Curt, 70
scholarships, 6–7
self-control, 36
Selig, Bud, 59
Shields, David, 93, 99
Skolnikoff, Jessica, 102–3
Smith, Galen, 37, 51
Smith, Tommie, 5
Smith, Yvonne, 35, 36, 45
Smoltz, John, 131
soccer moms, 164
Social Gospel, 114
South Eastern Conference college football, 72
Southern Baptist Convention, 116, 117
Southern Methodist University, 75
Special Olympics, 140
spiritual powers
    as creatures, 68
    as powers and principalities, 59, 60–61
    collusion of, 95, 98
    definition of, 56–58
    diversity of, 59
    language of, 62
    sports as, 63, 65, 67, 75, 139
Sportianity, 108, 129
sports
    as idol, 50, 54–55, 101
    as religion, 65, 72, 147
    balance in, 106, 133, 178
    church's relationship with, 8
    community and, 86–88, 135–36
    disability and, 140
    ego and, 50
    economics and, 73–74
    eschatology and, 85, 179
    ethics and, 36
    fun and, 87, 181
    gender and, 9
    higher education and, 74
    local church and, 172
    patriotism and, 71–72
    play and, 20, 82
    politics and, 70
    race and, 9
    self-discipline and, 88
    social cohesion and, 72–73
    soul of, 63, 69–70
    ties and, 37–38
    transcendence and, 83–85
    ubiquity of, 7, 10–12, 15, 25, 27
    virtues inherent in, 81–90
Sports Ambassadors, 117
sports ministry, 8, 52, 106–7, 129, 159, 168
    chaplaincy, 118
    evangelism and, 108–9, 115, 157
    mega-churches and, 118, 119
    parachurch and, 8, 52, 108–9, 115, 121, 122, 129, 140, 157, 178
    youth-sports industrial complex, 117–21
Sports Spectrum, 118
Spurber, Murray, 73
Stagg, Amos Alonzo, 113
standardized tests, 31, 35, 87
Starbuck, Margot, 128, 151, 152n14, 153
Stark, Jayson, 142
steroids. *See* PEDs
Stotz, Carl, 96, 134–35, 162
Stringfellow, William, 59, 68, 73
structures of existence, 59, 66
Sunday, Billy, 113, 115
Super Bowl, 34, 69
Sutton-Smith, Bryan, 26
Swinton, John, 140

"Take Me Out to the Ball Game," 28
Taub, Shais, 125
Tauer, John, 127–28, 154, 184
Tebow, Tim, 52, 159
Ten Commandments, 24, 133
Tertullian, 15
Texas A&M University, 143
Tickle, Phyllis, 158n2
Tinley, Josh, 83
Tom Brown's School Days, 113
Tressel, Jim, 49n40, 87

Name/Subject Index

Trump, Donald, 17–18

University of Arkansas, 143
University of Southern California, 143
Upward Sports, 9, 109, 118

video games, 19, 20, 25, 28, 81
Volf, Miroslav, 23–24

Warner, Gary, 23, 35, 37, 38, 49–50, 53–54, 87
Warren, Rick, 119
Washington Generals, 19
Watson, DeShaun, 47
Wesner, Brad, 110, 116
White, Matthew Brian, 118
Wink, Walter, 59, 61–65
winning, 17–18, 19, 33–34, 35–36, 37, 48, 49, 54, 101–2, 116, 163, 166
work, 23, 24
  and rest, 24–25, 28, 133
World Apple Pie Eating Championship, 34
World Series, 3, 34n1
worship, 24, 85
Wright, N. T., 132

Yoder, John Howard, 59
Young, Cy, 126–27
Young Life, 117

Young Men's Christian Association (YMCA), 9, 109, 114
Youth for Christ, 117
youth ministry, 11, 31, 104, 121, 176–77
youth sports
  administration, 168–69
  as entertainment, 42
  commodification of young athletes, 145–46
  competition and, 51
  complexes and facilities, 91–92, 102–4, 114
  "elite, select, travel," 97, 151, 178
  identity formation and, 143–56
  industrialization/ institutionalization of, 21, 40–41, 52, 69, 93–97, 111, 169–70
  justice and, 138–41
  lack of play in, 100
  percentage of participation, 95–96
  politics of, 4
  schedules, 105
  socio-economics factors and, 138–40, 151–52, 166, 172
  specialization in, 105–106
  tourism, 91, 98
  vices in, 93–107, 128

Zirin, Dave, 71

www.ingramcontent.com/pod-product-compliance
Lightning Source LLC
Chambersburg PA
CBHW021728220426
43662CB00008B/754